RETIREMENT ISSUES, PLANS AND LIFESTYLES

RETIREMENT SAVINGS AND SECURITY

RETIREMENT ISSUES, PLANS AND LIFESTYLES

Additional books and e-books in this series can be found on Nova's website under the Series tab.

RETIREMENT ISSUES, PLANS AND LIFESTYLES

RETIREMENT SAVINGS AND SECURITY

TREVOR BARTON
EDITOR

snova
New York

Library of Congress Cataloging-in-Publication Data

ISBN: 978-1-53615-647-8

Published by Nova Science Publishers, Inc. † New York

CONTENTS

PREFACE

The U.S. retirement system, and the workers and retirees it was designed to help, face major challenges. Traditional pensions have become much less common, and individuals are increasingly responsible for planning and managing their own retirement savings accounts, such as 401(k) plans. Yet research shows that many households are ill-equipped for this task and have little or no retirement savings.

Chapter 1 examines these challenges, drawing from prior work and others' research, as well as insights from a panel of retirement experts on how to better ensure a secure and adequate retirement, with dignity, for all. Chapter 2 examines key challenges U.S. participants face with: (1) unclaimed retirement accounts in the United States, and (2) complying with U.S. tax reporting requirements on their foreign retirement savings.

Chapter 1 - The U.S. retirement system, and the workers and retirees it was designed to help, face major challenges. Traditional pensions have become much less common, and individuals are increasingly responsible for planning and managing their own retirement savings accounts, such as 401(k) plans. Yet research shows that many households are ill-equipped for this task and have little or no retirement savings. In this special report, GAO examines these challenges, drawing from prior work and others' research, as well as insights from a panel of retirement experts on how to better ensure a secure and adequate retirement, with dignity, for all.

Chapter 2 - Saving for retirement can be difficult. However, when participants lose their workplace retirement accounts when they change employers or participate in a workplace retirement plan abroad they can encounter additional challenges in securing adequate retirement savings. GAO was asked to review steps federal agencies might take to assist participants with these challenges. This chapter examines key challenges U.S. participants face with: (1) unclaimed retirement accounts in the United States, and (2) complying with U.S. tax reporting requirements on their foreign retirement savings. GAO reviewed relevant federal laws and regulations, and reviewed selected tax treaties. GAO interviewed stakeholders in the United States and in Australia, Canada, Hong Kong, Switzerland, and the United Kingdom—chosen because these locations host relatively large populations of U.S. individuals and have well-developed workplace retirement systems.

In: Retirement Savings and Security
Editor: Trevor Barton
ISBN: 978-1-53615-647-8

Chapter 1

THE NATION'S RETIREMENT SYSTEM: A COMPREHENSIVE RE-EVALUATION IS NEEDED TO BETTER PROMOTE FUTURE RETIREMENT SECURITY*

United States Government Accountability Office

ABBREVIATIONS

BLS	Bureau of Labor Statistics
CFPB	Consumer Financial Protection Bureau
CMS	Centers for Medicare & Medicaid Services
CPS	Current Population Survey
CSIS	Center for Strategic and International Studies
DB	defined benefit
DC	defined contribution

* This is an edited, reformatted and augmented version of United States Government Accountability Office; A Report to Congress, Publication No. GAO-18-111SP, dated October 2017.

DOL	Department of Labor
EBRI	Employee Benefits Research Institute
ERISA	Employee Retirement Income Security Act of 1974
IRA	individual retirement account
IRC	Internal Revenue Code
IRS	Internal Revenue Service
NCS	National Compensation Survey
NEST	National Employment Services Trust
OASI	Old-Age and Survivors Insurance
OECD	Organisation for Economic Co-operation and Development
PBGC	Pension Benefit Guaranty Corporation
SCF	Survey of Consumer Finances
SIPP	Survey of Income and Program Participation
SSA	Social Security Administration
SSI	Supplemental Security Income
Treasury	Department of the Treasury
UK	United Kingdom

INTRODUCTION

The U.S. retirement system, and the workers and retirees it was designed to help, face major challenges. Traditional pensions have become much less common, and individuals are increasingly responsible for planning and managing their own retirement savings accounts, such as 401(k) plans. Yet research shows that many households are ill-equipped for this task and have little or no retirement savings. In this special report, GAO examines these challenges, drawing from prior work and others' research, as well as insights from a panel of retirement experts on how to better ensure a secure and adequate retirement, with dignity, for all.

Section 1. Landscape of U.S. Retirement System Has Shifted

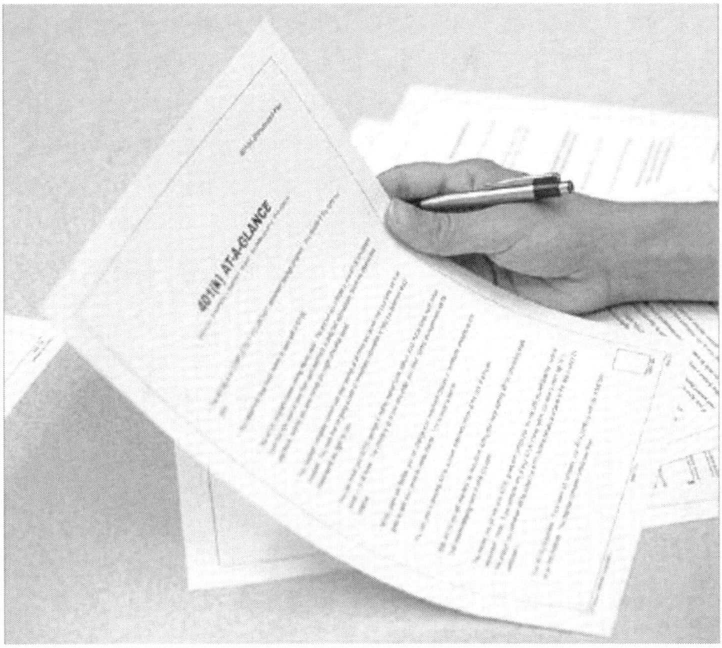

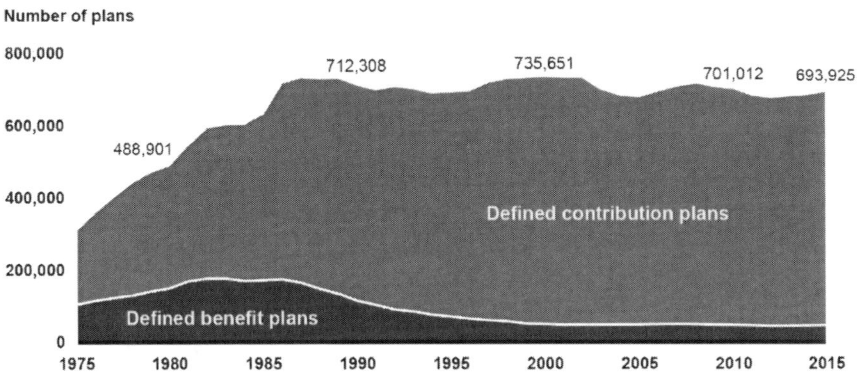

Source: GAO analysis of data from the U.S. Department of Labor. | GAO-18-111SP.

Trends in Private Sector Retirement Plans since 1975.

Fundamental changes have occurred over the past 40 years to the nation's current retirement system, made up of three main pillars: Social Security, employer-sponsored pensions or retirement savings plans, and individual savings. These changes have made it increasingly difficult for individuals to plan for and effectively manage retirement. In particular, there has been a marked shift away from employers offering traditional defined benefit (DB) pension plans to defined contribution (DC) plans, such as 401(k)s, as the primary type of retirement plan. This shift to DC plans has increased the risks and responsibilities for individuals in planning and managing their retirement. In addition, economic and societal trends—such as increases in debt and health care costs—can impede individuals' ability to save for retirement.

Section 2. Individuals Face Three Key Challenges in Planning and Managing Their Retirement

GAO's prior work has found that many individuals face the following challenges in their efforts to provide for a financially secure retirement at a time when increases in longevity further raise the risk of outliving their savings:

- Access: Accessing retirement plans through their employers.
- Saving: Accumulating sufficient retirement savings.
- Retirement: Ensuring accrued savings and benefits last through retirement.

Section 3. U.S. Retirement System Is Threatened by Fiscal Risks

The three pillars of the current retirement system in the United States are anticipated to be unable to ensure adequate benefits for a growing number of Americans due, in part, to the financial risks associated with certain federal programs.

- Social Security's retirement program (Old-Age and Survivors Insurance): Beginning in 2035, this program is projected to be unable to pay full benefits. Long-term fiscal projections show that, absent fiscal policy changes, the federal government is on an unsustainable path, largely due to spending increases driven by the growing gap between federal revenues and health care programs, demographic changes, and net interest on the public debt.
- Private employer-sponsored plans:
  - DB plans: On the decline; also, the Pension Benefit Guaranty Corporation (PBGC) which insures most DB plans, is at risk due to substantial liabilities, especially in its multiemployer program.
  - DC plans: On the rise, but with more risk and responsibility for individuals; many individuals are not saving enough in these plans to provide an adequate retirement.

- Individual savings: Outside of employer-sponsored plans, individuals' retirement savings are often low or nonexistent, which may increase their reliance on various federal and state safety net programs.

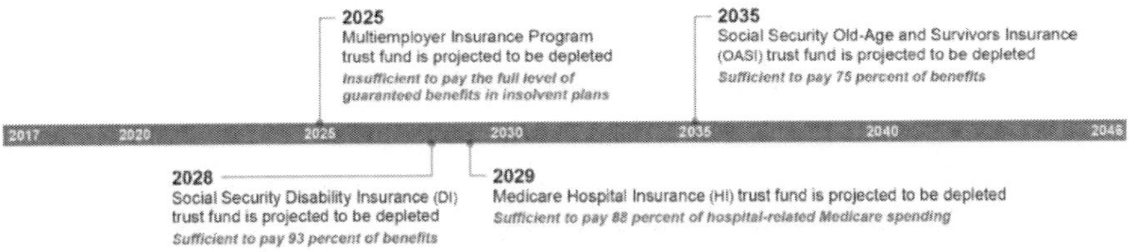

Source: GAO analysis of data from the Social Security Administration, the Centers for Medicare and Medicaid Services, and the Pension Benefit Guaranty Cooperation. | GAO-18-111SP.

Timeline of Projected Fiscal Risks for Certain Federal Programs.

Section 4. The Need to Re-Evaluate the Nation's Approach to Financing Retirement

Over the past 40 years, the nation has sought to address the issues facing the U.S. retirement system in a piecemeal fashion. This approach may not be able to effectively address the interrelated nature of the challenges facing the system today. Fundamental economic changes have occurred, as well as the shift from DB to DC plans, with important consequences for the system. Further, it has been nearly 40 years since a federal commission has conducted a comprehensive evaluation of the nation's approach to financing retirement. A panel of retirement experts convened by GAO in November 2016 agreed that there is a need for a new comprehensive evaluation. The experiences of other countries can also provide useful insights for ways to improve the system.

Matter for Congressional Consideration

Congress should consider establishing an independent commission to comprehensively examine the U.S. retirement system and make recommendations to clarify key policy goals for the system and improve how the nation promotes retirement security.

PREFACE

The nation's concern for the financial security of aging adults is as old as the nation itself. In 1778, the Continental Congress—in response to an appeal from General Washington at Valley Forge—unanimously voted in favor of a pension for officers continuing to serve at the end of the war.[1] Though the nation's initial retirement plans focused on military veterans, plans for state and local government workers emerged in the late 1800s—most prominently in 1878, when a retirement plan for New York City police officers began offering benefits based on years of service in addition to disability. Public sector retirement plans for other state and local government workers, such as firefighters and teachers, gradually followed, eventually spreading to virtually all federal, state, and local government employees nationwide.

Meanwhile, with the nation's transformation from an agrarian to an industrial society, private sector retirement plans also emerged in the late 1800s, reflecting the needs and interests of both employers and workers. Large employers viewed pensions as a tool to (1) remove from service elderly persons and others no longer able to perform their tasks efficiently; (2) reduce labor turnover; and (3) maintain their reputation by humanely meeting the needs of the elderly and incapacitated. Workers, who in the past likely would have been self-employed or part of a small family business that would have continued to provide for them as they aged, increasingly looked to their employers for continued support after they could no longer work.[2] The first private sector plans were primarily for railroad workers, but other industries soon followed.

---

[1] For a chronology of selected federal legislation and other milestones shaping retirement in the United States, see appendix I.

[2] See, for example, Steven A. Sass, *The Promise of Private Pensions, The First Hundred Years* (Cambridge, MA: Harvard University Press, 1997); and Murray Webb Latimer, *Industrial*

This early system of pension plans struggled with many of the same issues that continue to challenge plans today: limited access and participation, the cost and uncertainty of providing lifetime benefits, and sponsors becoming insolvent. Nevertheless, over the course of the 20th century, access to employer-sponsored retirement plans grew steadily and, by 1999, private sector employers were offering coverage to about 63 percent of working age individuals.[3] Since then, however, this percentage has increased only slightly: In 2016 (the most recent data available), about 66 percent of private sector workers were offered coverage.[4] Moreover, among those offered coverage in employer-sponsored retirement plans, not everyone participates. As the structure of plans has continued to evolve, many employers have come to require participants to assume more of the risk and responsibility for their retirement savings with a shift to account-based plans.

Many older adults in the United States rely primarily, if not completely, on another key source of income for their retirement: Social Security. In 1935, in the midst of the Great Depression, the Social Security Act was enacted, in part, to help ensure that older adults would have adequate retirement incomes and would not have to depend on welfare. While the program has been effective in helping to reduce poverty among older adults, it was not intended to be the sole source of retirement income. Yet many have come to rely almost completely on it for their retirement. In 2015 (the most recent data available), 34 percent of households age 65 or over received 90 percent or more of their income from Social Security.[5] In addition, the demographic shifts associated with the aging baby boom

Pension Systems in the United States and Canada (New York, NY: Industrial Relations Counselors, Inc.:1932).

[3] Alicia H. Munnell and Dina Bleckman, *Is Pension Coverage a Problem in the Private Sector?*, No. 14-7 (Chestnut Hill, MA: Center for Retirement Research at Boston College, April 2014). Analysis based on Current Population Survey (CPS) data that asks individuals if their employer offers a pension or other type of retirement plan, and if they are included in the plan.

[4] Bureau of Labor Statistics (BLS), *National Compensation Survey* (March 2016).

[5] Social Security Administration, *Fast Facts & Figures about Social Security, 2017*, SSA Publication No. 13-11785 (Washington, D.C.: September 2017).

generation and longer life expectancy have strained Social Security's finances.[6]

In this chapter, we explore what these trends in retirement security mean for the nation and why, if no action is taken, a retirement crisis could be looming.[7] In the first section, we examine the fundamental changes that have occurred in the landscape of the U.S. retirement system since enactment of the Employee Retirement Income Security Act of 1974 (ERISA). Traditional pensions have become much less common, and individuals are increasingly responsible for planning and managing their own retirement savings accounts, such as 401(k)s. Yet research shows that many households are ill-equipped for this task and have little or no retirement savings. In the second section, we summarize our recently published work on three key challenges facing workers in their efforts to plan for a secure retirement: obtaining access to workplace retirement savings plans, accumulating sufficient retirement savings, and ensuring financial resources throughout retirement.

In the third section, we examine how the three pillars of the current U.S. retirement system may be unable to ensure adequate benefits for a growing number of Americans, in part, due to the financial risks associated with certain federal programs. Finally, in the fourth section, we describe how the nation's piecemeal approach to addressing retirement security challenges may no longer be sufficient. Based on a distillation of findings and recommendations from prior federal commissions, the insights provided by a panel of retirement experts we convened in November 2016,[8] various international studies, and an assessment of our prior work and the work of other researchers and organizations, we identified five policy goals aimed at stabilizing the fiscal risks facing the U.S. retirement system and exploring ways to help more individuals plan and manage their retirement savings effectively for the future. We conclude that to address

---

[6] For a more detailed discussion of Social Security, see GAO, *Social Security's Future: Answers to Key Questions* GAO-16-75SP (Washington, D.C.: Oct. 27, 2015).

[7] This work was conducted in accordance with generally accepted government auditing standards. See appendix II for more details on the methods used.

[8] See appendix III for more on the panel, including a list of the experts who participated, the questions discussed, and a summary of the discussion.

these goals, Congress should consider establishing an independent commission to comprehensively examine the U.S. retirement system and make recommendations to clarify key policy goals for the system and improve how the nation can promote retirement security.

Gene L. Dodaro
Comptroller General of the United States

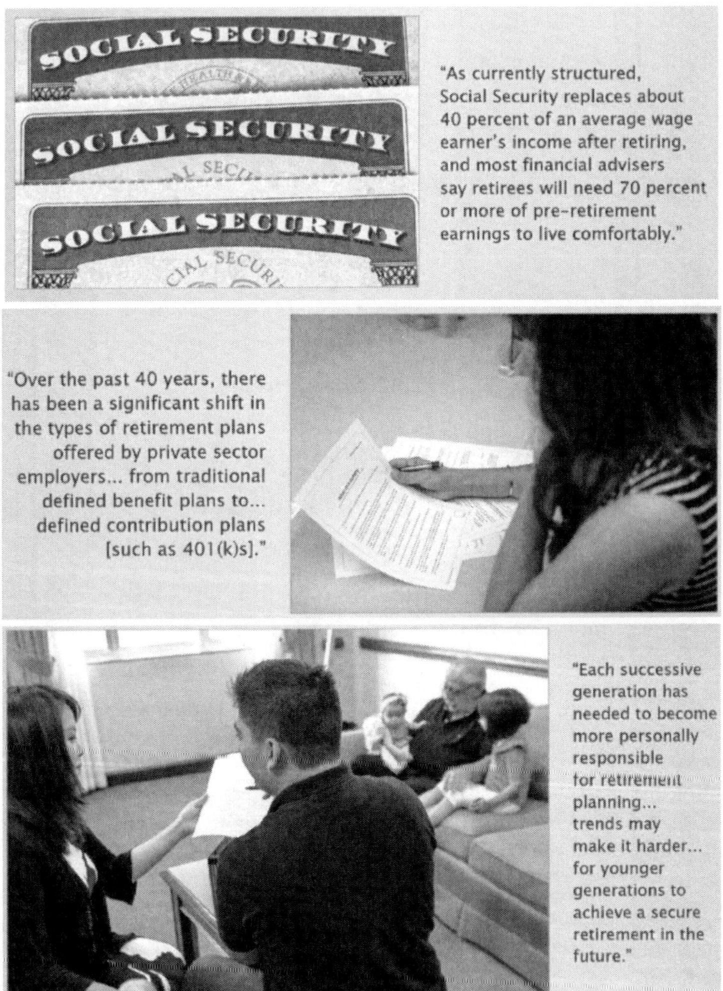

Section 1: Landscape of U.S. Retirement System Has Shifted

The current retirement system in the United States is supported by three main pillars: Social Security, employer-sponsored pensions or retirement savings plans, and individual savings. This three-pillar system, which is similar to the systems in other developed countries around the world, evolved gradually in the United States throughout the nation's history.[9] Despite progress in some ways over time, planning for retirement has always been challenging. However, fundamental changes have occurred over the past 40 years that have made it increasingly difficult for individuals to plan and manage their retirement effectively within this system.

The first pillar, Social Security, was established in 1935 to provide for the general welfare of older Americans by, among other things, establishing a system of federal old-age benefits, including a retirement program.[10] About 50 million retirees and their families were receiving Social Security retirement benefits at the end of 2016, based on the most recent data available from the Social Security Administration (SSA), which is responsible for administering the program.[11] But Social Security was never meant to be the only source of income for people when they retire. As currently structured, Social Security replaces about 40 percent of an average wage earner's income after retiring, and most financial advisors say retirees will need 70 percent or more of pre-retirement earnings to live comfortably.[12]

---

[9] See appendix I for a chronology of selected federal legislation and other milestones shaping retirement in the United States.

[10] Officially titled Old-Age and Survivors Insurance (OASI), the Social Security retirement program provides benefits to retired workers, their families, and survivors of deceased workers. For more about Social Security, see GAO-16-75SP.

[11] In addition, on the revenue side, about 171 million people were working and paying Social Security taxes in 2016. For more information, see The Board of Trustees, *The 2017 Annual Report of the Board of Trustees of the Federal Old-Age and Survivors Insurance and Federal Disability Insurance Trust Funds* (Washington, D.C.: July 13, 2017.)

[12] This comparison is imprecise because the 40 percent average cited for Social Security is relative to average indexed monthly earnings (or AIME, an element of the Social Security benefit formula), whereas the 70 percent cited by advisers is often relative to some measure of pre-retirement earnings closer to retirement. For more on replacement rates, see discussion in the next section of the report, in challenge 2, and GAO, *Retirement Security:*

The second pillar, employer-sponsored pensions or retirement savings plans, date back much further in U.S. history. Some private sector employers began sponsoring retirement plans in the 1800s, and efforts by the federal government to encourage plan sponsorship (and participation by employees) date back to shortly after enactment of the modern individual income tax in 1913.[13] Subsequently, during World War II, such efforts received a significant boost when the wage freeze in place at the time did not include certain pension, health, and other employee benefits.[14] This allowed employers to offer pensions as an alternative means to attract workers and avoid war-related increases in corporate taxes. Private sector plan sponsorship received another boost in 1948 when a federal appeals court upheld a National Labor Relations Board order requiring a company to bargain with respect to retirement and pension matters.[15] In 1940, 4.1 million private-sector workers (about 15 percent) were covered by a pension plan; by 1950, 9.8 million private-sector workers (about 25 percent) were covered.[16]

Over the course of the 20th century, numerous federal laws were enacted that amended parts of the Internal Revenue Code (IRC)[17] regarding the requirements for employer-sponsored retirement plans to qualify for favorable tax treatment.[18] For example, to be tax-qualified, employer-sponsored plans must meet certain requirements with respect to benefit limits, minimum required distributions, and nondiscrimination rules (that

---

Better Information on Income Replacement Rates Needed to Help Workers Plan for Retirement, GAO-16-242 (Washington, D.C.: Mar. 1, 2016).

[13] The Revenue Act of 1913 established an early framework for the current individual income tax, and although there was no explicit provision about pensions, in 1914, IRS issued a decision clarifying that employers may deduct, as ordinary and necessary expenses, amounts paid for pensions to retired employees, their families, or other dependents. Further, in 1919, IRS issued a tax ruling stating that contributions by a corporation to pension funds organized as separate and distinct entities from the corporation would also be deductible as an incident of business.

[14] In 1942, the president was authorized to freeze wages in an attempt to contain wartime inflation.

[15] See Inland Steel Co. v. NLRB, 170 F.2d 247, 248-55 (7th Cir. 1948).

[16] Employee Benefit Research Institute (EBRI), *History of Pension Plans* (1998).

[17] The IRC comprises federal tax laws and is codified in Title 26 of the United States Code.

[18] Being tax-qualified allows employers to deduct their contributions when they are made, within limits.

is, to provide contributions or benefits in a nondiscriminatory manner between highly-compensated employees and other workers).

Employee Retirement Income Security Act of 1974 (ERISA)

ERISA was enacted, in part, to address public concern about the prominent failure of a large private pension plan. The act, as amended, does not require any employer to establish a retirement plan, but those who do must meet certain requirements and minimum standards.

For example, ERISA establishes certain requirements for all employer-sponsored plans, including

- provision of information to participants on a regular basis about the plan's features and funding,
- responsibilities for plan fiduciaries (those who manage and control plan assets, among others),
- establishment of a grievance and appeals process (participants have the right to sue for benefits and breaches of fiduciary duty), and
- minimum funding standards, if the plan is a defined benefit plan.

ERISA also establishes certain minimum standards for employer-sponsored plans concerning:

- when an employee must be allowed to participate in a plan,
- how long participants have to work before having a non-forfeitable (i.e., vested) interest in their plan benefit,
- how long participants can be away from work before it might affect their plan benefit, and
- whether a participant's spouse has a right to plan benefits in in the event of the participant's death.

In addition, tax-qualified plans or their sponsors may have to pay insurance premiums to the Pension Benefit Guaranty Corporation (PBGC).

Source: Based on Department of Labor documents and provisions of ERISA, as amended. | GAO-18-111SP.

In addition, landmark legislation was enacted in 1974 that has played a major role in establishing the structure for private sector employers' involvement in the current U.S. retirement system: the Employee Retirement Income Security Act of 1974 (ERISA). (See text box.) ERISA is a complex law administered by multiple federal agencies including the Department of Labor (DOL), the Internal Revenue Service (IRS) within the Department of the Treasury (Treasury), and the Pension Benefit Guaranty Corporation (PBGC), a government corporation established to protect the pension benefits of American workers. Since the law was enacted, both the IRC and ERISA have been amended, partly in response to the significant shift in the types of retirement plans offered by private sector employers and the transfer of considerable risk and responsibility from employers to individuals.

Finally, as part of this three-pillar system, individuals are expected to augment their retirement income from Social Security and employer-sponsored plans with their own savings, which would include any home equity and other non-retirement savings and investments.[19] However, economic and societal trends—such as slow wage growth, high levels of household debt, and increased longevity—are making it more difficult for many individuals to save for and manage their retirement.

Shift in Types of Retirement Plans Offered by Private Sector Employers

Employers play an important role in the current U.S. retirement system by sponsoring retirement plans and, in many cases, providing employer contributions to those plans.[20] However, over the past 40 years, there has been a significant shift in the types of retirement plans offered by private sector employers, who have increasingly moved from offering traditional defined benefit (DB) plans to offering defined contribution (DC) plans as

---

[19] For discussion of the various sources of potential income in retirement, see section 2.

[20] While not all employers contribute to the plans they sponsor, surveys conducted by various organizations indicate that most do. See, for example, Deloitte, *Annual Defined Contribution Benchmarking Survey, 2015 Edition* (New York, NY: Deloitte Development LLC, 2015); and Plan Sponsor Council of America, *58th Annual Survey of Profit Sharing and 401k Plans* (Chicago, IL: PSCA, 2015).

their primary retirement plans, which are, essentially, employer-sponsored individual retirement savings accounts.[21]

Defined benefit (DB) plan: an employer-sponsored retirement plan that traditionally promises to provide a benefit for the life of the participant, based on a formula specified in the plan that typically takes into account factors such as an employee's salary, years of service, and age at retirement.

Defined contribution (DC) plan: an employer-sponsored account based retirement plan, such as a 401(k) plan, that allows individuals to accumulate tax-advantaged retirement savings in an individual account based on employee and/or employer contributions, and the investment returns (gains and losses) earned on the account.

Source: GAO (see glossary). | GAO-18-111SP.

As shown in Figure 1.1, DC plans (which today are primarily 401(k) plans) have become the dominant employer-sponsored plan type in the private sector. In the past, many employers offered DC plans as a supplemental way for employees to save for retirement in addition to their primary DB plan. But over time, DC plans have become the primary retirement plans for many workers. In 1975, there were about 103,300 DB plans, compared with about 207,700 DC plans. By 2015, the number of DB plans had decreased to about 45,600, while the number of DC plans had increased to more than 648,300. These data illustrate the shift in types of plans offered, but neither the number of plans, nor data on the number of participants across all plans, accurately reflect the extent of coverage.[22]

---

[21] Public sector employees—i.e., employees of federal, state, and local governments— generally still have access to DB plans. According to data collected by BLS as part of the 2015 National Compensation Survey (NCS), 93 percent of full-time state and local government workers had access to a DB plan, while only 18 percent of private sector workers had access to a DB plan in 2015. All federal workers also generally have access to a DB plan. As of fiscal year 2014, the primary plan for about 8 percent of federal workers (those hired before 1984) was a DB plan, and the primary plan for the remaining 92 percent (those hired in 1984 and after) included both a smaller DB, with lower benefits, and a DC component.

[22] The number of plans is an imperfect indicator of the relative breadth of coverage of DC plans versus DB plans, because some plans cover a very small number of participants, whereas other plans cover hundreds of thousands of participants. However, totaling the number of

There has also been a significant increase in the amount of assets held in individual retirement accounts (IRA), which are funded mostly by assets rolled over from DB and DC plans when individuals change jobs or retire.[23] In the private sector, total assets in DC plans and IRAs, which place responsibility on individuals for making investment decisions, far exceed those in DB plans, which place responsibility on plan officials for making investment decisions. In 2015, DC plans and IRAs held about $12.6 trillion in assets while DB plans only held about $2.9 trillion.

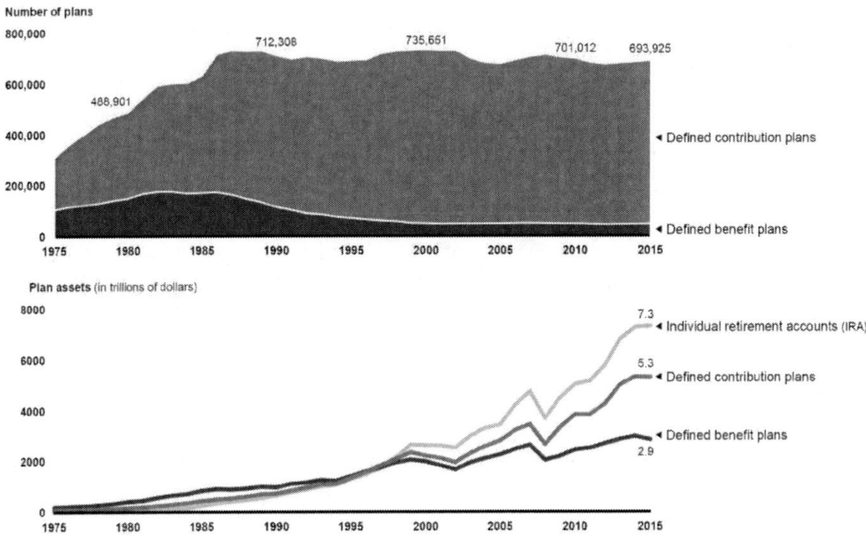

Source: GAO analysis of data from the U.S. Department of Labor and the Investment Company Institute. | GAO-18-111SP.

Figure 1.1. Trends in Private Sector Retirement Plans and IRAs since 1975.

participants across all plans would also produce an inaccurate indicator of coverage because often the same individuals would be counted multiple times. For example, if an employer offers both a DB and DC plan, workers may participate in both plans. In addition, a worker may have changed employers and have DC accounts with both the old and new employers' plans. (For further discussion of the issues related to access and participation, see section 2.)

[23] According to Investment Company Institute, about $424 billion of the funds going into traditional IRAs in 2014 were rollovers from employer-sponsored DC or DB plans. See ICI, "The Role of IRAs in US Households' Saving for Retirement, 2016," *ICI Research Perspective*, vol. 23, no. 1 (January 2017). Rollovers accounted for approximately 92 percent of asset growth in IRAs in 2014.

Table 1. Key Characteristics of Private Sector Defined Contribution and Defined Benefit Plans

Defined contribution (DC) plans		Defined benefit (DB) plans
Employer contributions and/or matching contributions [a]	There is no requirement that the employer contribute [to individuals' DC accounts], except for certain types of plans.[b] The employer may choose to match a portion of the employee's contributions or to contribute without employee contributions. In some plans, employer contributions may be in the form of employer stock.	Employer funded. Federal rules set amounts that employers must contribute to plans in an effort to ensure that plans have enough money to pay benefits when due. There are penalties for failing to meet these requirements.
Employee contributions	Many plans require the employee to contribute in order for an account to be established.	Generally, employees do not contribute to these plans.[c]
Managing the investment	The employee often is responsible for managing the investment of his or her account, choosing from investment options offered by the plan. In some plans, plan officials are responsible for investing all the plan's assets.	Plan officials manage the investment and the employer is responsible for ensuring that the amount it has put in the plan plus investment earnings will be enough to pay the promised benefit.
Amount of benefits paid upon retirement	The benefit depends on contributions made by the employee and/or the employer, performance of the account's investments, and fees charged to the account.	A promised benefit is based on a formula in the plan, often using a combination of the employee's age, years worked for the employer, and/or salary.
Type of retirement benefit payments	The retiree may transfer the account balance into an individual retirement account (IRA) from which the retiree withdraws money, or may receive it as a lump-sum payment. Some plans also offer monthly payments through an annuity.	Traditionally, these plans pay the retiree monthly annuity payments that continue for life. Plans may offer other payment options [such as lump sums].
Guarantee of benefits	No federal guarantee of benefits.	The federal government, through the Pension Benefit Guaranty Corporation (PBGC), guarantees some amount of benefits.

Table 1. (Continued)

Defined contribution (DC) plans		Defined benefit (DB) plans
Leaving the company before retirement age	The employee may transfer the account balance to an IRA or, in some cases, another employer plan, where it can continue to grow based on investment earnings. The employee also may take the balance out of the plan, but will owe taxes and possibly penalties, thus reducing retirement income.[d] Plans may cash out small accounts.[e]	If an employee leaves after vesting in a benefit but before the plan's retirement age, the benefit generally stays with the plan until the employee files a claim for it at retirement. Some defined benefit plans offer early retirement options. [Plans may also cash out small accounts.]

Source: Department of Labor pamphlet (August 2013). | GAO-18-111SP.

[a] ERISA provides plan sponsors some flexibility in designing their plans' eligibility and vesting policies. In DC plans, sponsors may require an employee to work a certain length of time to become eligible, and participants may need to work up to 6 years to fully vest in the funds added to their accounts derived from employer contributions. In DB plans, eligibility and participation are typically automatic upon employment but participants may need to work up to 7 years to fully vest in the accrued benefits derived from employer contributions.

[b] Exceptions include SIMPLE and safe harbor 401(k) plans, money purchase plans, Savings Incentive Match Plan for Employees Individual Retirement Accounts (SIMPLE IRA), and Simplified Employee Pension Plans (SEP). The employer may also have to contribute in certain automatic enrollment 401(k) plans.

[c] In private sector DB plans, contributions are typically made by employers only. But in public sector DB plans, contributions are typically made by both employers and employees. (Also, because public sector plans are not governed by most of the substantive requirements under ERISA, there can be more variability with regard to many of the provisions described in this table.)

[d] There are exceptions to the tax penalties for early withdrawal of funds from a qualified retirement plan, such as for certain medical expenses or total disability.

[e] Either upon retirement, or when leaving employment before retirement, employees may also have the option of leaving their account balances in the employer's DC plan.

Retirement experts have posited a variety of reasons for employers' switch to DC plans. One oft-cited reason is that the structure of DC plans gives employers better control over how much they spend on wages and benefits packages. With DC plans, employers may or may not choose to make contributions to participants' individual accounts rather than promising a certain future monthly benefit in retirement (see Table 1). As a result, when economic conditions fluctuate, the cost of sponsoring DC plans is not affected in the same way as DB plans. For example, during the 2007-2009 recession, even as the market downturn caused DC plan participants' account balances to plummet, DC plan sponsors had the flexibility to suspend or reduce their contributions. In contrast, when DB plan sponsors experienced large declines in their plan assets due to market losses, and increases in liabilities due to low interest rates, many were required to increase their contributions in response to these changing conditions.[24]

Pension Protection Act of 2006 (PPA)

The PPA made several important revisions to ERISA, including:

- strengthened minimum plan funding standards for defined benefit plans,
- enhanced protections for spouses,
- strengthened plan asset diversification requirements,
- included provisions to improve the portability of pension plans,
- facilitated the adoption of automatic enrollment and target date funds for defined contribution plans, and
- increased the breadth and complexity of pension plan sponsors' reporting and disclosure requirements.

Source: GAO and Congressional Research Service. | GAO-18-111SP.

Another reason retirement experts cite for the switch to DC plans was the introduction of 401(k) accounts in the Internal Revenue Code in 1978, which they credit with fostering the adoption of account-based plans by sanctioning the use of salary deferrals as a source of contributions. In contrast, over time, new requirements have been placed on DB plans that, according to some retirement experts, added to their costs and made reporting and funding the plans more burdensome. For example, some

[24] Because DB plan sponsors bear most of the financial risks for their plans, DB plan sponsorship exposes employers to more risks than DC plan sponsorship, including risks such as poor investment returns, decreases in interest rates, increases in longevity, and globalization of the economy. For a more detailed discussion of the factors and decisions affecting the shift from DB to DC plans, see, for example, Teresa Ghilarducci, *When I'm Sixty-Four: The Plot Against Pensions and the Plan to Save Them* (Princeton, NJ: Princeton University Press, 2008), Chapter 3, "When Bad Things Happen to Good Pensions—Promises Get Broken."

experts have cited the additional reporting requirements enacted under the Pension Protection Act of 2006 (PPA) and increases in PBGC premiums as contributing to the costs and burden on DB plan sponsors.[25]

Some retirement experts have also suggested that employees' preferences and demands have changed over time, making DC plans more feasible and, in some respects, more appealing. For example, some analysts have noted that the portability of an account-based plan can be better suited to meet the needs of a more mobile workforce.[26] Meanwhile, some experts have noted that the declining presence of unions and collective bargaining has reduced the ability of workers to negotiate access to pensions, especially DB plans. In 1983, just over 20 percent of the workforce belonged to a union; by 2016, the percentage had dropped by almost half, to 10.7 percent.[27]

Economic and Societal Trends That May Impede Individuals' Ability to Save for Retirement

Since 1974, different generations have faced different responsibilities and decisions when planning for and managing their retirement, in part because of the shift to a DC-centered retirement system, but also because of economic and societal changes that may impede individuals' ability to save for retirement. Each successive generation has needed to become more personally responsible for retirement planning to ensure sufficient income in retirement. Experts vary in their views on the extent to which those retiring now have saved enough to last through retirement, but most agree that future retirees will need to save more to maintain their desired standards of living in light of the range of risks they face, including

---

[25] PBGC officials noted, however, that most premium increases have occurred since 2012, following passage of the Moving Ahead for Progress in the 21st Century Act (MAP-21), so the long-term decline in DB plans arguably has little to do with premiums (increases or otherwise).

[26] At the same time, as discussed in section 2, portability can also be a source of leakage—that is, funds being taken out of retirement savings and used for non-related expenses. For more on this topic, see GAO, *401(k) Plans: Policy Changes Could Reduce the Long-term Effects of Leakage on Workers' Retirement Savings,* GAO-09-715 (Washington, D.C.: Aug. 28, 2009).

[27] BLS statistics-based data from CPS on union affiliation of wage and salary workers, age 16 or older.

employment risk, investment risk, economic risk, health risk, and longevity risk.[28] Yet, economic and societal trends may make it difficult for current working-age individuals to contribute to DC plans and retirement savings accounts and plan effectively for all these risks. The more time a generation is subject to these economic and societal trends, the more these trends continue to place pressure on income security and widen disparities, the harder it may be for younger generations to achieve a secure retirement in the future.

Economic Trends

Deferring current consumption and saving for retirement is difficult, but several economic trends such as slow wage growth, high levels of household debt, and rising health care costs could make it even more difficult, in different ways. First, average real wages remain near the levels they were in the 1970s for most individuals, adding to the difficulty of increasing their level of saving.[29] As shown in Figure 1.2, while mean household income has increased for the top 20 percent of households (and for the top 5 percent, in particular), it has stayed relatively constant for the bottom 80 percent of households. If wages continue to stagnate for most workers, future generations of retirees will continue to find it challenging to provide for a secure retirement.[30]

---

[28] For further discussion of savings adequacy, the amount of income needed to be replaced in retirement, the increasing cost of retirement, and the range of risks individuals face in managing their retirement savings, see section 2 as well as GAO, *Retirement Security: Most Households Approaching Retirement Have Low Savings*, GAO-15-419 (Washington, D.C.: May 12, 2015); and *Retirement Security: Low Defined Contribution Savings May Pose Challenges*, GAO-16-408 (Washington, D.C.: May 5, 2016).

[29] Level real wages are a concern because a variety of factors—including reduced support from DB plans, higher health care costs, longer life spans, and lower interest rates—make financing retirement more expensive than in the past, so that higher real wages might be needed to finance a secure retirement. See Alicia H. Munnell, *Falling Short: The Coming Retirement Crisis and What to Do About It* (Chestnut Hill, MA: Center for Retirement Research at Boston College, April 2015).

[30] In addition, our prior work suggests that, in the aftermath of the 2007-2009 recession, more workers may have alternative employment arrangements (i.e., work in temporary, contract, or other forms of non-standard employment arrangements) in which they may not receive employer-provided retirement and health benefits. We also found that many of these workers (referred to as contingent workers) receive lower wages and benefits than workers in standard employment arrangements. See GAO, *Contingent Workforce: Size, Characteristics, Earnings, and Benefits*, GAO-15-168R (Washington, D.C.: Apr. 20, 2015).

In addition, according to the 2016 Survey of Consumer Finances, the median real value of debt held by households has risen significantly since 1989 and may affect households' financial security in retirement (see Figure 1.3).[31] While this statistic fell between 2010 and 2016 for three of the four age groups we examined, the median real value of debt was still much higher than it was in 1989. For example, from 1989 to 2016, the median real value of debt grew 67 percent (in constant 2016 dollars) for households headed by someone age 35 through 44, and by 104 percent for households headed by someone age 45 through 54. Also, according to analysts at the Federal Reserve, the make-up of debt has changed over time, with declining home ownership and rising education debt, which increased substantially between 2013 and 2016.[32] The increase in debt loads could impede these households' ability to save for retirement during an important stage of their prime working years.

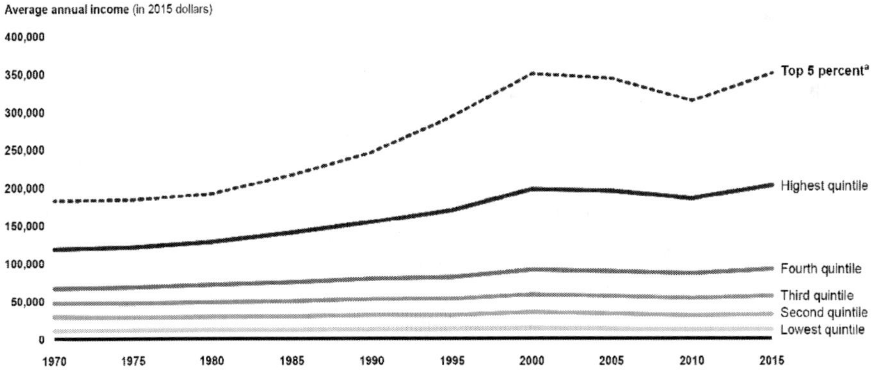

Source: GAO analysis of U.S. Census Bureau data. | GAO-16-111SP.

Note: The changes over time are cross-sectional comparisons, not longitudinal ones—that is, the households in a particular quintile in one year may not be the same households in that quintile in another year.

[a] The top 5 percent is also included in the highest quintile.

Figure 1.2. Mean Household Incomes, by Quintiles and Top 5 Percent, 1970–2015.

[31] We use 1989 as a starting point because the data summarized in the Survey of Consumer Finances (SCF) chartbooks begin with this year. See Board of Governors of the Federal Reserve System, *2016 SCF Chartbook* (Washington, D.C.: Sept. 27, 2017).

[32] Jesse Bricker et al. "Changes in U.S. Family Finances from 2013 to 2016: Evidence from the Survey of Consumer Finances," *Federal Reserve Bulletin*, vol. 103, no. 3 (September 2017).

Individuals must also contend with rising health care costs as they strive to save for retirement.[33] Paying for rising health care costs during one's working years can make it more difficult to allocate income to save for retirement.[34] In addition, rising health care costs can increase the overall amount individuals may need to save to ensure they have an adequate income once they retire. Research indicates that many retirees spend large shares of their income on health-related expenses, including out-of-pocket costs and premiums, and that out-of-pocket spending generally rises as people age.[35]

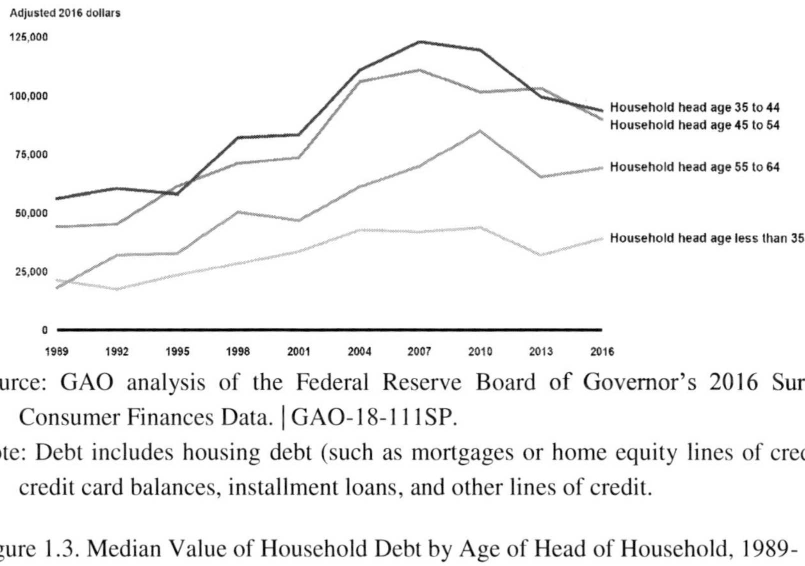

Source: GAO analysis of the Federal Reserve Board of Governor's 2016 Survey Consumer Finances Data. | GAO-18-111SP.

Note: Debt includes housing debt (such as mortgages or home equity lines of credit), credit card balances, installment loans, and other lines of credit.

Figure 1.3. Median Value of Household Debt by Age of Head of Household, 1989-2016.

---

[33] For further discussion of the challenges related to accumulating sufficient retirement savings, see section 2.

[34] Further, some research has shown that health care costs have continued to increase while median inflation-adjusted wages have stagnated. See Harriet Komisar, *The Effects of Rising Health Care Costs on Middle-Class Economic Security* (Washington, D.C.: AARP Public Policy Institute, 2013).

[35] Health care premiums have risen more quickly than inflation over time. However, out-of-pocket health spending among retirees varies according to a number of factors, including whether the retiree is covered by Medicare, has purchased Medicare supplemental coverage (such as Part D prescription coverage), or is dually eligible for Medicaid. In our previous work, we analyzed consumption for households in various age groups. We found that older retiree households (those headed by individuals age 80 or older) spent 15 percent of their total spending on health care, which was more than double the share spent by mid-career households (those headed by individuals age 45 through 49). See GAO-16-242.

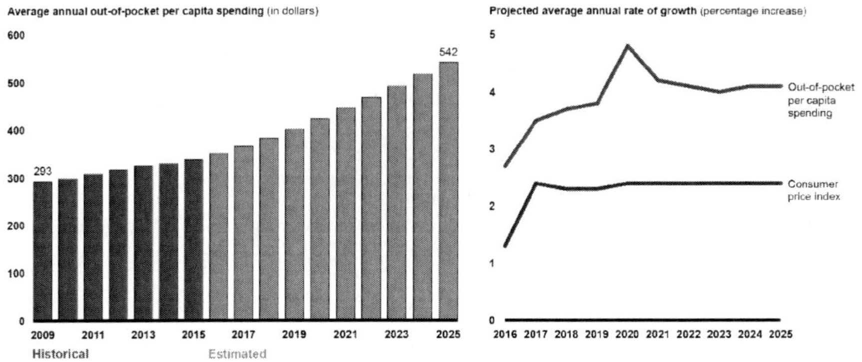

Source: GAO analysis of data from the Centers for Medicare and Medicaid Services and the Bureau of Labor Statistics. | GAO-18-111SP.

Note: Out-of-pocket spending includes direct spending by consumers for all health care goods and services, including coinsurance, deductibles, and any amounts not covered by insurance; however, premiums paid by individuals for private health insurance are not included. Amounts are in nominal dollars, not adjusted for inflation.

Figure 1.4. Projected Growth in Out-of-Pocket Health Care Spending.

For example, according to data from the Centers for Medicare & Medicaid Services (CMS) from 2002 to 2012, out-of-pocket health care spending per capita has grown at a faster rate than overall inflation—an average 2.9 percent versus 2.4 percent per year.[36] Going forward, CMS projections estimate that the annual growth rate for out-of-pocket health care spending per capita will accelerate to about 4.8 percent by 2020 and remain at or above 4.0 percent through 2025 (see Figure 1.4).[37] While these costs are projected to rise for the population as a whole, individuals age 65 or older face the highest health-related expenses. On a per person basis, CMS data show that out-of-pocket health care spending was nearly 3.5 times higher for individuals age 65 or older compared to those age 19 to 64 in 2012. The rising cost of health care later in life could be particularly

[36] The average annual rate of change in inflation is based on Consumer Price Index data from DOL's BLS. BLS research using Consumer Expenditure Survey data also found that health care spending has grown as a share of household expenditures from 2005 to 2014. See Ann C. Foster, "Household Healthcare Spending in 2014," *Beyond the Numbers*, vol. 5, no. 13 (BLS: August 2016).

[37] CMS, Office of the Actuary in the Centers for Medicare & Medicaid Services, *National Health Expenditure Projections 2016-2025*.

daunting for younger generations given increases in average life expectancy and health care needs in a person's final years, making retirement planning even more important.

Societal Trends

> ***Longevity risk*:** the risk that individuals may outlive their retirement savings.
>
> Source: GAO (see glossary). | GAO-18-111SP.

As greater responsibility is shifting to individuals for assuring their own retirement security, some societal trends—such as increases in life expectancy and changes in household composition—have the potential to increase economic vulnerability for retirees. For example, life expectancy for those age 65 or older has increased significantly over the past century and is projected to continue to increase (see Figure 1.5). A man born in 1915, once reaching age 65, could expect to live to age 79.7, on average, but a man born in 2015, once reaching age 65, can expect to live to age 86.1 on average—an increase of about 6.4 years.[38] Similarly, a woman born in 1915, once reaching age 65, could expect to live to age 83.7, on average, but a woman born in 2015, once reaching age 65, can expect to live to age 88.7—an increase of about 5.0 years. Thus, people retiring at age 65 are now exposed to retirement risks for longer periods than previous generations. As a result, rising life expectancy after age 65 may exacerbate the challenge of achieving economic security throughout retirement (referred to as longevity risk), requiring that individuals engage in more planning and saving to support longer retirements.

[38] Based on Social Security Administration, Office of the Chief Actuary, "Life Tables for the United States Social Security Area 1900 to 2100," Actuarial Study number 120, SSA pub. No. 11-11536 (August 2005). However, lower-income groups' life expectancy has not increased as much as higher-income groups' life expectancy. For further discussion of issues surrounding disparities in life expectancy and the implications for retirement planning, see GAO, *Retirement Security: Shorter Life Expectancy Reduces Projected Lifetime Benefits for Lower Earners*, GAO-16-354 (Washington, D.C.: Mar. 25, 2016).

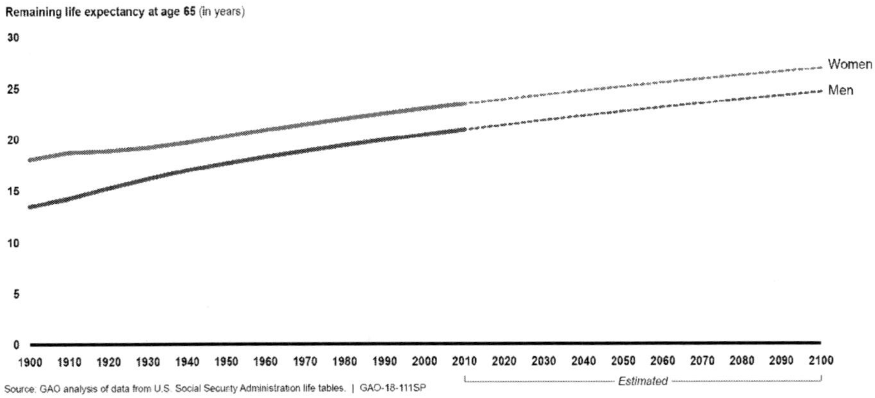

Note: Cohort life expectancy at age 65 by year of birth based on the death rates for those age 65 and all older ages that were, or are projected to be, experienced for those born in that specific year.

Figure 1.5. Increasing Life Expectancy in the United States, 1900-2100.

Additionally, fewer people are getting married, and those who do get married often do so later in life and stay married for shorter periods of time. Specifically, from 1980 to 2016, the proportion of the population age 15 or older that is not married (i.e., never married, divorced, or widowed) has increased from 39 to 48 percent (see fig 1.6). These trends have disproportionately occurred within the nation's most vulnerable populations: low-income, less-educated individuals, and some minorities. Among low-income individuals, the proportion of the population that is not married has been decreasing, but is still much larger than for the population overall. For example, in 2016, 62 percent of low-income individuals were not married, compared with 48 percent of the overall population.[39]

These societal trends have consequences for economic security in retirement. Unmarried individuals are unable to take advantage of the economic benefits of marriage and may therefore be at greater risk of poverty in old age.

[39] For further details on these trends, see GAO, *Retirement Security: Trends in Marriage and Work Patterns May Increase Economic Vulnerability for Some Retirees*, GAO-14-33 (Washington, D.C.: Jan. 15, 2014).

For example, single households may be more vulnerable to economic and health shocks because they cannot pool resources with a spouse against risks of job loss, illness or disability. In addition, never married individuals are also unable to take advantage of some federal benefits and other protections that are conferred through marriage, such as Social Security and DB plan survivor benefits.

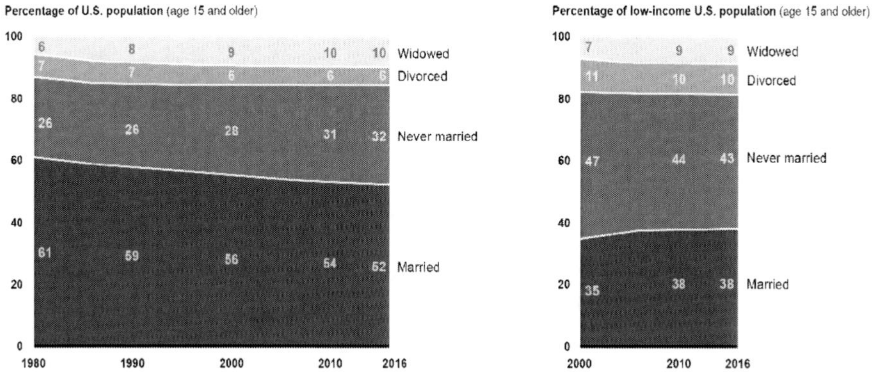

Source: GAO analysis of data from the U.S. Census Bureau. | GAO-18-111SP.

Note: Low-income includes individuals with earnings less than $15,000 annually, in nominal dollar values. Totals may not add to 100 percent due to rounding.

Figure 1.6. Marital Status in the United States over Time, 1980-2016.

Other Trends Affecting Women in Retirement

At the same time, women's participation in the workforce has been rising, which generally improves retirement income security. See GAO-14-33.

Also, family size has been decreasing. In 1975, families with children under age 18 had, on average, 2.09 children. By 2016, the average number of children had fallen to 1.89. (U.S. Census Bureau, Current Population Survey, 2016.)

Source: GAO and Census. | GAO-18-111SP.

"Having access to an employer-sponsored retirement plan makes it easier to save, and more likely that an individual will have another source of income in retirement beyond Social Security."

"When seeking to accumulate financial resources for retirement, the challenges that individuals face vary by whether they have access to an employer-sponsored plan, and if so, the type of retirement plan they have access to."

"As individuals enter retirement, they face the challenge of ensuring that their accumulated resources last throughout retirement, whatever their mix of resources might be."

Section 2: Individuals Face Three Key Challenges in Planning and Managing Their Retirement

When trying to plan or manage their retirement to provide for a financially secure future, individuals face three key challenges. First, they may not have access to a retirement plan through their employer. Second, even if they have access to an employer-sponsored plan, they may have difficulty accumulating retirement savings or benefits due to constraints on their income, or the plan's structure and policies. Third, individuals may have difficulty making accrued savings and benefits last with the increases in longevity that further raise the risk of outliving their savings.[40]

Regardless of whether they have access to an employer-sponsored plan and the structure of that plan, individuals are likely to face a series of complex financial decisions over how to manage a myriad of potential sources of retirement income (see Figure 2.1)—decisions that they may be ill-equipped to make, and that could have significant consequences for their financial security throughout retirement.

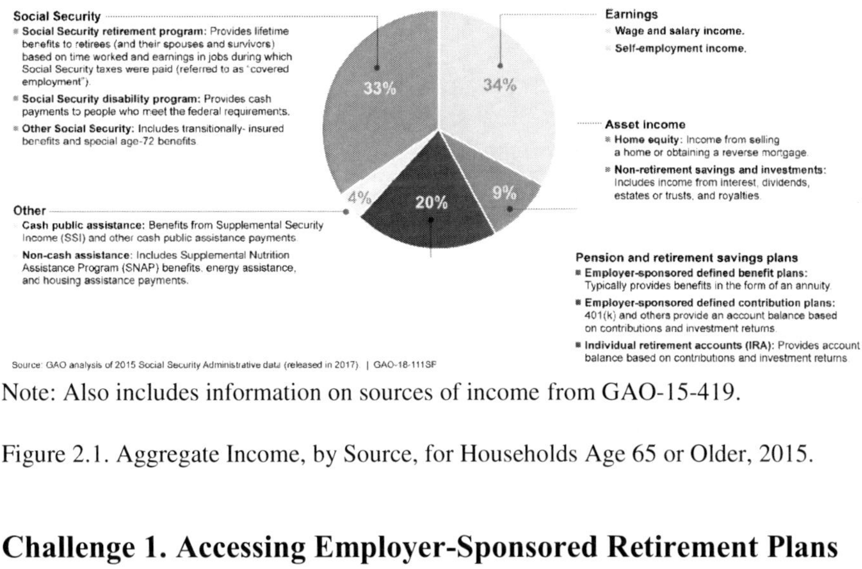

Note: Also includes information on sources of income from GAO-15-419.

Figure 2.1. Aggregate Income, by Source, for Households Age 65 or Older, 2015.

Challenge 1. Accessing Employer-Sponsored Retirement Plans

About two-thirds of private-sector workers in the United States had access to an employer-sponsored retirement plan in 2016,[41] and about a

[40] The challenges discussed in this section are applicable primarily to private sector workers, as the challenges faced by public sector workers are somewhat different. Virtually all public sector workers have access to employer-sponsored retirement plans, in most cases, DB plans. However, public sector plans are not governed by most of the substantive requirements under ERISA, including PBGC insurance.

[41] Bureau of Labor Statistics, *National Compensation Survey, Retirement benefits: Access, participation, and take-up rates, private industry* (Washington, D.C.: July 2016). In this

third did not.[42] Although individuals without access to an employer-sponsored plan can save for retirement on their own, having access to an employer-sponsored retirement plan makes it easier to save, and more likely that an individual will have another source of income in retirement beyond Social Security. In addition, certain U.S. workers are more likely to lack access than others. For example, those working for smaller firms and in certain industries are less likely to have access. Similarly, low-income workers are less likely to have access to an employer-sponsored plan, even when working for an employer that offers a plan, due to eligibility requirements. The federal government has taken various steps to encourage greater access, primarily by offering tax incentives, but with limited success.

Smaller Firms and Firms in Certain Industries Are Less Likely to Offer Plans

In a 2015 report, we analyzed data from the Census Bureau's (Census) Survey of Income and Program Participation (SIPP) and found that those who are employed by smaller firms were less likely to have access to an employer-sponsored retirement plan.[43] Also, our analysis of BLS data found that workers in certain industries were less likely to have access to an employer-sponsored retirement plan.

Employed by Smaller Firms

We have previously found that those who worked for firms with 50 or fewer workers were more than 9 times less likely to have access to an

---

report, we use the phrase "access to an employer-sponsored retirement plan" to mean that a worker's employer is offering a plan and that the worker is eligible to participate in the plan.

[42] In our 2015 report on retirement plan coverage, we found similar results using Survey of Income and Program Participation (SIPP) data matched with W2 tax data. We calculated that 61 percent of private sector workers had access to an employer-sponsored retirement plan, while 39 percent did not. In addition, in our 2015 report, we estimated that another 15 percent chose not to participate, even though they had access, so that overall, about half of private sector workers lacked coverage from a workplace plan. See GAO, *Retirement Security: Federal Action Could Help State Efforts to Expand Private Sector Coverage,* GAO-15-556 (Washington, D.C.: Sept. 10, 2015).

[43] GAO-15-556.

employer-sponsored retirement plan compared to workers at the largest firms, after controlling for other factors (see Figure 2.2).[44] Smaller firms were not sponsoring plans for a variety of reasons, such as the administrative burden of sponsoring a plan and lack of financial resources.[45]

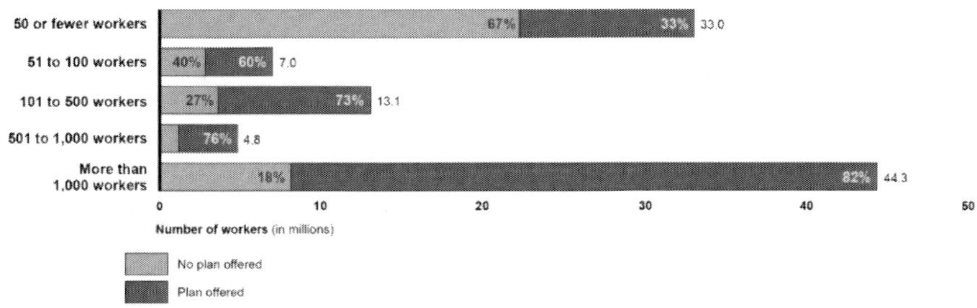

Source: GAO analysis of weighted Survey of Income and Program Participation (SIPP) data for private sector workers, 2012. | GAO-18-111SP.

Note: Based on data from GAO-15-556, Table 10. The 95 percent confidence intervals for estimates in this graph are within +/- 12.0 percent of the estimates themselves.

Figure 2.2. Workers' Access to Employer-Sponsored Retirement Plans by Firm Size, 2012.

For example, we found that small employers could be less willing or less able to sponsor a retirement plan because of the one-time costs to start a plan and the ongoing costs of maintaining the plan.[46] Additionally, small employers we interviewed stated that general economic uncertainty made them reluctant to commit to such long-term expenses and explained that they needed to reach a certain level of profitability before they would consider sponsoring a plan.[47]

---

[44] GAO-15-556.

[45] According to our analysis of SIPP data in prior work, 33 million workers were employed by businesses with 50 or fewer workers in 2012, which was approximately 32 percent of the private sector labor force. See GAO-15-556.

[46] See GAO, *Private Pensions: Better Agency Coordination Could Help Small Employers Address Challenges to Plan Sponsorship,* GAO-12-326 (Washington, D.C.: Mar. 5, 2012).

[47] In 2012, we reported that according to several experts, a firm's age could also affect the likelihood of plan sponsorship, with newer employers less likely to sponsor a plan. Small firms often had limited financial resources and faced a high probability of failure during their first several years before they were stable enough to sponsor a plan, and may hesitate before adding additional fixed costs. See GAO-12-326.

Work in Certain Industries

BLS data also show that workers' access to employer-sponsored retirement plans varies based on the industry in which they work (see Figure 2.3).[48] For example, in 2016, 89 percent of workers in information services had access to an employer-sponsored plan, compared with 32 percent of workers in the leisure and hospitality industry—the lowest percentage of workers in any industry.[49] In the next lowest industry, other services, 47 percent of workers had access to a plan.[50] Also, while union membership has been declining overall, it remains somewhat stronger among workers in the industry with the most access to an employer-sponsored plan (information services) compared to workers in the industry with the least access (leisure and hospitality). Union membership is 8.6 percent in information services versus 3.2 percent in leisure and hospitality.[51]

---

[48] *National Compensation Survey*, 2016. Although there are different surveys that provide data on access by type of employment, we chose the National Compensation Survey (NCS) for this part of our analysis because the data are publicly available and allowed us to examine access by industry, a topic not explored in our past work prior to this report. Other surveys with data on access by type of employment include the CPS and the SIPP. Estimates of participation rates vary across studies because the study sample varies (e.g., whether the study includes full and part-time workers, or is based on household, firm-level, or industry-level data). Nevertheless, research has shown a persistent gap in access among private sector workers across a number of different categories. For more information on the differences in estimates across these three surveys, see GAO-15-556.

[49] In the NCS, BLS' definition of retirement benefits includes DB pension plans and DC retirement plans. BLS defines leisure and hospitality as consisting of the arts, entertainment and recreation sector, which includes a wide range of establishments that operate facilities or provide services to meet varied cultural, entertainment, and recreational interests of their patrons, and the accommodation and food service sector, which is comprised of establishments providing customers with lodging and/or preparing meals, snacks, and beverages for immediate consumption.

[50] The average weekly earnings of workers in the leisure and hospitality industry were about half those of workers in the next closest category, other services: $393 compared with $745. BLS defines the other services sector as establishments primarily engaged in activities such as equipment and machinery repair, promoting or administering religious activities, grant making, advocacy, and providing dry cleaning and laundry services, personal care services, death care services, pet care, photo finishing, temporary parking services, and dating services. The other services sector does not include public administration.

[51] According to BLS, in 2016 10.7 percent of wage and salary workers (a total of 14.6 million workers) were members of unions. In 1983, the first year for which comparable union data are available, 20.1 percent of wage and salary workers (a total of 17.7 million workers) were members of unions. BLS defines union membership rate as the percent of wage and salary workers who were members of unions. Bureau of Labor Statistics, *Union affiliation*

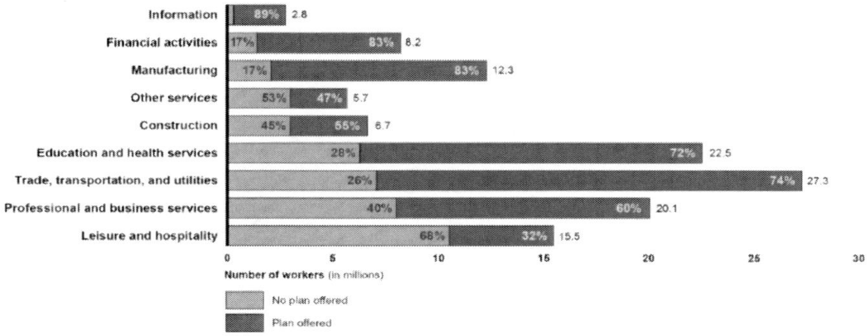

Source: GAO analysis of data from the Bureau of Labor Statistics, National Compensation Survey and Current Employment Statistics, March 2016. | GAO-18-111SP.

Note: Data on private sector worker's access from the National Compensation Survey; data on number of workers by industry from the Current Employment Statistics. The 95 percent confidence intervals for estimates in this figure are within +/- 16.2 percent of the estimates themselves.

Figure 2.3. Workers' Access to Employer-Sponsored Retirement Plans by Industry, 2016.

Lower-Income Workers Have Less Access to Employer-Sponsored Plans

Compared to workers in the highest income quartile, our 2015 report found that workers in the lowest income quartile were nearly four times less likely to work for an employer that offered a retirement plan, based on our analysis of 2012 SIPP data, controlling for other factors (see Figure 2.4).[52]

Even when employers offer a plan, as we noted in a 2016 report, some individuals may lack access due to various eligibility requirements.[53] For example, employers can establish minimum service eligibility policies which require employees to work for an employer for a certain period of

---

of employed wage and salary workers by occupation and industry (Washington, D.C.: January 2016).

[52] GAO-15-556.

[53] See GAO, *401(k) Plans: Effects of Eligibility and Vesting Policies on Workers' Retirement Savings,* GAO-17-69 (Washington, D.C.: Oct. 21, 2016). Individuals whose employers offer DB plans are less likely to face barriers due to age and service-related eligibility requirements, when compared to individuals in DC plans, as enrollment in DB plans is generally automatic.

time, generally up to one year, before they can enroll and participate in a 401(k) plan.

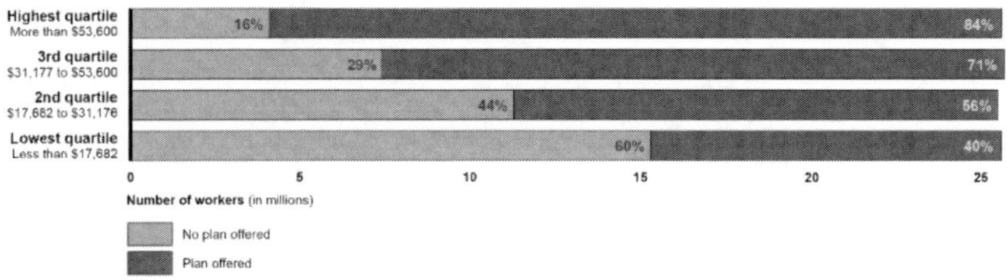

Source: GAO analysis of weighted Survey of Income and Program Participation (SIPP) data for private sector workers, 2012. | GAO-18-111SP.

Note: Based on data from GAO-15-556, Table 10. The 95 percent confidence intervals for estimates in this figure are within +/- 7.0 percent of the estimates themselves.

Figure 2.4. Workers' Access to Employer-Sponsored Retirement Plans by Income Level, 2012.

According to a 2014 report from the Center for Retirement Research at Boston College, one reason lower-income workers lack access to employer-sponsored retirement plans is that they struggle to meet plan eligibility requirements related to sufficient tenure and hours worked.[54] In addition, low-income workers tend to have weaker labor force attachment and higher unemployment rates.[55] Our prior work supports these observations. For example:

- Insufficient tenure and hours worked: In a recent report, we found that employer-established eligibility policies, such as tenure and hours worked requirements, can affect whether employees qualify

---

[54] BLS data also suggest that the extent of part-time employment in certain industries affects access to retirement benefits. Specifically, BLS determined that access rates for retirement benefits are 21 percentage points greater for industries in which employees tend to work more hours per week (such as health care, information, and construction) than industries in which employees work fewer hours (such as accommodation and food services, arts, entertainment, recreation, and retail). See Bureau of Labor Statistics, "The Relationship between Access to Benefits and Weekly Work Hours," *Monthly Labor Review* (June 2015).

[55] April Yanuyan Wu, Matthew S. Rutledge, and Jacob Pengalse, *Why Don't Lower-Income Individuals Have Pensions?* (Chestnut Hill, MA: Center for Retirement Research at Boston College, April 2014).

to participate in a plan.[56] Because of these policies, part-time workers were about 2.6 times less likely than full-time workers to be eligible for a retirement savings program offered by their employer, after controlling for other factors.[57]

- Irregular (or contingent) work: In a 2015 report, we found that, compared to standard workers, workers who have temporary, contract, or other forms of non-standard employment receive lower wages and benefits. Further, we found that the odds of participating in a work-provided retirement plan were an estimated 67.6 percent lower for such workers (referred to as contingent workers) than for standard workers.[58] While estimates on the size of the contingent workforce vary, our prior work suggests it has grown since the 2007-2009 recession.

Federal Efforts to Expand Access

> ***Nondiscrimination rules***: rules that generally require contributions or benefits provided under a pension or retirement savings plan not to discriminate in favor of highly-compensated employees in order for the plan to qualify for preferential tax treatment.
>
> Source: GAO (see glossary). | GAO-18-111SP.

Despite various federal efforts since 1975, there has been little improvement in increasing access to employer-sponsored retirement

[56] See GAO-17-69. In this report, we used the term eligibility policies to refer to 401(k) plan policies that require employees to reach a minimum age (minimum-age policies) or work for a minimum length of time (minimum-service policies) before they can participate and save their earnings in a plan.

[57] GAO-17-69 and GAO-15-556. ERISA provides the legal framework for eligibility policies used by private sector employers sponsoring retirement plans. For example, ERISA allows sponsors to require their employees to work up to 1,000 hours per year and to be at least age 21 to be eligible to join their retirement plan. In GAO-17-69, we surveyed 80 401(k) plan sponsors and plan professionals and found that 33 had policies that did not allow workers younger than age 21 to participate in the plan. Assuming a minimum age policy of 21, GAO projections estimated that a medium-level earner who does not save in a plan or receive a 3 percent employer matching contribution from age 18 to 20 could have $36,422 (in 2016 dollars) less savings by their retirement at age 67.

[58] See GAO-15-168R.

plans.[59] The primary way that the federal government has tried to encourage greater plan formation is through increased tax incentives.[60] In structuring these tax incentives, Congress sought to help ensure that lower-paid employees have equitable access to plan benefits, in part through nondiscrimination rules. However, our prior work has found that plan formation has not resulted in any significant expansion of access, even with these incentives and rules in place.[61] For example, despite several legislative efforts that increased the tax qualified contribution limits to 401(k) plans during this period, the number of plans actually declined between 2000 and 2011.[62]

***Safe harbor 401(k) plan*:** a safe harbor 401(k) is similar to a traditional 401(k) plan, but the employer is required to make contributions for each employee. The safe harbor 401(k) eases administrative burdens on employers by eliminating some of the rules ordinarily applied to traditional 401(k) plans.

Source: GAO (see glossary). | GAO-18-111SP.

---

[59] For previously issued GAO recommendations for executive action and matters for congressional consideration in this area see, appendix IV.

[60] In 2001, the Economic Growth and Tax Relief Reconciliation Act (EGTRRA) created a tax credit for small employers to offset pension plan startup costs. The credit for small employer pension plan startup costs applies to certain startup costs in connection with the establishment of a new qualified DB plan, DC plan (including 401(k) plans), SIMPLE IRA plan, or SEP IRA plan. To be eligible, an employer must have no more than 100 employees who received at least $5,000 of compensation in the preceding year. The credit equals 50 percent of qualified startup costs, which include administration costs and employee education, up to a maximum of $500 per year (for the first three years of the plan). The Pension Protection Act of 2006 made these EGTRRA provisions permanent. For more information, see GAO-12-326.

[61] See GAO, *Private Pensions: Some Key Features Lead to an Uneven Distribution of Benefits*, GAO-11-333 (Washington, D.C.: Mar. 30, 2011). Another study also noted that nondiscrimination rules may not lead to greater access. See Peter Brady, "Pension Nondiscrimination Rules and the Incentive to Cross Subsidize Employees," Investment Company Institute, *PEF* vol. 6, no. 2 (July, 2007). For more information about the history of nondiscrimination rules, dating back to 1937, see appendix I.

[62] Increasing the contribution limits could spur plan formation to the extent that a firm's owners and highly-compensated employees find it attractive to save more for retirement on a tax-deferred basis. Other factors, for example the 2007-2009 recession, likely contributed to the lack of plan formation during this period. However, plan formation did not increase even in the immediate years following legislation in 2001 that increased the contribution limits and made other changes to spur plan formation. See GAO, *Private Pensions: Pension Tax Incentives Update*, GAO-14-334R (Washington, D.C.: Mar. 20, 2014).

In addition, in response to concerns from employer organizations and small employers that fear of litigation was a key reason for choosing not to sponsor plans, federal agencies have also established safe harbor regulations to encourage sponsorship by helping protect employers from such risk. For example, in 2007, DOL created a regulatory safe harbor to limit plan sponsor liability for investing contributions on behalf of employees into default investments when employees do not otherwise make an election. In addition, DOL identified three examples of default investment options that, if selected by sponsors, would qualify the plan for safe harbor protection.[63] Nevertheless, there has been little improvement in the number of employers offering new retirement plans in recent decades.

The federal government also tried to increase access by developing a new savings vehicle, called *my*RA, for those without access to employer-sponsored plans. A type of Roth IRA account, *my*RA was created by Treasury in 2014 to help people take the first step toward saving for retirement. In *my*RA accounts, contributions are invested in a no fee, risk free bond. However, on July 28, 2017, Treasury announced that it is phasing out *my*RA accounts because the program has not been cost-effective.

In light of the relatively limited effect federal efforts have had in significantly increasing access, some states have taken the initiative to create alternative retirement savings programs for private sector workers without access to employer-sponsored plans within their states. In a 2015 report, we found that at the time of our review, 29 states had enacted, or were considering, state level retirement savings plan options for private sector workers.[64] For example, in 2012, Massachusetts enacted a law that authorized the state to sponsor a state-run 401(k) plan that can be adopted

---

[63] These default investment options, known as qualified default investment alternatives (QDIA), include: (1) target date funds; (2) balanced funds; and (3) managed account services. If 401(k) plan fiduciaries default participants who do not provide investment directions with respect to their plan contributions into one of these three options, and they satisfy all other requirements of the QDIA regulation, they can limit their liability under the law. See GAO, *401(K) Plans: Improvements Can Be Made to Better Protect Participants in Managed Accounts,* GAO-14-310 (Washington, D.C.: June 25, 2014); and *401K Plans: Clearer Regulations Could Help Plan Sponsors Choose Investments for Participants,* GAO-15-578 (Washington, D.C.: Aug. 25, 2015).

[64] GAO-15-556.

by not-for-profit employers with fewer than 20 employees. Also, Washington was planning to create a state-facilitated small business retirement marketplace that would list a variety of approved retirement plans through which employers with fewer than 100 employees could choose to offer their workers a retirement savings plan, to be implemented in 2017. However, the future of these state efforts is unclear. In the past, some employer groups and financial services firms have raised concerns about how such arrangements could affect employers that already offer retirement plans. In February 2017, Congress passed two joint resolutions disapproving DOL's final rule providing a safe harbor to states and political subdivisions related to savings arrangements they establish for non-governmental employees.[65]

Challenge 2. Accumulating Sufficient Retirement Savings

Some individuals face greater challenges accumulating retirement savings than others, depending on their type of retirement plan, if any. While retirement savings may often be adequate for those with higher incomes, those with lower incomes face many challenges trying to save. The federal government has taken various steps to encourage individuals to save more for retirement through new rules and guidance for employers sponsoring retirement plans, and initiatives to improve financial literacy.

> ***Financial literacy***: the ability to make informed judgments and take effective actions to improve one's present and long-term financial well-being.
>
> Source: GAO (see glossary). | GAO-18-111SP.

Savings Challenges Differ by Type of Plan

The challenges faced by individuals when seeking to accumulate financial resources for retirement vary by whether they have access to an employer-sponsored retirement plan and if so, the type of plan. Challenges

[65] The joint resolutions have since been enacted. See Pub. L. No. 115-24 and Pub. L. No. 115-35.

are greatest for workers with no employer-sponsored plan, and are also significant for those with DC plans. Workers with DB plans can also face certain challenges, but to a lesser extent. In 2016, 34 percent of private sector workers had no employer-sponsored plan, 44 percent had DC plans, and 15 percent had DB plans.[66]

Individuals with No Employer-Sponsored Plans

Individuals who do not have access to an employer-sponsored plan often face the greatest challenges trying to save for retirement. As discussed in challenge 1, individuals without access to an employer-sponsored plan may contribute to various types of IRAs which provide tax-advantaged savings, similar to the advantages available to those with an employer-sponsored plan (see text box).[67] However, for individuals to take advantage of these options, they generally are required to take more action on their own, starting with learning about various IRA options, making a selection, signing up, and then actually saving.

> ***Tax-advantaged***: able to defer the payment of taxes on income earned now until some point in the future, such as when the funds are withdrawn from a qualified retirement savings account.
>
> Source: GAO (see glossary). | GAO-18-111SP.

Not only do those without employer-sponsored plans have to take more initiative to open an IRA, they face other drawbacks, as well. For example unlike those with an employer-sponsored plan, individuals saving on their own generally are not provided any employer contributions to augment their savings.

---

[66] *National Compensation Survey*, 2016. The NCS does not distinguish between workers who have DB plans exclusively and DC plans exclusively. As such, workers with DC plans may also have DB plans and vice-versa.

[67] In addition to savings accumulated through IRAs, individuals may also accumulate assets through personal savings, and investments such as owning a home and building home equity, for example.

Individual Retirement Accounts (IRA)

There are two basic types of IRAs:

- Traditional IRA: A traditional IRA allows individuals to make contributions to their accounts with taxes deferred on investment earnings until distribution, when distributions are generally taxed as ordinary income. For traditional IRAs, deductions for contributions are subject to limits based on income, filing status, and pension coverage for an individual and his or her spouse. Distributions made prior to age 59%, other than under specific exceptions, are generally subject to an additional 10 percent tax.
- Roth IRA: A Roth IRA allows eligible individuals to make after-tax contributions to their accounts. Distributions (based on both contributions and investment earnings) are generally tax free once individuals are age 59% or older, if at least 5 years have elapsed since the individual initially opened an account.[a]

Individuals can contribute to IRAs on their own, or through one of two types of employer-sponsored IRA plans, depending on the size and capacity of the employer:

- Savings Incentive Match Plan for Employees (SIMPLE) IRAs: SIMPLE IRAs are a means by which employers with 100 or fewer employees can more easily provide a retirement savings plan to their employees rather than through a 401(k) or defined benefit (DB) plan. Under such a program, eligible employees can direct a portion of their salary, within limits, to a SIMPLE IRA and employers must either (1) match the employees' contribution up to 3 percent of the employee's salary, or (2) make contributions of 2 percent of each employee's salary for all employees making at least $5,000 for the year, regardless of whether the employee makes contributions on his or her own.[b]
- Payroll Deduction IRAs: Through a payroll deduction IRA program, individuals may establish either traditional or Roth IRAs and make contributions by authorizing payroll deductions, which are forwarded by the employer to their IRAs.

Sources: GAO-15-556 and GAO, *Automatic IRAs: Lower-Earning Households Could Realize Increases in Retirement Income*, GAO-13-699 (Washington, D.C.: Aug. 23, 2013). | GAO-18-111SP.

[a] Another type of Roth IRA is *my*RA, which Treasury launched in 2014 for those individuals who did not have access to an employer-sponsored retirement plan. In 2017, Treasury announced it was discontinuing the program.

[b] Prior to 1997, employers could establish Salary Reduction Simplified Employee Pension Plans (SARSEP), an employer-sponsored IRA plan. The introduction of SIMPLE IRA plans were intended to replace SARSEPS. Employers can no longer establish new SARSEPs; however, employers who established SARSEPs prior to January 1, 1997, can continue to maintain them and new employees of the sponsoring employer remain eligible to participate.

In addition, the annual contribution limit for IRAs is lower than for employer plans, IRAs are not subject to the ERISA protections that are provided for employer-sponsored plans, and the fees to maintain IRAs are generally higher than those charged participants in employer-sponsored plans.[68] Moreover, individuals saving on their own also face many of the same challenges that those with employer-sponsored DC plans face, such as having to make decisions about how to manage their accounts, as discussed below.

Individuals with DC Plans

Individuals who work for employers that offer DC plans are provided ready access to a vehicle for saving, but they still face many key decisions and risks in accumulating retirement savings. The process involves several steps and each one may be complex. Participants must decide whether to participate, how much to contribute, and how to manage their investments to strike the right balance between risk and returns. Participants also must make decisions that can have an impact on their retirement accounts when other needs arise or life circumstances change, such as when leaving a job mid-career. DC plan sponsors are required to provide a variety of reports and disclosures to help their plan participants make these decisions and to

[68] For statutory annual contribution limits for 1974 through 2014, see GAO, *Individual Retirement Accounts: IRS Could Bolster Enforcement on Multimillion Dollar Accounts, but More Direction from Congress Is Needed*, GAO-15-16 (Washington, D.C.: Oct. 20, 2014).

act in the best interest of plan participants, but as we have previously reported, the materials they provide are often difficult for participants to understand.[69]

Deciding Whether and How Much to Contribute

> ***Employer match*:** when an employee contributes to an employer-sponsored retirement savings account, an employer may make a matching contribution, which is typically a percentage of the employee's contributions, up to a certain limit.
>
> Source: GAO (see glossary). | GAO-18-111SP.

When individuals are deciding whether to participate in their employers' plans, and if so, how much to contribute, they may be confused or overwhelmed by the information provided and put off making a decision. Sponsors are required to provide eligible employees certain information about the plan, such as the requirements for receiving employer matching funds, and the limitations on amounts that can be contributed on a tax-deferred basis. However, participation in the plan is often optional and, for the most part, sponsors do not provide advice about how much to contribute. Our prior work has found that many DC plan sponsors are reluctant to provide much advice because they are concerned that it could inadvertently lead to a violation of their fiduciary responsibilities to act in the best interest of the participant, leaving them vulnerable to litigation.[70] (See text box.)

---

[69] See GAO, *Private Pensions: Clarity of Required Reports and Disclosures Could Be Improved*, GAO-14-92 (Washington, D.C.: Nov. 21, 2013). We identified more than 60 different disclosures that retirement plan sponsors may be required to provide to participants, depending on the plan's type, size, and circumstances.

[70] GAO-15-578. In April 2016, DOL issued a final rule defining who is a fiduciary as a result of giving investment advice to plan officials, plan participants, and beneficiaries and IRA owners. The final rule describes the kinds of communications that would constitute investment advice and describes the types of relationships in which such communications give rise to fiduciary investment advice responsibilities. Implementation of the rule was set to begin in April 2017. However, in February 2017, President Trump issued a memo asking DOL to postpone its implementation for several months to determine whether the rule may adversely affect the ability of Americans to gain access to retirement information and

Retirement Plan Fiduciaries

Under the Employee Retirement Income Security Act of 1974, a fiduciary is a sponsor, trustee, investment advisor, service provider, or other person who:

- exercises any discretionary authority or control over plan management;
- exercises any authority or control over the management or disposition of plan assets;
- renders investment advice respecting plan money or property for a fee or other compensation; or
- has discretionary authority or responsibility for plan administration.

Fiduciaries are expected to act prudently, and in the best interest of participants.

Source: 29 U.S.C. §§ 1002(21)(A) and 1104(a). | GAO-18-111SP.

***Auto-enrollment*:** plan feature whereby eligible workers are enrolled into a plan automatically, or by default, unless they explicitly choose to opt out.

***Auto-escalation*:** plan feature that increases employee contributions automatically on a predetermined schedule, such as annually, up to a pre-set maximum.

Source: GAO (see glossary). | GAO-18-111SP.

One way to encourage enrollment in DC plans is by putting mechanisms in place to automatically enroll new employees in the plan—commonly referred to as auto-enrollment. Moreover, auto-enrollment typically includes a default contribution rate for participants who do not specify an alternative contribution level (including an election to not contribute).

financial advice. In May 2017, DOL announced a temporary enforcement policy related to the final rule, with a phased implementation period from June 2017 until January 2018, while it reviews the issues raised by the President's February 2017 memo.

Decision-Making and Behavioral Economics

Behavioral economics studies the effect of emotional, social and cognitive factors on economic decision-making and the financial consequences of these decisions. It combines economics and psychology to offer an alternative to the traditional economic theory that individuals always act rationally and in their own self-interest. According to behavioral economics, for example, people face a big challenge overcoming inertia when making an affirmative decision to participate in a retirement plan, partly because it requires forgoing consumption now for a distant future goal. As a result, framing the choice differently by making participation the default option, as with auto-enrollment, helps to increase participation rates in retirement plans.

Behavioral economics has also shown that individuals tend to be overwhelmed by too many choices or information overload. To deal with complex problems, people use simplification heuristics (i.e., mental shortcuts), such as allocating savings equally across all fund options offered in their retirement plan.

Insights from behavioral economics have helped plan sponsors design strategies to help individuals reach their financial goals. Such strategies include auto-enrollment, auto-escalation, and target date funds (an investment option that automatically shifts to lower-risk, income-producing investments as a 'target' retirement date approaches). These strategies recognize the realities of human psychology, including procrastination and inertia, as well as difficulty in processing complex information, and steer individuals in directions designed to increase their financial well-being.

Sources: Amos Tversky and Daniel Kahneman, "The Framing of Decisions and the Psychology of Choice," *Science, New Series*, vol. 211, no. 4481 (Jan. 30, 1981); Bridgitte C Madrian and Dennis F. Shea, "The Power of Suggestion: Inertia in 401(k) Participation and Savings Behavior," *The Quarterly Journal of Economics*, vol. 116, no. 4. (November 2001); and Richard H. Thaler and Cass R. Sunstein, "Libertarian Paternalism," *The American Economic Review*, vol. 93, no. 2 (May 2003). | GAO-18-111SP.

Note: For further discussion of this topic, see GAO-15-556.

Sponsors can also adopt an auto-escalation policy, which triggers an employee's contribution rate to be increased automatically—typically 1 percent a year—till a pre-set maximum is reached, unless the employee opts out. In our previous work, we found that auto-enrollment policies can result in considerably increased participation rates, reaching as high as 95 percent in certain plans.[71] For example, one study we reviewed followed groups of employees hired before and after a company adopted auto-enrollment for new employees only, and compared the participation rates of the two groups. The participation rate for those hired before auto-enrollment was 37 percent at 3 to 15 months of tenure, compared with an 86 percent participation rate for the group hired after auto-enrollment with a similar amount of tenure.[72] (For more on how the use of behavioral economics can encourage participation and contributions in DC plans, see text box).

***Target replacement rate*:** the percentage of pre-retirement income needed to maintain a certain standard of living in retirement. Source: GAO (see glossary). | GAO-18-111SP.

At the same time, retirement experts and researchers disagree about how much individuals need to save to maintain their desired standard of living through the remainder of their lives after retirement. In previous work, we found that calculating an appropriate percentage of pre-retirement income needed to maintain a certain standard of living in retirement, referred to as a target replacement rate, can be complex, and there is considerable debate about what the right target rates should be (see text box).[73] Some researchers and financial industry professionals

---

[71] The findings in this prior report were not based on a random sample and thus were not generalizable to all 401(k) plan sponsors. Also, we noted that while auto-enrollment can increase participation in 401(k) plans, it does not expand the portion of the workforce saving for retirement that does not have access to such plans. See GAO, *Retirement Savings: Automatic Enrollment Shows Promise for Some Workers, but Proposals to Broaden Retirement Savings for Other Workers Could Face Challenges,* GAO-10-31 (Washington, D.C.: Oct. 23, 2009).

[72] Brigitte C. Madrian and Dennis F. Shea, "The Power of Suggestion: Inertia in 401(k) Participation and Savings Behavior," *The Quarterly Journal of Economics*, vol. 116, no. 4 (November 2001).

[73] GAO-16-242.

recommend using a standard rule of thumb for everyone, while others recommend customizing the rates for different people based on individual preferences and circumstances. In addition, once a target replacement rate is determined, it must be converted into a savings plan, such as how much to set aside from each paycheck over a number of years, which is also a complicated exercise.

Debate on Replacement Rates

Researchers are not in agreement about the range of factors that should be used in the calculations of replacement rates, or the percentage of pre-retirement income that needs to be maintained for adequate income in retirement. A literature review we conducted in 2016 found that use of different factors resulted in target replacement rates that ranged from 43 percent of pre-retirement income to 476 percent. For example, in their calculations of pre-retirement earnings, some researchers used final average earnings, which is based on average annual earnings for a fixed period of time leading up to retirement, while others used average annual earnings over the course of an individual's career. Researchers also used a wide range of assumptions about spending patterns, with variations based on income level, personal circumstances, and age, and of different baskets of expenses, which included some or all of the following: housing, health care, entertainment, and consumer goods. Researchers also varied in the degree to which they included certain household characteristics in their calculations about the amount of income needed in retirement. We found that those analyses which accounted for factors such as longevity, catastrophic health care costs, and investment risk posited a need for higher replacement rates, while those which did not account for such factors posited a need for lower replacement rates.

Source: GAO. | GAO-18-111SP.
Note: For further discussion of this topic, see GAO-15-419 and GAO-16-242.

While researchers do not agree on what percentage of income individuals should strive to replace at retirement, many agree that a sizeable portion of the population is not saving enough.[74] In addition, our analysis indicates that the cost of funding retirement is increasing. For example, we found that in 1977, a married couple retiring at age 65 with accumulated savings of 8.9 times their income at retirement could expect to replace 50 percent of that income throughout their retirement in real terms. In contrast, in 2017, a married couple retiring at age 65 may need to accumulate 12.1 times their income at retirement in order to have the same expectation.[75]

Deciding How to Invest

Making decisions on how to manage and invest the funds in a DC account can also be a complicated and daunting task for many participants. The disclosures plan sponsors must provide are not required to assist participants in making optimal investment decisions, but rather are primarily intended to provide participants and beneficiaries information about their rights and obligations under the plan. Moreover, participants may find that disclosures contain complex content that is difficult to understand, even though notices are generally required to be written in a manner calculated to be understood by the average participant. Based on a study of reporting and disclosures and associated costs, as well as the

---

[74] See, for example, Alicia H. Munnell, Wenliang Hu, and Geoffrey T Sanzenbacher, *Do Households Have a Good Sense of Their Retirement Preparedness?* (Chestnut Hill, MA: Center for Retirement Research at Boston College, February 2017); Jack Van Derhei, "Retirement Savings Shortfalls: Evidence from EBRI's Retirement Security Projection Model," *EBRI Issue Brief No. 410* (Employee Benefit Research Institute, February 2015); and Fidelity Investments, *America's Retirement Score: In Fair Shape-But Fixable* (2016). Other studies have questioned the extent of the savings shortfall, but are nevertheless uncertain about the retirement security of future retirees. For example, see Adam Bee and Joshua Mitchell, "Do Older Americans Have More Income Than We Think?" *SESHD Working Paper #2017-39* (July 2017). While the study found that retired households did not experience substantial declines in income upon retirement, the authors noted that the results could not easily be extrapolated to future generations of retirees, in part because of demographic and labor market changes, as well as retirement policy changes, such as the rise of DC plans.

[75] Our analysis also shows that a single male individual retiring at age 65 in 1977 would have needed to accumulate savings of about 7.0 times his income at retirement, compared to 10.1 times in 2017. A single female at age 65 in 1977 would have needed to accumulate savings of about 8.9 times her income at retirement, compared to 12.1 times in 2017. Estimated savings are based on historical demographic and economic data, and assumptions about future outcomes.

testimony of various financial services representatives, researchers and agency officials, the ERISA Advisory Council (EAC) concluded in 2009 that disclosures often go unread because participants feel overwhelmed by too much information.[76] For example, one DOL official testifying before the EAC noted that the quantity of disclosures creates communication challenges as participants struggle with what they must or should read.

Providing participants with access to advisors is one way to help them manage their accounts. But sponsors may be reluctant to provide such support because of the cost or concerns about potential legal liability. In a 2016 report, our analysis of industry research found that only a minority of plan sponsors were making advisors available to plan participants.[77] In interviews conducted for the 2016 report, one industry stakeholder told us plan sponsors were reluctant to provide access to investment advice, in part because of concerns about the costs. In addition, attorneys representing 401(k) plans told us they counsel their clients against providing participants access to advice because of potential legal liability regarding whether they are acting in the best interest of their participants.[78] In our past work, 401(k) plan attorneys we interviewed said that, in part to avoid this potential liability, many plan sponsors relied on third party service providers for consulting and financial advice for retirement plan participants.[79]

Alternatively, sponsors can help participants better manage their DC investments by providing an automatic mechanism for allocating funds. For example, for those plans that have incorporated an auto-enrollment feature, if participants do not direct how to invest their funds, sponsors can

---

[76] ERISA established an Advisory Council on Employee Welfare and Pension Benefit Plans, known as the ERISA Advisory Council (EAC). The duties of the EAC are to advise the Secretary of Labor and submit recommendations regarding the Secretary's functions under ERISA.

[77] See GAO, *401(K) Plans: DOL Could Take Steps to Improve Retirement Income Options for Plan Participants,* GAO-16-433 (Washington, D.C.: Aug. 9, 2016).

[78] GAO-16-433.

[79] In addition to providing consulting and financial advice, third party retirement plan service providers can also provide investment management services, recordkeeping, and customer service for participants. See GAO, *Private Pensions: Changes Needed to Provide 401(k) Plan Participants and the Department of Labor Better Information on Fees,* GAO-07-21 (Washington, D.C.: Nov. 16, 2006).

invest their funds automatically. To promote automatic enrollment, DOL has provided a safe harbor for sponsors who use certain types of default investment arrangements including: (1) target date or life cycle funds; (2) balanced funds; and (3) managed accounts.[80] Among the most popular of these options are target date funds.[81] Target date funds can help participants manage their investments over time by allocating investments among various asset classes, and then shifting this allocation automatically to lower-risk asset classes over time as a "target" retirement date approaches.

While certain plan features, such as auto-enrollment, are designed to increase participation and savings in DC plans, our prior work has found that other aspects of how plans operate may work against this goal and can erode accumulated savings.[82] For example, those who participate in DC plans may pay fees which, although generally lower than IRA fees, can slow the growth of their balances over time. Such fees vary by plan sponsor and by plan size, but are generally referred to as investment management, administrative, and recordkeeping fees (see text box).[83] While plan sponsors often paid these fees in the past, we have found that participants are bearing these costs in a growing number of plans.[84] In addition, despite DOL's efforts to improve participant disclosures about

---

[80] DOL has designated three default investment options (known as QDIAs) that may be used when 401(k) plan participants do not provide direction on plan contributions to their accounts: (1) an investment product or model portfolio that is designed to become more conservative as the participant's age increases, such as a target date fund; (2) an investment product or model portfolio that is designed with a mix of equity and fixed income exposures appropriate for the participants of the plan as a whole, such as a balanced fund; and (3) an investment management service that uses investment alternatives available in the plan and is designed to become more conservative as the participant's age increases such as a managed account. See 29 C.F.R. § 2550.404c-5; see also GAO-14-310 and GAO-15-578.

[81] Over the past decade, target date funds have received net inflows of $509 billion. In 2016, target date funds had net inflows of $65 billion and ended the year with assets of $887 billion. See: ICI, *2017 Investment Company Fact Book*, 57th edition (2017).

[82] See GAO, *Private Pensions: Alternative Approaches Could Address Retirement Risks Faced by Workers but Pose Trade-offs,* GAO-09-642 (Washington, D.C.: July 24, 2009).

[83] ERISA requires plan fiduciaries to, among other things, ensure the services provided to the plan are necessary and that the cost of those services are reasonable. See GAO, *401(k) Plans: Increased Educational Outreach and Broader Oversight May Help Reduce Plan Fees,* GAO-12-325 (Washington, D.C.: Apr.12, 2012).

[84] See GAO, *Defined Contribution Plans: Approaches in Other Countries Offer Beneficial Strategies in Several Areas,* GAO-12-328 (Washington, D.C.: Mar. 22, 2012); and GAO-14-310.

these fees, participants may not always be aware of the different fees they pay.[85] In our prior work, we found that participants typically do not receive the simple, useful, and targeted information they need about such fees to make informed decisions about their investment options.[86]

Investment and Administrative Fees

Participants with 401(k) accounts generally pay investment management fees and administrative fees to providers or record keepers to maintain their accounts. Investment management fees, which can vary by investment option, are generally charged as a percentage of assets and indirectly charged against participants' accounts because they are deducted from investment returns. Administrative fees, on the other hand, may be assessed as an overall percentage of total plan assets regardless of participants' investment choices. In addition, there may be a flat rate for some fixed services, such as printing plan documents. The sponsor has the option of passing along some or all of the administrative fees to participants.

Source: GAO. | GAO-18-111SP.
Note: For further discussion of this topic, see GAO-14-310.

Managed account: services under which providers manage participants' 401(k) savings over time by making investment and portfolio decisions for them.

Source: GAO (see glossary). | GAO-18-111SP.

---

[85] In 2010, Labor published final regulations to improve U.S. participant fee disclosures. These regulations require that plan sponsors provide participants core information about investments available under the plan, including performance and fee information, prior to investing and at least on an annual basis thereafter, in a chart or similar format designed to facilitate investment comparisons. Fiduciary Requirements for Disclosure in Participant-Directed Individual Account Plans, 75 Fed. Reg. 64,910 (Oct. 20, 2010) (codified at 29 C.F.R. § 2550.404a-5). A revised and delayed effective date for this regulation was published on July 19, 2011. Requirements for Fee Disclosure to Plan Fiduciaries and Participants—Applicability Dates, 76 Fed. Reg. 42,539 (July 19, 2011).

[86] We found that according to industry professionals, participants had often been unaware that they pay any fees associated with their 401(k) plan. In fact, we found that studies showed that 401(k) participants often lacked the most basic knowledge that there were fees associated with their plans. See GAO-12-328.

Some DC plan participants have managed accounts, a service in which a provider actively manages the 401(k) plan participant's account for a fee.[87] Participants may elect to enroll in a managed account service, if available, or they may be defaulted into it if auto-enrolled into their plan. Managed account providers typically decide how to invest 401(k) contributions and then manage these investments over time to help participants reach their retirement savings goals. In our prior work, providers and sponsors described how managed accounts can have advantages for participants.[88] For example, they noted that managed accounts can provide increased diversification of portfolios to better manage risk and increase returns, encourage participants to save more for retirement compared to those who are not enrolled in the service, and provide access to retirement readiness statements that allow participants to assess if they are on track to meet their retirement goals. However, although managed accounts can offer advantages to 401(k) participants, there can also be disadvantages, depending on the overall performance of the account—and performance is not guaranteed. For example, in certain circumstances, the advantages can be offset by paying additional fees for the services provided. In addition, we found that other retirement vehicles, such as target date funds, can provide similar rates of return without requiring the payment of additional managed account fees.[89]

Understanding the Implications of Changing Employers

Finally, DC plan participants can also face challenges keeping their savings in their retirement accounts when other needs arise or their life circumstances change, such as when leaving an employer mid-career. When an individual changes employers and a DC account is cashed out

---

[87] The Plan Sponsor Council of America found in its *49th* and *56th Annual Profit Sharing and 401(k) Surveys* that about 25 percent of sponsors offered managed accounts in 2005, but by 2012 this number had grown to about 36 percent. In a prior report, we estimated that the total amount of defined contribution plan assets in managed accounts exceeded $100 billion at the end of 2012. See GAO-14-310.

[88] GAO-14-310.

[89] Managed account fees can vary substantially by provider. As a result, some participants pay no fees, others pay a flat fee each year, and still others pay a comparatively large percentage of their account balance for generally similar services from managed account providers. For further details, see GAO-14-310.

and not rolled over, it means that the funds are distributed from the retirement plan. Once the funds are no longer in a DC plan, individuals may use their savings for non-retirement-related purposes, also referred to as leakage (see text box).

***Rollover*:** plan savings that are moved to a new qualified employer plan or an individual retirement account when a plan participant is separating from an employer.

Source: GAO (see glossary). | GAO-18-111SP.

Leakage of Retirement Plan Savings

Leakage, or the use of retirement savings for nonretirement purposes, adversely affects account accumulation for those with defined contribution (DC) accounts or individual retirement accounts (IRA), particularly for those with small account balances. Cashing out a portion or all of a DC account balance reduces retirement savings immediately. The participant also forgoes any long-term investment growth for the amount withdrawn. Participants who withdraw money from a DC plan before age 59% generally pay standard income taxes on the distributions, plus an additional 10 percent tax in most circumstances. However, the additional 10 percent tax does not apply to early withdrawals for certain immediate or heavy financial needs. Such hardship allowances include withdrawals to cover certain medical and higher education expenses.

Source: GAO. | GAO-18-111SP.

Note: For further discussion of this topic, see GAO, *Private Pensions: Low Defined Contribution Plan Savings May Pose Challenges to Retirement Security, Especially for Many Low-Income Workers*, GAO-08-8 (Washington, D.C.: Nov. 29, 2007); GAO-09-715; and GAO-16-408.

When leaving an employer mid-career, those with DC plans may benefit from the plan's portability, but their retirement savings can still be adversely affected by leakage and in other ways, as well. In particular, when changing employers, a participant's savings may be negatively affected by the plan's rollover and vesting policies. Further, participants may find it difficult to track various retirement savings accounts over time.

> ***Portability of defined contribution (DC) account balances*:** in a DC plan, portability is a plan feature that allows participants to take their account contributions and any account earnings when changing jobs, and move the funds to a new employer's DC plan or to an individual retirement account (generally with no tax penalty), or take as a cash lump sum (which would be taxed as income with a corresponding early withdrawal penalty, if before age 59%).
>
> Source: GAO (see glossary). | GAO-18-111SP.

We have found that the information participants receive about their plan's rollover and vesting policies is often too generic, leaving participants without a clear understanding of the implications of changing employers, and the key factors they need to know to make decisions about their retirement savings.[90] For example, we found that some plan sponsors have processes or policies that make it easier for a participant leaving an employer to cash out or roll over an account balance into an IRA rather than into a new employer's 401(k) plan, even though such choices may not be the best options for participants.[91] Participants may not even be aware of all the options for their retirement savings when they change employers (see Figure 2.5). Also, IRA accounts can have complex fee structures that may be difficult for participants to find and understand, making comparisons of different options a challenge.

The rollover policies that some plan sponsors have put in place not only make it easier to cash out or move retirement savings to an IRA, they can force the employee into these options if the account balance is $5,000 or less. For example, our prior work has found that some sponsors have policies that if a participant is separating from the company and has a vested account balance of $5,000 or less in the plan, and does not instruct

[90] See GAO, *401(K) Plans: Labor and IRS Could Improve the Rollover Process for Participants,* GAO-13-30 (Washington, D.C.: Mar. 7, 2013).

[91] GAO-13-30.

the plan on what to do with the money, the participant's account balance may be forced to cash out or into an IRA (also referred to as a forced transfer).[92]

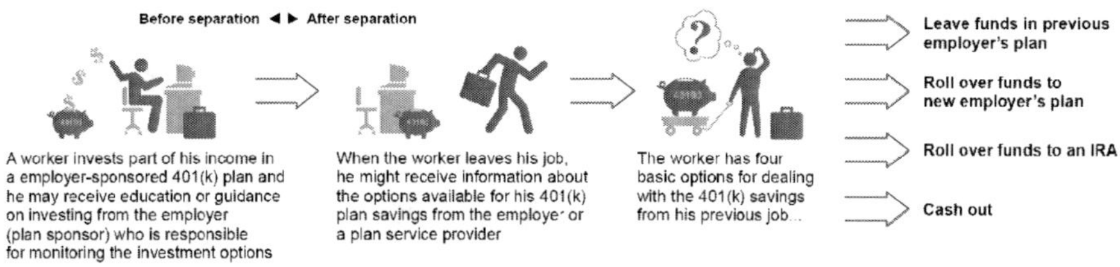

Source: GAO analysis. | GAO-18-111SP.

Note: Plans are not always required to permit participants to leave funds in the plan once they separate from employment, for example, if the balance is less than $5,000 or if the participant attains the later of age 62 or the normal retirement age. Plans are also not required to accept rollovers. For more details, see GAO-13-30.

Figure 2.5. Separating 401(k) Plan Participants Generally Have Up to Four Options for Their Plan Savings.

Rollover policies and processes on the part of a new employer can also make it easier to cash out or roll funds into an IRA instead of initiating a plan-to-plan rollover when changing employers. For example, when seeking to initiate a plan-to-plan rollover, participants may face waiting periods to roll a DC account balance from a previous employer into their new employer's plan, complex verification procedures to ensure that savings are tax-qualified, wide divergence in plans' paperwork, and inefficient practices for processing such rollovers. In contrast, the option of rolling over the account to an IRA can be facilitated by IRA providers who offer assistance to plan participants. As a result, participants may roll over their accounts to an IRA, despite the fact that, as noted earlier, the higher fees in IRAs compared to employers' plans may reduce their account balances over time.

---

[92] See GAO, *401(K) Plans: Greater Protections Needed for Forced Transfers and Inactive Accounts,* GAO-15-73 (Washington, D.C.: Nov. 21, 2014).

***Vesting of defined contribution (DC) account balances*:** in a DC plan, vesting is a plan feature that determines when participants can keep the employer contributions to their accounts (and the investment returns based on those contributions) if they leave a job. Three common types of DC plan vesting are:

- ***Immediate vesting*:** employer contributions and the investment returns based on those contributions are vested without having to work for a minimum length of time.
- ***Cliff vesting*:** no employer contributions and no investment returns based on those contributions are vested until the full vesting period is satisfied, whereupon 100 percent is vested all at once (after no more than 3 years of service).
- ***Graduated vesting*:** an increasing percentage of employer contributions and the investment returns based on those contributions are vested over time: at least 20 percent after 2 years of service, with the percentage increasing by at least 20 percent for each additional year of service thereafter, reaching 100 percent vested after no more than 6 years.

(Different criteria apply for vesting in a defined benefit (DB) plan.)

Source: GAO (see glossary). | GAO-18-111SP.

When individuals leave their employers mid-career, they can also be adversely affected by certain features of a plan's vesting policies. For example, as we recently reported, under ERISA plan sponsors are allowed to establish vesting policies that affect the extent to which DC plan participants can earn and keep employer contributions in their accounts.[93] Sponsors have a range of options, from immediate vesting to requiring up to 6 years of service before all employer contributions (and the investment returns based on those contributions) fully vest.[94] Sponsors are also

[93] See GAO-17-69.

[94] The minimum percentage that must be vested at a given time depends on the type of vesting policy used by the plan. For further details on vesting, see GAO-17-69. DB plans have different vesting rules than DC plans, and participants in DB plans also face challenges when leaving a job mid-career.

allowed to use a last day policy, requiring the participant to be employed on the last day of the year in order to earn the employer contribution for that year. As a result of these policies, the amount of employer contributions participants can receive and keep when leaving a job may be negatively affected. Our previously reported projections suggest that the loss of an employer's matching contributions can be significant over time and that the impact on retirement savings can increase with each job change (see Figure 2.6).

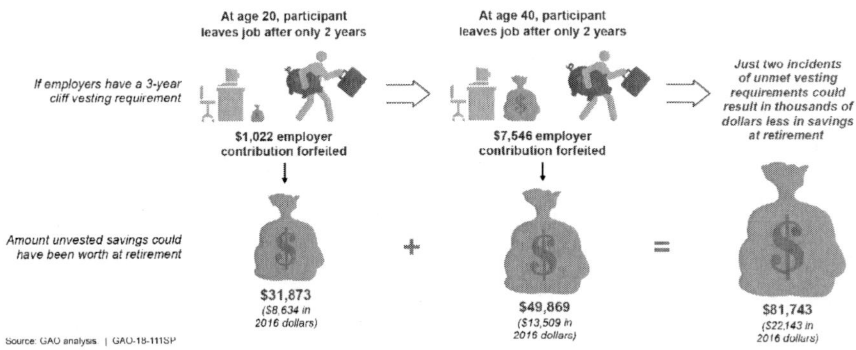

Note: This figure reflects hypothetical projections formulated by GAO for illustrative purposes. Assumptions include a 3-year cliff vesting policy, and that the participant worked during ages 19-20, and 39-40. For more details on projection assumptions and methods, see GAO-17-69.

Figure 2.6. Potential Value of Lost Retirement Savings Due to 401(k) Vesting Policies When Leaving an Employer.

When DC plan participants change jobs multiple times, they also may find it difficult to keep track of all their accounts and savings. Key information on accounts may be held by different plans, service providers, or government agencies, and participants may not know where to turn for information. Plan sponsors may lose track of former employees and be unable to contact them or otherwise reunite them with their accounts. Our prior work found that from 2005 through 2015, 25 million participants in workplace plans separated from an employer and left at least one account behind. Millions more left two or more accounts behind.[95] To the extent that more participants are auto-enrolled into retirement savings plans, there is the potential for a greater number of accounts to be unclaimed during a participant's retirement years because auto-enrollment can contribute to participants having multiple small accounts that may be onerous to track and, as a result, may be forgotten.

Individuals with DB Plans

Although DB plan participants have a less complicated arrangement for accumulating retirement savings in their plans, they, too, face certain risks. DB plans offer lifetime income benefits generally determined by a formula specific to the plan, which typically takes into account factors such as years of service, age at retirement, and, often, salary or wage levels.[96] Under a DB arrangement, the employer is usually responsible for funding the plan and investing and managing the plan's assets, bearing all the management risk. Nevertheless, DB participants still face certain challenges accumulating accrued benefits (the DB counterpart to savings in DC plans). For example, as discussed in our prior work, when DB plan participants change employers, their accrued benefits are less portable than accrued savings in a DC plan.[97] If the change in employers takes place before they have met vesting requirements, DB plan participants can lose all the benefits accumulated to that point.[98] Moreover, even if participants are vested, DB plans generally do not allow participants to take

[95] Based on SSA's analysis of Form 8955-SSA data. SSA data include benefits left behind by separating participants in all defined contribution plans, including 401(k) plans, as well as in defined benefit plans, which are not subject to forced transfers. GAO assessed the reliability of the data and found that it met our standards for our purposes. See GAO-15-73.

[96] A DB plan can be either more or less generous than a DC plan, depending on the particular provisions of the plans and the particular characteristics of any participant. In addition, a plan's value may vary with demographic and economic developments, such as improving human longevity and shifts in financial market expectations. Thus, such comparisons of plans involve complex actuarial measurement issues.

[97] GAO-09-642.

[98] ERISA requires that retirement plan participants' rights to their accrued benefit derived from their own contributions be nonforfeitable. However, as noted earlier, employees with private sector DB plans generally do not contribute to these plans, so, in most instances, all unvested accrued benefits would be lost when a change of employment takes place.

distributions from their plan until they are eligible for retirement.[99] As a result, while the accrued benefits are preserved and the participant will still receive benefits at retirement age, for many types of DB plans, participants' benefit levels stay frozen based on their salary and years of service at the time they leave their jobs, and inflation may erode the value of their pension income over time.[100]

Types of Defined Benefit (DB) Plans

- Single-employer DB plan: a DB plan sponsored by one employer.
- Multiemployer DB plan: a DB plan created through a collective bargaining agreement typically between two or more employers and a union. The employers are usually in the same or related industries, such as transportation, construction, mining, or hospitality.
- Multiple employer DB plan: a DB plan that, as with a multiemployer DB plan, covers employees of more than one employer, but that is generally treated as a single-employer plan with respect to certain reporting, auditing and funding requirements, and for PBGC insurance coverage. For example, a multiple employer plan is allowed to file a single annual report and to pay a single-employer insurance premium to PBGC for the plan as a whole. Also, unlike multiemployer plans, multiple employer plans are not collectively bargained.

Source: PBGC documents. | GAO-18-111SP.

---

[99] DB plans covered by ERISA generally must offer an annuity payout option. Recently, some DB plans have begun offering plan participants who have separated from employment with vested benefits the option of taking a lump-sum payment in exchange for their future annuity. For further discussion of lump-sum payments, see discussion to follow in challenge 3.

[100] DB plans whose benefit formulas are based on years of service and final average salary are sometimes referred to as traditional DB plans. The value of the benefit accrual under such plans has a back loaded pattern, meaning that the biggest years of benefit accrual are late in a participant's career. As a result, even if a participant changing jobs is vested, the participant may miss out on the biggest benefit accruals. Certain types of DB plans, such as cash balance DB plans, have a flatter benefit accrual pattern, so early years of participation provide comparatively greater benefits. Typically, cash balance DB plans offer a lump-sum feature (as do some traditional DB plans). However, whether a cash balance DB plan is more or less costly or generous than a traditional DB plan depends on the particular terms of each plan and a participant's particular circumstances.

In addition, DB plan participants' pensions can be dependent on the financial well-being of their employers. For example, an individual's pension could be eroded if his or her employer encounters financial difficulties, and chooses to freeze the plan, in which case the participant's future pension accruals may be limited.[101] If the plan is underfunded and is terminated or is nearing insolvency, the participant's future pension benefits could also be limited.[102]

Savings Challenges Are Often More Acute for Low-Income Individuals

Unlike higher-income individuals who have more disposable income, low-income individuals face a significant retirement challenge as they are the least able to afford saving for retirement and must spend a larger percentage of take-home earnings for food, clothing, and shelter.[103] In previous work, we defined low-income households as those in the lowest income quartile, i.e., the bottom 25 percent of the income distribution. These households earned $39,200 or less in 2013.[104]

According to a 2015 federal survey of household economic well-being, 35 percent of workers earning less than $40,000 a year report that they do not participate in a DC plan that is offered by their employer because they cannot afford to make contributions.[105] Moreover, some households may

---

[101] As offering a pension is a voluntary decision on the part of the employer, the employer may decide to freeze or close a DB plan at any time for financial as well as non-financial reasons. See GAO, *Defined Benefits Pensions: Plan Freezes Affect Millions of Participants and May Pose Retirement Income Challenges,* GAO-08-817 (Washington, D.C.: July 21, 2008). According to the most recent data available from PBGC, the percentage of DB plans that have frozen or limited benefit accruals has continued to grow, increasing from 27.9 percent in 2008 to 37.1 percent in 2014.

[102] For further discussion of the potential implications for DB plan participants' benefits if ld their plans become underfunded and terminated, or if plans are nearing insolvency, see challenge 3.

[103] At the same time, it has been argued that low-income individuals have less need to save, as they will have a higher percentage of their income replaced by Social Security given the program's progressive benefit structure. For further discussion of this topic, see challenge 3 and Andrew G. Biggs and Sylvester Schieber, "Is There a Retirement Crisis?" *National Affairs* (Summer 2014).

[104] GAO-16-408.

[105] Board of Governors of the Federal Reserve System, *Report on the Economic Well-Being of U.S. Households in 2014* (Washington, D.C.: May 2015).

be unwilling to save for retirement without first saving for emergencies, such as loss of employment. In the same survey, over half the households reported they did not have emergency funds to cover 3 months of expenses, and nearly a quarter reported experiencing a financial hardship in the previous year.[106] In our past work, we have also found that low-income households with DC plans had significantly smaller account balances than other income groups (see Figure 2.7).

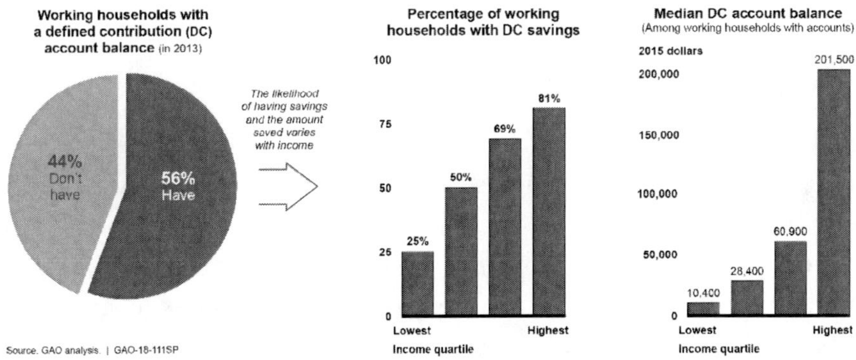

Note: Working households are defined as households with at least one person working, but not self-employed, and the household head is age 25 through 64. All percentage estimates in this figure have 95 percent confidence intervals within +/- 3.1 percent. Thus the amount and percentage for each income group, or quartile, of household income is statistically different from the others. For more details see GAO-16-408.

Figure 2.7. Defined Contribution (DC) Plan Savings by Household Income among Working Households, 2013.

Women and some minorities also appear to face greater challenges when trying to accumulate savings in DC plans because they have, on average, lower incomes.[107] For example, while women's plan participation

[106] *Ibid*. These results represent responses from households across income groups. The percentage of low-income households without emergency funds is likely larger.

[107] Income data from Census and others show large gender and racial wage gaps in the United States. For example, the Pew Research Center's analysis of 2015 Current Population Survey (CPS) data on full- and part-time U.S. workers shows that women earned 83 percent of men's median earnings, and that blacks earned 75 percent of whites' median hourly earnings. See Eileen Patten, *Racial, Gender Wage Gaps Persist in U.S. Despite Some Progress*, July 1, 2016, accessed Sept. 11, 2017, http://www.pewresearch.org/fact-

has improved relative to men, women continue to contribute to their DC plans at lower levels. As we have previously reported, among those reporting their DC plan contributions in dollar amounts, women's annual contributions were consistently around 30 percent lower than men's contributions between 1998 and 2009.[108]

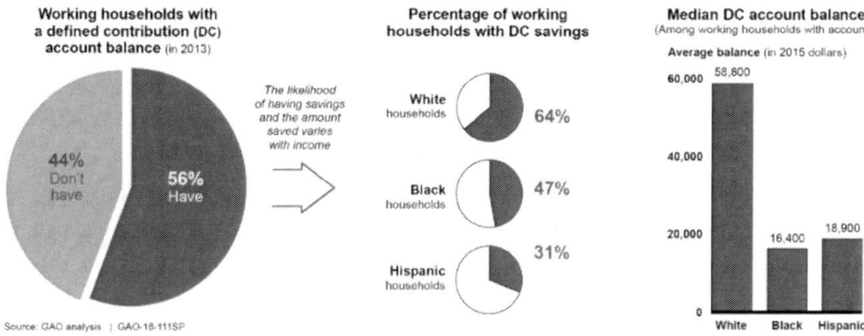

Note: Working households defined as households with at least one person working, but not self-employed, and the household head is age 25 through 64. All percentage estimates in this figure have 95 percent confidence intervals within +/- 3.8 percent. For more details see GAO-16-408.

Figure 2.8. Defined Contribution (DC) Plan Savings by Race/Ethnicity among Working Households, 2013.

Similarly, some minority households had median DC retirement savings that were less than a third of those of white households (see Figure 2.8). In addition, some minority households experienced declines in DC plan participation in the years following the 2007-2009 recession.[109] For

---

tank/2016/07/01/racial-gender-wage-gaps-persist-in-u-sdespite-some-progress/. Also, women and some minorities are like less likely, on average, to own homes, and as such, they are generally less able to draw on home equity in retirement. For example, another research group's analysis of 2011 SIPP data found large racial and ethnic minority disparities in homeownership rates—73 percent of white households owned homes compared to 47 percent of Hispanic and 45 percent of black households. See Demos and Institute on Assets and Social Policy, *The Racial Wealth Gap: Why Policy Matters* (New York: 2015).

[108] See GAO, *Retirement Security: Women Still Face Challenges,* GAO-12-699 (Washington, D.C.: July 19, 2012).

[109] For example, there was a decline in plan access for both Hispanic and black households, which may have been due to an increase in unemployment for both groups due to the 2007-2009 recession. See U.S. Bureau of Labor Statistics, *BLS Spotlight on Statistics: The Recession of 2007-2009* (February 2012).

example, the percentage of Hispanic working households with DC plan access decreased by 12 percentage points from an estimated 47 percent in 2007 to 35 percent in 2013, while the percentages of black and white working households remained unchanged.[110]

Federal Efforts to Encourage More Saving

As responsibility for saving for retirement has shifted increasingly to individuals, the federal government has taken various steps to support individuals' efforts to save more. Key tools used by the federal government to promote more saving are increased tax incentives, requirements for improved guidance from plan sponsors, various financial literacy initiatives, and efforts to encourage DC plan sponsors to adopt automatic mechanisms for workers to enroll and contribute to their plans.[111]

The federal government has taken various steps to increase tax incentives to encourage greater retirement savings. For example, under the Economic Growth and Tax Relief Reconciliation Act of 2001 (EGTRRA), limits for tax-advantaged contributions to employer-sponsored plans were increased. EGTRRA also included a so-called catch-up provision, allowing persons age 50 or older to make additional tax-deferred contributions, in excess of other applicable statutory limits, to 401(k) and similar DC plans.[112] The provision was intended to encourage older workers who had not previously been able to save sufficiently to make larger catch-up

---

[110] See GAO-16-408. The analysis in this prior report was based on the Survey of Consumer Finances (SCF), which does not provide data on Asian Americans as a separate group. However, using a different data set (SIPP), we have previously reported that Asian working men and women had higher DC plan participation rates compared to other races. See GAO-12-699.

[111] For previously issued GAO recommendations for executive action and matters for congressional consideration in this area see appendix IV.

[112] Pub. L. No. 107-16, § 631, 115 Stat. 38, 111-13 (codified as amended at 26 U.S.C. § 414(v)). This provision was designed to help workers with brief or intermittent work histories, such as nonworking spouses. The contribution limit for an employee who participates in a 401(k) plan, or similar DC plan, is $18,000. The catch-up contribution limit for an employee who is 50 years of age or older and who participate in a 401(k) plan, or similar DC plan, is $6,000. The contribution limit for IRAs is $5,500, while the catch-up contribution limit for those age 50 or older is $1,000. All contribution limits current as of 2017. For statutory annual contribution limits for 1974 through 2014, see GAO-15-16.

contributions in order to reach adequate levels of retirement savings.[113] However, in prior work analyzing data from the Survey of Consumer Finances (SCF), we found that over the past two decades, DC participants with high incomes and other assets benefited the most from increases to limits for tax-advantaged contributions.[114]

Federal law also allows individuals to defer taxes on retirement savings outside of employer sponsored plans, such as on contributions to IRAs and the income earned on IRA assets. To encourage saving for retirement for those without employer-sponsored plans, in 2001, EGTRRA also authorized creation of the Saver's Credit, which allows certain low- and middle-income individuals to receive a nonrefundable federal income tax credit of up to $2,000 for qualified retirement savings.[115] Subsequent research suggested that 60 to 67 percent of eligible taxpayers claimed the credit during the first couple of years it was available.[116] More recent Treasury data indicate that in 2014, over 8.4 million federal income tax filers claimed the credit on their tax returns. (The creation of *my*RA in 2014 was another federal effort to extend tax incentives for retirement savings to those without employer-sponsored retirement plans, as discussed earlier with respect to access.)

Another way that the federal government has tried to encourage more saving is through requiring improved reporting and disclosure information from plan sponsors. Multiple laws and regulations since 1974 have expanded the reporting and disclosure requirements regarding information that plan sponsors must provide participants. We previously identified

---

[113] EGTRRA provisions had been scheduled to expire on December 31, 2010. But, the Pension Protection Act of 2006 made permanent higher contributions for IRAs and DC plans, and catch-up contributions for workers age 50 or older that were included in EGTRRA.

[114] For example, in 2014 we reported that high-earning DC participants accounted for a larger share of those reaching or exceeding contribution limits, based on an analysis of 2010 SCF data on participant contributions. We estimated that 76 percent of participants who contributed at or above any of the 2010 contribution limits were in the top 10 percent of earners and 47 percent were in the top 5 percent. See GAO-14-334R, which was an update of a prior, more comprehensive report on the same topic: GAO-11-333.

[115] A nonrefundable tax credit can reduce current-year tax liability to zero, whereas a refundable credit in excess of tax liability results in a cash refund. Individuals can also claim the Saver's Credit for contributions to employer-sponsored retirement plans if they meet certain income eligibility requirements.

[116] For further details, see GAO-12-699.

more than 130 reports and disclosures stemming from ERISA provisions and the IRC.[117] For example, DC plan sponsors have been required to provide participants more information about fees and expenses. DB plan sponsors have been required to provide participants more information about the benefits they have accrued and the funded status of their plans.

However, all this information reflects the increased complexity of planning for retirement. As complexity increased, a number of federal agencies have also taken steps to improve financial literacy by supporting financial education in the workplace and financial literacy more broadly. In 2014, we reported that federal agencies had 12 significant financial literacy programs or activities underway.[118] For example, as early as 1995, DOL established a Retirement Savings Education Campaign and developed tools and materials to help workers plan how much they need to save for retirement. In 2003, the Financial Literacy and Education Commission (FLEC) was established, chaired by the Secretary of the Treasury and comprised of DOL and 21 other federal entities as of 2016, with a vision to enhance financial literacy, financial capability, and individual financial well-being, including planning for longevity and long-term financial security. As part of its initiative on financial inclusion, Treasury has worked with FLEC to update thc National Strategy for Financial Literacy.[119] The Consumer Financial Protection Bureau (CFPB) also has a broad mandate to help educate individuals on basic financial literacy, by helping consumers navigate their financial choices across different life phases, including retirement.[120] For example, CFPB offers financial

[117] GAO-14-92.

[118] GAO, *Financial Literacy: Overview of Federal Activities, Programs, and Challenges*, GAO-14-556T (Washington, D.C.: Apr. 30, 2014).

[119] In 2011, FLEC issued "Promoting Financial Success in the United States: National Strategy for Financial Literacy," which outlined several goals for improving individuals' financial literacy and financial well-being. FLEC updated the National Strategy in 2016. Additionally, in September 2016, Treasury co-hosted a Financial Security Research Symposium which highlighted research and identified policy implications on a range of issues relating to Americans' financial security and retirement readiness, including an understanding of Social Security, workplace savings and other assets.

[120] CFPB was created after the 2007-2009 recession and regulates the offering and provision of consumer financial products or services under federal consumer financial laws. CFPB also works to protect older adults from predatory practices by financial advisers. Before its creation, these responsibilities were divided across multiple agencies. For more on the

educational programs and tools, such as a retirement planning webinar to help with complicated decisions about retirement. GAO also has facilitated knowledge transfer among key players in the arena of financial literacy, including through Comptroller General forums in 2004 and 2011.[121] While all these efforts have striven to help individuals better plan and manage their retirement savings, some agency officials have noted that the programs are disjointed and it is unclear which approaches are most effective.

Yet another way that the federal government has promoted individual retirement saving is through changes in the law that encourage DC plan sponsors to adopt default plan features, such as automatic enrollment.[122] For example, in 2006, Congress amended the IRC and ERISA through the PPA to provide a safe harbor for sponsors implementing automatic enrollment in DC plans.[123] DC plan sponsors that adopt this safe harbor automatic enrollment plan feature for plan participants must use auto-escalation to increase employee contributions until a pre-set maximum of six percent is reached, unless a participant elects a higher deferral rate.[124] In 2009, Treasury announced further IRS actions to promote automatic enrollment by providing sample plan language for sponsors to adopt or use in drafting individualized plan amendments concerning autoenrollment.[125] More recently, the IRS took additional steps to encourage the adoption of auto-enrollment by providing new procedures that reduce penalties for

---

CFPB, see GAO, *Consumer Financial Protection Bureau: Observations from Small Business Review Panels*, GAO-16-647 (Washington, D.C.: Aug. 10, 2016).

[121] See GAO, *Highlights of a GAO Forum: The Federal Government's Role in Improving Financial Literacy*, GAO-05-93SP (Washington, D.C.: Nov. 15, 2004); and *Highlights of a Forum: Financial Literacy: Strengthening Partnerships in Challenging Times*, GAO-12-299SP (Washington, D.C.: Feb. 9, 2012).

[122] As noted earlier, default plan features such as auto-enrollment are intended to increase individual participation by defaulting eligible participants into employer-sponsored plans, while plan features such as auto-escalation aim to increase plan savings by automatically increasing participant contribution rates over time.

[123] See Pension Protection Act of 2006, Pub. L. No. 109-280, § 902, 120 Stat. 780, 1033- 40; see also 26 U.S.C. § 401(k)(13).

[124] Under this safe harbor design, the minimum elective contribution starts at 3 percent of the participant's salary, unless the participant elects an alternative amount. The minimum elective contribution increases to 4 percent, 5 percent, and 6 percent in subsequent years.

[125] Internal Revenue Service, *Adding Automatic Enrollment to Section 401(k) Plans – Sample Amendments*, Notice 2009-65 (Washington, D.C.: Sept. 28, 2009).

employer errors related to the implementation of automatic contributions.[126]

Challenge 3. Ensuring Financial Resources throughout Retirement

As individuals enter retirement, they face the challenge of ensuring that their accumulated resources last throughout retirement, whatever their mix of resources might be. Most workers will have Social Security available to them in retirement and will need to decide when to start claiming their benefits (see text box).[127] For many, Social Security will be their primary source of retirement income, with continued work often their only option to have additional income in retirement. Others who have been able to accumulate resources in employer-sponsored retirement plans or on their own during their working years face a different set of challenges, depending on the type and extent of resources accumulated. For example, those with DC accounts must determine how best to manage and spend down their funds over their remaining lifetime. In contrast, those with lifetime annuities from DB plans may face concerns about the financial health of their plans or plan sponsors; or, if they are offered and accept a lump-sum payment in place of a lifetime annuity, they may face similar concerns as those with DC accounts about how best to manage and spend down their funds. Federal efforts to help individuals deal with these challenges have focused on educating individuals on when to claim Social Security, and placing requirements on private sector plan sponsors to provide better information to guide participants in their decision making at and during retirement.

---

[126] Internal Revenue Service, *Revenue Procedure 2015-28* (Washington, D.C.: Apr. 2, 2015).

[127] Social Security covers about 96 percent of all U.S. workers. Nearly all of the rest are certain state and local government employees, and some federal employees who do not pay Social Security taxes on the earnings from their government jobs and will not receive Social Security when they retire. See GAO-16-75SP.

Deciding When to Claim Social Security

Many individuals face a complex challenge when deciding at what age to file for Social Security, and many are unclear on key program rules and details. For example, individuals may be unclear on how Social Security's claiming age affects the amount of monthly benefits, how earnings (both before and after claiming) affect benefits, the availability of spousal benefits, and other factors that may influence their claiming decision. This information is central to individuals' ability to make informed decisions about when to claim Social Security benefits because such decisions often concern tradeoffs between claiming benefits earlier versus waiting to claim later to increase the amount of the monthly benefit they receive.

While the Social Security Administration (SSA) defines full retirement age as the age at which an individual is entitled to unreduced benefits, individuals who choose to delay claiming beyond their full retirement age receive credits, until age 70, that increase their benefit amount. For those born in 1943 or later, these credits amount to 8 percent a year. Those individuals who elect to claim Social Security benefits earlier than full retirement age, at age 62, will receive a smaller monthly payment throughout their retirement compared to what they would receive if they waited to claim benefits until reaching full retirement age. Despite higher monthly benefits for those who delay, many people still claim Social Security retirement benefits at age 62, the earliest age of eligibility. According to SSA, for men and women born in 1945, 42 percent of eligible men and 48 percent of eligible women claimed benefits at age 62.

Source: GAO. | GAO-18-111SP.

Note: For further discussion of this topic, see GAO, *Social Security: Improvements to Claims Process Could Help People Make Better Informed Decisions about Retirement Benefits*, GAO-16-786 (Washington, D.C.: Sept. 14, 2016); and *Retirement Security: Challenges for Those Claiming Social Security Benefits Early and New Health Coverage Options*, GAO-14-311 (Washington, D.C.: Apr. 23, 2014).

Many Will Have to Rely Primarily on Social Security

At some point during their retirement, many individuals without adequate retirement savings will likely have to rely primarily on Social Security. This includes individuals who have not been able to save in an employer-sponsored plan or other retirement savings vehicles, such as an IRA, as well as those with DC plans whose account balances are low at retirement. In addition, certain groups, including women and minorities, are likely to rely more on Social Security than others.

Those individuals who worked all or most of their careers for employers that did not sponsor a retirement plan are most likely to have low levels of retirement savings and be dependent on Social Security. Social Security benefits are calculated using a progressive formula which replaces a greater percentage of earnings for lower earners than for higher earners. As a result, for example, retired workers with relatively lower average career earnings receive monthly benefits that, on average, equal about 50 percent of what they made while working, while workers with relatively higher career earnings receive benefits that equal about 30 percent of prior earnings.[128] In a 2015 report, our analysis of 2013 SCF data found that 27 percent of households age 65 through 74 had no DB plan or retirement savings (such as from DC plans or IRAs).[129] Our analysis found that about 41 percent of households in this age range rely on Social Security for over half their income; while 14 percent rely on Social Security for more than 90 percent of their income. According to Census data, about 43 percent of people age 65 or older would have incomes below the poverty line if they did not receive Social Security.[130] The most recent data available from SSA indicate that in 2014, the poverty rate among those age 65 or older was 7.3 percent if a Social Security recipient, but 22.2 percent if not a recipient.[131]

---

[128] This example is based on hypothetical workers born in 1985 and retiring at age 65 in 2050. The career-average level of earnings for each hypothetical worker was based on a percentage of Social Security's national average wage index. The low and higher earners had earnings about 45 percent and 160 percent of the national average wage index ($21,054 and $74,859, respectively, for 2014). See GAO-16-75SP.

[129] GAO-15-419.

[130] U.S. Census Bureau, "Impact on Poverty of Alternative Resource Measures by Age: 1981 to 2013," *Current Population Survey, Annual Social and Economic Supplements* (Sept. 16, 2014).

[131] Social Security Administration, *Income of the Population 55 or Older, 2014,* SSA Publication No. 13-11871 (Washington, D.C.: April 2016).

Those retiring with DC plan accounts may also face risks in retirement, particularly those who have small balances in their accounts.[132] Low-income individuals are the most at risk of having low levels of retirement savings. In a 2016 report, our analysis of 2013 SCF data found that 25 percent of working, low-income households had savings in a DC account compared to 81 percent of working, high-income households.[133] More recent data from the 2016 SCF show that the median retirement account balance for those in the lowest income quintile was $7,800, and for the next lowest income quintile the median account balance was $17,000.[134] This suggests that many of these households would likely need to depend primarily on Social Security in retirement.[135] In addition, individuals from low-income groups often experience less stable employment, which may ultimately translate into a smaller Social Security benefit, when compared to individuals who have experienced consistent employment.

Those with little or no retirement savings may decide to work longer to delay or supplement their Social Security benefits. In a 2015 report, we found that labor force participation among workers age 55 or older had increased during the last decade.[136] We also found that, compared to current retirees, workers age 55 or older were more likely to expect to retire later and to work during retirement. More specifically, surveys indicate that workers age 55 or older generally plan to retire at an older age and work more in retirement than current retirees actually did. However, these expectations for retiring later may prove unrealistic or may not come to fruition for a variety of reasons, such as declining health or barriers in the workplace.[137] In such cases, workers may find their retirement security

---

[132] See earlier figure 2.1 for an overview of the sources of income for households age 65 or older.

[133] GAO-16-408.

[134] Board of Governors of the Federal Reserve System, *2016 SCF Chartbook*.

[135] GAO-16-408. Our findings were based on an analysis of 2013 Survey of Consumer Finance data.

[136] GAO-15-419. Also, in an earlier report, we found that older workers' labor force participation had continued to increase despite the worst labor market in decades. See GAO, *Unemployed Older Workers: Many Experience Challenges Regaining Employment and Face Reduced Retirement Security,* GAO-12-445 (Washington, D.C.: Apr. 25, 2012).

[137] Our prior work identified a number of possible barriers to older workers staying in or rejoining the workforce. For example, a decade ago, participants in a GAO forum noted that, in their view, employers' perceptions about the cost of hiring and retaining older workers, age discrimination, and legal and regulatory requirements can be key obstacles to

at risk, since they may have fewer years to work and save for retirement than they had planned on working.

Certain groups, such as women, may be particularly vulnerable as they enter retirement. Women age 65 or older have less retirement income, on average, and higher rates of poverty than men in this age group, and were nearly twice as likely to be living in poverty as men. In prior work, we found that women—especially widows and those age 80 or older— depend on Social Security benefits for a larger percentage of their income than men.[138]

Similarly, as noted earlier, we found that some minority households face challenges in retirement and are likely to depend on Social Security for a larger percentage of their income than white households.[139] For example, the median DC account balances of the estimated 47 percent of black households and 31 percent of Hispanic households that had DC accounts in 2013 were less than one third as much as white households.[140] Even after accounting for Social Security benefits, some minority groups were more likely to live in poverty compared with whites. As we reported in 2015, poverty rates for black and Hispanic older adults were 18 and 20 percent, respectively, compared to 8 percent for whites.

Moreover, some groups may receive only a small Social Security monthly benefit, depending on their work history or access to spousal benefits. For example, the SSA data indicate that in 2014, the poverty rate among those age 65 or older was 5.0 percent if married, but 16.4 percent if

---

older workers' continued employment. See GAO, *Highlight's of a GAO Forum: Engaging and Retaining Older Workers,* GAO-07-438SP (Washington, D.C.: Feb. 28, 2007). More recently, our work found that perceived employer reluctance to hire older workers has been a continuing challenge faced by older workers in finding reemployment. Once laid off, older workers were unemployed for much longer periods and if they were rehired, it was often at significantly lower pay. See GAO-12-445.

[138] We found that, compared with men, women who were divorced or separated after age 50 experienced detrimental effects on their total household assets and income. Women's income fell by 41 percent, nearly twice that of men's (23 percent). In addition, the effects of widowhood were more pronounced for women than for men. For example, while men's income fell 22 percent after becoming widowers, women's income after becoming widows fell by 37 percent. See GAO-12-699.

[139] GAO-16-408.

[140] See earlier figure 2.8 for DC plan savings for working households by race and ethnicity. See GAO-16-408.

not married. Another reason Social Security recipients can have incomes below the poverty threshold is due to reductions (referred to as offsets) to their benefits for various types of debts owed the federal government.[141]

Those with Significant Resources Also Face Challenges

Individuals who have been able to accumulate substantial resources in employer-sponsored retirement plans, or on their own in an IRA, also may face challenges making their resources last through their retirement.[142] The nature of those challenges varies based on the type and extent of resources accumulated.

DC Plan Retirees

Individuals retiring with significant retirement savings in DC plans face a series of complex decisions about how best to draw down their accumulated assets so that they do not risk outliving their savings. However, our prior work has found that participants often receive plan disclosures that can be difficult to understand, which may hinder participants' ability to assess how much income their DC savings will provide in retirement.[143] In addition, DC plan retirees may face difficulties because most DC plans do not provide options that can help them draw down their retirement funds in a systematic way.[144] DC plan retirees may also be encouraged to roll over their accounts into an IRA, which may or may not be in their best interest, depending on individual circumstances.

---

[141] In particular, there is a growing number of older Americans who have defaulted on their student loan debt and are having their Social Security benefits offset or reduced to repay their loans. In a 2017 report, we found that retirees with student loan debt who are subject to Social Security offsets increasingly receive benefits below the federal poverty guideline because the threshold to protect benefits—implemented by regulation in 1998— is not adjusted for increases in the cost of living. While this was a small group of people at the time, the rapid increase in student loans and defaults among older Americans suggested that this could become a greater problem in the future. See GAO, *Social Security Offsets: Improvements to Program Design Could Better Assist Older Student Loan Borrowers with Obtaining Permitted Relief*, GAO-17-45 (Washington, D.C.: Dec. 19, 2016).

[142] In addition to any retirement accounts and any accrued benefits, if available, individuals may also use personal savings, investments and the value of their home as assets to draw down in retirement.

[143] GAO-14-92.

[144] GAO-16-433.

Table 2. External Risk Factors Affecting Individuals' Financial Security in Retirement

Risk factor	Description
Inability to continue working	Individuals face the risk that unemployment later in their careers may lead them to stop saving for retirement earlier than planned, draw down retirement savings early, and compel some to claim Social Security benefits early. For example, individuals who experience unemployment later in their careers may find it difficult to find a new job. Those who experience health issues may also find it difficult to continue working. Long-term underemployment can have a similar effect, causing individuals to take money out of savings or retirement funds to pay bills.
Poor investment returns	DC plan participants face the risk that poor investment returns will lead to lower than expected savings during both their working and retirement years. Additionally, relatively poor investment returns just prior to or just after retirement can substantially affect how long their savings will last. This is known as sequence of returns risk, and it can have a serious effect on retired participants who have less ability to make up for lost savings through increased DC plan contributions or longer employment. Lack of investment knowledge can compound these issues.
Unexpected costs	Individuals face the risk that rising and unpredictable health care or long-term care costs may lead them to draw down retirement savings faster than expected.
Inflation	Individuals face the risk that even modest inflation could erode the purchasing power of retirement income and savings over the course of an extended retirement.
Diminished capacity	Individuals face the risk that cognitive decline may affect their ability to manage their savings, especially later in retirement
Longevity risk	Individuals face the risk that they may live beyond their life expectancy[a] , and exhaust their retirement assets. Longevity risk can also be thought of as including the overarching risk that the longer an individual lives in retirement, the greater the risk. For example, increased longevity can mean there is a greater range of potential future investment outcomes and a longer period over which inflation may erode the purchasing power of available savings.

Source: GAO. | GAO-18-111SP.

Note: For further discussion of these risks, see GAO-12-445 and GAO-16-433.

[a] Longevity risk is a concept distinct from life expectancy. Life expectancy is a particular longevity statistic that measures how long a particular population of people might expect to live on average; individuals within the population may live longer or shorter lives than this average life expectancy.

In previous reports, we have found that DC plan participants may face challenges managing their resources through retirement because they may lack basic account information, have difficulty understanding complex account information, and have limited or no access to plan advisors.[145]

[145] GAO-14-92 and GAO-16-433.

Researchers we interviewed commented that without access to an advisor, participants tend to overestimate their ability to generate investment returns and underestimate their longevity risk.[146] Many people do not understand their life expectancy, the number of years they might spend in retirement, or the amount they should save for retirement. For example, a survey conducted by the Society of Actuaries showed that there is a greater tendency for retired respondents to underestimate rather than overestimate their life expectancy.[147] Further, participants may not fully understand longevity risk—that is, the possibility that they could live well beyond their life expectancy. To ensure that their funds last through retirement, DC plan participants must identify longevity risks, among other risks (see Table 2), and strive to allocate the use of their assets accordingly.

DC plan retirees may face additional challenges if their plans have not adopted financial products–such as lifetime income options–to help them draw down their accumulated assets over time. These products can reduce the difficulties and uncertainties of managing an investment portfolio as a retiree ages. In a 2014 survey, we found that many plans did not provide such products.[148] However, agency officials noted that, since then, qualified longevity annuity contracts (QLACs) have become increasingly available as a hedge against longevity risk.[149]

---

[146] One researcher we spoke with warned that participants tend to look to potentially misleading regulatory cues to inform retirement planning decisions. For example, the researcher commented that participants might interpret statutory provisions providing that the tax penalty on premature 401(k) distributions cease at age 591/2 as a signal to start drawing down their savings at this age, even if they would be better served by staying invested in their plan until a later date. For more information, see GAO-16-433.

[147] However, people with lower incomes can expect to live fewer years as they approach retirement than those with higher incomes, on average, according to studies we reviewed in a prior report. For more information, see GAO-16-354.

[148] We conducted a non-generalizable survey of 11 401(k) plan record keepers in December 2014, and found that most of the plans surveyed had not adopted products and services that could help participants turn their savings into an income stream to last through retirement (referred to as a lifetime income option). Plan record keepers that responded to our survey accounted for approximately 42 percent of the 401(k) plan market as measured by plan assets, 46 percent as measured by participants, and 26 percent as measured by the number of plans, as of December 2014. For more details, see GAO-16-433.

[149] In 2014, IRS finalized a rule allowing for the use of QLACs in certain tax-qualified defined contribution plans including 401(k) plans. See Longevity Annuity Contracts, 79 Fed. Reg. 37,633 (July 2, 2014). Under the regulations, minimum distribution requirements do not

Lifetime income options: products or services that can turn participant savings into a retirement income stream for the rest of a participant's life.

Annuity: provides a payment for life; with payments distributed at a determined and fixed interval, such as monthly.

Source: GAO (see glossary). | GAO-18-111SP.

In addition, although access to lifetime income products may not be facilitated by their plans, DC plan participants still have the option of purchasing an annuity from an insurance provider on their own with all or a portion of their account. However, they generally must make the purchase on the retail market and may find the cost of the annuity expensive for the amount of the monthly benefit received.[150] Some experts we spoke with also noted that there is commonly a psychological hurdle involved in the decision to exchange a large payment today for an unknown number of small monthly payments in the future. DC plan participants may be reluctant to purchase annuities because the funds would no longer be available to cover large unplanned expenses (like a health emergency), would not be available as a bequest to heirs without an additional fee, or because the monthly benefit could lose value over time if it does not include inflation protection.

Required minimum distribution: participants age 701/2 or older who have defined contribution plans or individual retirement accounts must receive minimum annual payments from their plan savings based on their account balance and remaining life expectancy.

Source: GAO (see glossary). | GAO-18-111SP.

DC plan retirees who remain in their plans beyond age 701/2 are subject to required minimum distribution provisions—that is, under the IRC, an automatic annual payment must be made to these retirees.[151] (See

apply to the assets used to purchase a QLAC until payments begin, which can be as late as age 85.

[150] See GAO, *Retirement Income: Ensuring Income throughout Retirement Requires Difficult Choices,* GAO-11-400 (Washington, D.C.: June 7, 2011).

[151] See 26 U.S.C. § 401(a)(9)(A), (C).

Figure 2.9.) However, some plan sponsors adopt methods to meet the provisions that may not be in the retirees' best interests. In our prior work, we found that plan sponsors have several ways to meet relevant required minimum distribution provisions.[152] For example, plan sponsors can issue a minimum annual payment based on the retiree's account balance and life expectancy, which may approximate a systematic withdrawal option. Alternatively, plan sponsors can offer a retiree the option of a lump-sum withdrawal of the entire account balance, which would also allow a plan sponsor to meet these requirements. Industry research has shown that many plans do not allow retired participants to take partial withdrawals; instead, retirees generally must either withdraw their entire account balance or forgo withdrawing any funds.[153] Further, according to a record keeper we spoke to, some plans may require participants to take lump-sum distributions of their entire account balance before reaching age 701/2 to avoid the plan having to administer the minimum distribution requirements.[154] However, none of these alternative practices help to provide participants with lifetime retirement income.

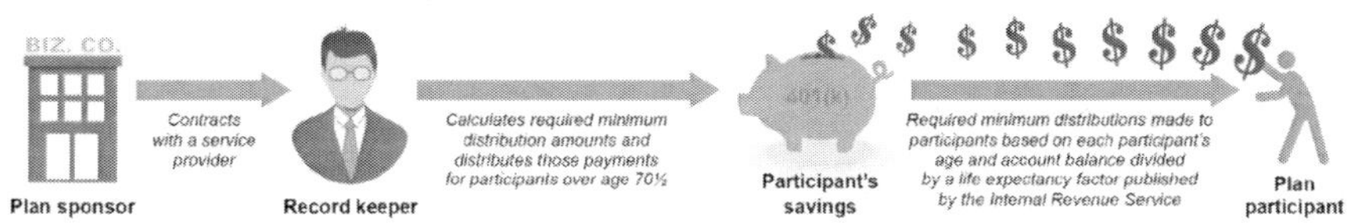

Source: GAO. | GAO-18-111SP.

Note: Based on analysis of agency and industry documents and stakeholder interviews. For more details, see GAO-16-433.

Figure 2.9. Plan Administration of Required Minimum Distributions for 401(k) Plans.

---

[152] GAO-16-433.

[153] According to a 2015 study by Vanguard, 87 percent of plans for which they serve as record keeper require terminated participants to take a distribution of their entire account balance if a partial distribution is desired. The same study reported that fewer than 1 in 5 retired participants remain in their plan 5 years after they left their employer and cited the influence of plan rules for partial distributions on participant behavior. Jean A. Young, *Retirement Distribution Decisions Among DC Participants—An update* (Vanguard, September 2015).

[154] One record keeper indicated that some plans impose a 701/2 and out rule; that is, they require participants to take a full lump-sum distribution by age 701/2 to avoid having to calculate and pay required minimum distributions to participants that could lead to errors resulting in legal liability and plan disqualification.

When retiring, DC plan participants also may be encouraged to roll over their accounts to IRAs, the same as when employees change jobs. As discussed earlier, this may or may not be in the participant's best interest for a variety of reasons, depending on an individual's circumstances, and may be due to poor advice and result in higher fees.[155]

DB Plan Retirees

Since DB plans generally provide a lifetime annuity, individuals who work all or most of their careers for employers that sponsor DB plans may be, for the most part, less vulnerable to longevity risk. But they, too, may still face challenges in certain situations. For example, some DB plan participants may be offered a lump-sum payment in exchange for their annuity and, if taken, would need to be managed the same as DC account balances and IRAs. However, annuity benefits are dependent on the continued financial health of the plan and its sponsor. If a participant's former employer encounters financial difficulties and fails to adequately fund the plan, benefits could be at risk of being reduced, despite the protection provided by PBGC. Although both of these scenarios have been relatively uncommon in the past, they can pose challenges to DB participants when they occur, and may be more prevalent in the future.[156] Finally, like DC plan participants, DB plan participants may find plan disclosures complex and difficult to understand, which may lead participants to be unclear on the value of the benefit when making decisions about how to manage their sources of retirement income.

---

[155] For more details, see earlier discussion in the previous challenge and GAO-13-30.

[156] For example, the amount of DB benefits guaranteed by PBGC could change in the future if the agency's financial difficulties are not addressed. PBGC's financial future remains uncertain, due in large part to a long-term decline in the number of traditional DB plans and the collective financial risk of underfunded pension plans that PBGC insures (especially the risk related to a few very large plans, according to PBGC officials) . GAO designated PBGC's single-employer program as high risk in July 2003 and added the multiemployer program in January 2009. For more information on PBGC's financial challenges see section 3.

Lump-Sum Payments

> ***Lump sum*:** one immediate payment based on the estimated present value of the participant's lifetime benefit.
>
> Source: GAO (see glossary). | GAO-18-111SP.

One potential challenge for some DB plan participants occurs if they are offered a lump-sum payment in exchange for their lifetime annuity. Some DB plans offer participants a lump-sum option, at retirement or termination of employment, as an ongoing plan feature. Some other plans may occasionally offer a one-time lump-sum option during a time-limited window period. In a 2015 report, we identified 22 plan sponsors who had made such lump-sum window offers to retirees in 2012, involving approximately 498,000 participants and resulting in lump-sum payouts totaling more than $9.25 billion.[157] We found that participants who accepted such offers potentially faced a reduction in their retirement assets and that key information provided about the offer was often unclear.[158] In addition, while participants who accept a lump-sum offer have the ability to control and manage the funds, they also take on the risks and challenges associated with that decision, the same as those with DC plans or IRAs. Partially in response to our 2015 report, Treasury limited such offers to only those participants who are not yet retired.[159] In other prior work, we

---

[157] See GAO, *Private Pensions: Participants Need Better Information When Offered Lump Sums That Replace Their Lifetime Benefits,* GAO-15-74 (Washington, D.C.: Jan. 27, 2015). In this report, we also noted that experts in the field of retirement pensions, including DOL's EAC, generally maintained that since 2012 an increasing number of sponsors had used lump-sum window offers to pay down plan liabilities. However, we found little public data were available on the number of DB plan sponsors that had offered lump-sum payments to replace participants' lifetime annuities.

[158] Our 2015 report identified eight key types of information that DB plan participants need when weighing their options and determining what is in their best interest when faced with a lump-sum offer. For further details see GAO-15-74.

[159] On July 9, 2015, IRS issued Notice 2015-49 indicating it intended to amend, effective the same day, the required minimum distribution regulations under 26 U.S.C. § 401(a)(9) to generally prohibit qualified defined benefit plans from replacing any form of annuity currently being paid with a lump-sum payment or other accelerated form of distribution. That is, plan sponsors would be limited to making lump-sum offers only to those participants who had not yet retired and were not yet receiving an annuity.

identified at least 38 companies that offered individuals lump-sum payments or "advances" in exchange for receiving part or all of the individual's pension payment streams.[160] Some companies targeted financially vulnerable consumers nationwide who had poor or bad credit. Our undercover investigators solicited lump-sum offers from these 38 companies, and found that the amounts of the offers received ranged from 46 to 77 percent of the amounts that would have to be paid if the lump-sum offers were subject to ERISA and IRC requirements (i.e., if they were lump-sum offers from private sector DB plans). Partially in response to our report, the Consumer Financial Protection Bureau (CFPB) and Federal Trade Commission (FTC) undertook consumer advisory and education efforts, and the CFPB undertook enforcement actions against two of the companies included in our review.

PBGC's Guarantees for Underfunded DB Plans

Another potential challenge for some DB plan participants occurs when their plans are underfunded, the employers sponsoring their plans face financial difficulties, and their retirement benefits become subject to the limits under PBGC's single-employer or multiemployer insurance programs.[161] PBGC was created under ERISA to serve as the insurer of promised DB plan benefits, up to certain legal limits, for participants in most private sector DB plans.[162] As of 2016, PBGC insured the pension

---

[160] See GAO, *Pension Advance Transactions: Questionable Business Practices Identified,* GAO-14-420 (Washington, D.C.: June 4, 2014); and *Pension Advance Transactions: Questionable Business Practices and the Federal Response,* GAO-15-846T (Washington, D.C.: Sept. 30, 2015).

[161] PBGC is also responsible for locating participants who may be owed benefits by a terminated DB plan, but whom the sponsor can no longer locate. While PBGC's program to locate missing participants is required for the DB plans PBGC insures, PBGC issued proposed regulations on Sept. 20, 2016, as authorized by PPA, to establish similar voluntary programs for plans beyond those that it insures, such as terminating DC plans. See Missing Participants, 81 Fed. Reg. 64,700 (Sept. 20, 2016) and Pub. L. No. 109-280, § 410, 120 Stat. 780, 934-35. The changes authorized by PPA will only become effective after PBGC implements final regulations. PBGC plans to have the expanded program operational in 2018.

[162] While PBGC insures most private sector DB pension plans, PBGC does not insure public sector DB plans, such as federal, state, and local/municipal government plans and military plans. Within the private sector, Congress has also defined exceptions, including DB pension plans associated with religious institutions (including hospitals and schools with

benefits of nearly 40 million U.S. workers and retirees who participate in nearly 24,000 private sector DB plans. For those participating in single-employer DB plans, if the sponsoring employer is unable to fund its plan because, for example, the company is going out of business, PBGC may assume trusteeship of the plan. For those participating in a multiemployer DB plan, if the plan is nearing insolvency PBGC may provide financial assistance to keep the plan operational. But should either of these events occur, a participant's benefits would be subject to the guarantee limits specified by law, which can be an amount considerably less than the benefit amount promised by the plan (see text box).

As of 2016, of the 40 million participants in DB pension plans insured by PBGC, 1.5 million (less than 4 percent) were in plans that had been in financial distress and were subject to PBGC guarantees (either in a single-employer plan taken over by PBGC, or a multiemployer plan receiving PBGC assistance). Even among these 1.5 million participants, most did not experience benefit reductions. According to studies conducted by PBGC, when PBGC takes over a single-employer plan due to the employer's financial distress, most participants still receive the full amount of the benefits they have earned under the plan (see text box). Nevertheless, for those affected, an unexpected benefit reduction can result in a participant having to make painful financial adjustments in retirement.

The increase in financial distress among multiemployer plans has become concerning for many more participants. In its 2016 annual report, PBGC estimated that plans covering about 10 to 15 percent of the participants insured by its multiemployer insurance program are at risk of running out of money over the next 20 years, and PBGC's benefit guarantee under the multiemployer program is much lower than under the single-employer program.[163]

---

religious affiliation) and plans for small professional practices (a doctor, lawyer, or other professional groups with fewer than 25 employees).

[163] For further discussion of the multiemployer insurance program, see GAO, *Private Pensions: Timely Action Needed to Address Impending Multiemployer Plan Insolvencies,* GAO-13-240 (Washington, D.C.: Mar. 28, 2013).

PBGC's Two Insurance Programs

- *Single-Employer Insurance Program*: The larger of the two programs, as of 2016, this program protects about 29.8 million workers and retirees in about 22,300 pension plans. When an underfunded single-employer plan terminates and the sponsor is unable to fund all promised benefits (either as a distress termination or an involuntary termination) PBGC takes over the plan's assets, administration, and payment of plan benefits. In such circumstances, participants' benefits may be reduced based on the guaranteed limits, which are set by law and automatically adjusted yearly, unless there are sufficient plan assets available to pay more than those limits. For plans that ended (or whose sponsors entered bankruptcy) in 2017, the maximum guarantee set by law for workers who retire at age 65 is $64,432 yearly ($5,369.33 monthly).[a] Single-employer plans can also end in a standard termination, which occurs when the sponsoring employer decides that it no longer wishes to operate the plan, provided the plan has enough money to pay all benefits owed to participants, among other things.[b]
- *Multiemployer Insurance Program*: A much smaller program than the single-employer program, as of 2016, this program protected about 10.6 million workers and retirees in about 1,400 pension plans. When multiemployer plans are nearing insolvency, PBGC provides financial assistance and offers technical assistance to multiemployer plan administrators, service providers and other stakeholders to keep the plan in operation. As with the single-employer program, PBGC's benefit guarantee for a multiemployer plan participant is set by law. However, it is not adjusted on a yearly basis, is generally less than 100 percent of a participant's accrued benefit, and is considerably less than in the single-employer program. For example, since 2000, the maximum guarantee for a person who had 30 years of service has been $12,870 yearly ($1,072.50 monthly).[c]

Source: Pension Benefit Guaranty Corporation (PBGC) documents. | GAO-18-111SP.

[a] The maximum guarantee is lower for those who retire before age 65 or when there is a benefit for a survivor. The guarantee is increased for those who retire after age 65.

[b] In a standard termination, PBGC reviews the termination to make sure that the plan administrator follows all required steps to ensure proper notification to workers and retirees and proper arrangements for payment, but PBGC does not become

responsible for benefit payments; instead, a group annuity contract is purchased from an insurance company, which becomes responsible for benefit payments.

[c] The maximum guarantee is lower for participants who worked fewer than 30 years and higher for those who worked more than 30 years. Prior to 2000, the maximum benefit for participants with 30 years' work was $5,850 yearly, set in 1980.

PBGC Studies on Impacts of Benefit Limitations

PBGC does not systematically track the number of participants affected by guaranteed benefit limits or how much these limits affect benefit amounts; however, PBGC has periodically conducted studies on the impact of these limitations. For example:

- In 1999, and again in 2008, PBGC analyzed a sample of single-employer plans that had been terminated and taken over by PBGC. In both studies, PBGC found that the vast majority of participants received 100 percent of the benefits they had earned under their plans.
- In the 1999 study of 22 plans, 5.5 percent of the 90,000 participants were adversely affected by the limits.
- In the 2008 study of 125 plans, 15.9 percent of the 525,700 participants were adversely affected by the limits.
- See PBGC, *PBGC's Guarantee Limits—an Update* (Washington, D.C.: Sept. 2008).
- According to PBGC officials, another study of the impact of single-employer limits is also currently underway.
- More recently, in 2015, PBGC issued a study on the impact of guarantee limits on 109 multiemployer plans that had become insolvent as of the end of fiscal year 2013. Almost half of the participants in these plans were excluded from the study due to insufficient data, but of the 78,557 participants with sufficient data to be included, the study found that 21 percent had been or would be adversely affected by the limits. The study also projected that the impact of limits would increase substantially, up to 51 percent, for participants in multiemployer plans that become insolvent in the future. See PBGC, *PBGC's Multiemployer Guarantee* (Washington, D.C.: Mar. 2015).

Source: Pension Benefit Guaranty Corporation (PBGC) sources, as cited above. | GAO-18-111SP.

Further, PBGC's report noted that insolvency of PBGC's multiemployer insurance program is projected as likely by 2025, which would affect not only the retirement benefits of those in these at-risk plans, but all participants in multiemployer plans that are currently receiving financial assistance from PBGC.[164]

Federal Efforts to Help Individuals Manage Their Finances through Retirement

Federal efforts to help individuals manage their finances through retirement have focused primarily on providing information and tools to help individuals decide when to claim Social Security, and on placing additional requirements on private sector plan sponsors to provide individuals with more complete, clear, and objective information to guide their decision-making at and during retirement.[165] For example, SSA provides comprehensive written information to help people decide when to claim retirement benefits. This information includes details on how claiming age affects monthly benefit amounts, how benefits are determined, details on spousal and survivors benefits, the retirement earnings test, information about life expectancy and longevity risk, and the taxation of benefits.[166] The agency makes this information available through its website, publications on various topics (available in electronic and paper form), interactive tools such as online calculators, and a

---

[164] Pension Benefit Guaranty Corporation, *Annual Report 2016* (Washington, D.C.: Nov. 15, 2016). GAO designated PBGC's single-employer program as high risk in July 2003, and added the multi-employer program in January 2009. See GAO, *High-Risk Series: Progress on Many High-Risk Areas, While Substantial Efforts Needed on Others,* GAO-17-317 (Washington, D.C.: Feb. 15, 2017). For further information of the fiscal risks faced by PBGC, see section 3.

[165] GAO-16-786. For previously issued GAO recommendations for executive action and matters for congressional consideration in this area see appendix IV.

[166] Individuals who claim benefits before their full retirement age, but continue to work for pay face a retirement earnings test, with earnings above a certain limit resulting in a temporary reduction of monthly benefits. Benefits withheld under the earnings test are not forfeited, but are instead deferred, and are, on average, paid back at a later time with interest. When a beneficiary reaches full retirement age, SSA recomputes the benefit level for future months, permanently removing such portion of the original early-retirement reduction as corresponds to the number of months in which any part of the benefit was withheld due to the earnings test. See GAO-16-786.

personalized benefit statement mailed to individuals and made available online.

Nevertheless, we have found previously that most individuals do not understand important rules and details about when to claim Social Security that could affect their retirement benefits or the benefits of their spouses and survivors. In addition, we have found that Social Security claims specialists did not consistently provide key information to potential claimants, or ensure individuals were aware of such information when they applied for benefits.[167]

Other federal efforts to help individuals better manage their retirement have focused on the information provided by private sector plan sponsors. Changes in the law have encouraged or required both DC and DB plan sponsors to provide more complete, clear, and objective information to guide plan participants in their decision-making at and during retirement. For example, in April 2016, DOL promulgated regulations describing the kinds of communications that would constitute investment advice and the types of relationships in which such communications give rise to fiduciary responsibilities.[168] Also, since 2006, DB plans have been required to provide plan participants with annual funding notices so that they can be better informed about the financial status of their plans.

Section 3. U.S. Retirement System Is Threatened by Fiscal Risks and Benefit Adequacy Concerns

Fiscal exposures: responsibilities, programs, and activities that may legally commit or create expectations for future federal spending based on current policy, past practices, or other factors.

Source: GAO (see glossary). | GAO-18-111SP.

---

[167] Observation based on a nongeneralizable sample of 30 face-to-face claims interviews at 7 SSA field offices. For more information see GAO-16-786.

[168] In February 2017, the President issued a memo asking DOL to postpone the fiduciary rule's implementation while DOL determines whether the rule may adversely affect the ability of Americans to gain access to retirement information and financial advice. In May 2017, DOL announced a temporary enforcement policy related to the final rule, with a phased implementation period from June 2017 through January 2018, while it reviews the issues raised by the President's February 2017 memo.

The current retirement system in the United States may be unable to ensure adequate benefits for a growing number of Americans, in part due to the financial risks associated with certain federal programs. Current research suggests that all three main pillars of the system—Social Security, employer-sponsored retirement plans, and individual savings— face various risks and, if left unchanged, present significant potential fiscal exposures for the federal government.[169] The Social Security Old-Age and Survivors Insurance (OASI) program (Social Security's retirement program), together with Social Security's Disability Insurance program and Medicare, are key contributors to an unsustainable fiscal path for the federal government (see Figure 3.1). In addition, employer-sponsored retirement plans provide less assurance of an adequate income in retirement with the decline of private sector DB plans, growing risks facing PBGC, and the low amount of savings that many have in their DC accounts. Outside of employer-sponsored plans and IRAs, individuals' savings are often low or nonexistent, which may further increase individuals' reliance on various safety net programs.

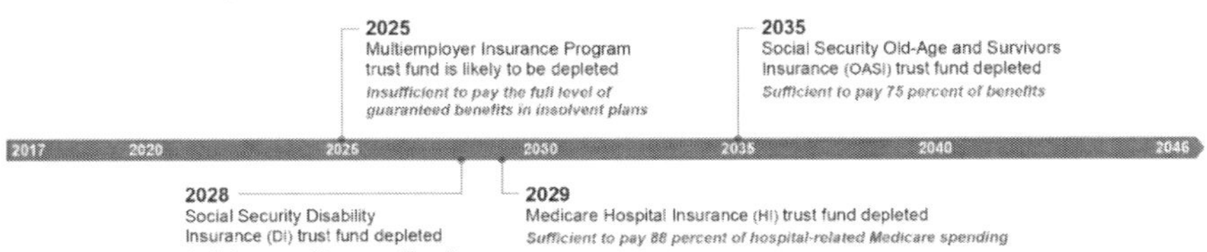

Source: GAO analysis of data from the Social Security Administration, the Centers for Medicare and Medicaid Services, and the Pension Benefit Guaranty Corporation. | GAO-18-111SP.

Figure 3.1. Timeline of Projected Fiscal Risks for Certain Federal Programs.

[169] Long-term fiscal projections show that, absent fiscal policy changes, the federal government is on an unsustainable path, largely due to spending increases driven by the growing gap between federal revenues and health care programs, demographic changes, and net interest on the public debt. For more information on the nation's fiscal exposure and fiscal health more generally, see GAO, *The Nation's Fiscal Health: Action Is Needed to Address the Federal Government's Fiscal Future,* GAO-17-237SP (Washington, D.C.: Jan. 17, 2017).

Social Security Retirement Program

The first pillar, Social Security, remains the bedrock of retirement security in the United States, helping to reduce poverty among beneficiaries, many of whom rely on Social Security for the majority of their income.

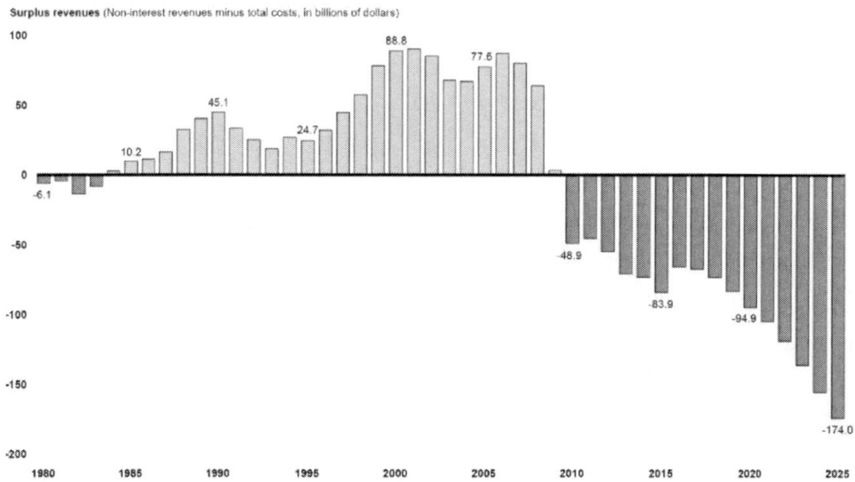

Source: GAO analysis of Social Security Administration data. | GAO-18-111SP.

Note: Non-interest revenues are revenues from payroll taxes, taxation of benefits, and reimbursements from the general fund of the Department of the Treasury. Total costs include benefit payments, administrative costs, and Railroad Retirement Board interchange costs. For more details, see GAO-16-354.

Figure 3.2. Trend in the Annual Net Cash Flow of Social Security's Combined Old-Age and Survivors Insurance and Disability Insurance Trust Funds, 1980-2025 (Projected).

But the Social Security retirement program is facing financial difficulties that, if not addressed, will affect its long-term stability. For many years Social Security's revenues for the retirement program have exceeded costs and the program has built up reserves in the trust fund. However, starting in 2010, this situation reversed as Social Security began paying out more in benefits than it received (see Figure 3.2).

If no changes are made, current projections indicate that by 2035, the retirement program trust fund will only be sufficient to pay 75 percent of scheduled benefits.[170] The escalating retirement of the baby-boom generation (individuals born between 1946 and 1964) and the general aging of the U.S. population are the primary drivers underlying Social Security's financial difficulties. For example, our analysis indicates that the number of baby boomers turning age 65 has been growing and is projected to grow further, from an average of over 9,000 per day in 2015 to more than 11,000 per day in 2029 (see Figure 3.3).

Other demographic changes also add to the strain on Social Security's finances. For example, life expectancy at age 65 has increased continually since the 1940s and is expected to continue to do so, although not equally for all groups.[171] Lower fertility rates compound the rise in Social Security's projected net costs by further increasing the portion of the population age 65 or older relative to the portion under age 65 who are contributing to the system.[172] In 2015, older adults (people age 65 or older) constituted 15 percent of the population, but by 2045, they are projected to account for an estimated 21 percent of the population. As a result of all these demographic changes, there will be fewer workers per retiree, increasing the gap between revenues and costs.

---

[170] The Board of Trustees, *The 2017 Annual Report of the Board of Trustees of the Federal Old-Age and Survivors Insurance and Federal Disability Insurance Trust Funds* (Washington, D.C.: July 13, 2017). Because the future is uncertain, the Trustees present several measures to illustrate and quantify the uncertainty inherent in these predictions. This projection is based on an intermediate set of assumptions that represent the Trustees' best estimate of the likely future course of the population and economy. For further discussion, see GAO-17-237SP and GAO-16-75SP.

[171] For more on disparities in life expectancy and the implications for retirement security, see GAO-16-354.

[172] Immigration has been a somewhat countervailing force to lower fertility rates, as immigration is projected to overtake births as the major driver of future population growth. See GAO, *GAO Strategic Plan: Serving the Congress and the Nation 2014-2019*, GAO-14-1SP (Washington, D.C.: Feb. 28, 2014), pp. 65-66. Also, research has found that immigrant families tend to have more children: Immigrant women have had higher birth rates than U.S.-born women since the 1970s. See G. Livingston, *Births Outside of Marriage Decline for Immigrant Women* (Pew Research Center, Oct. 26, 2016).

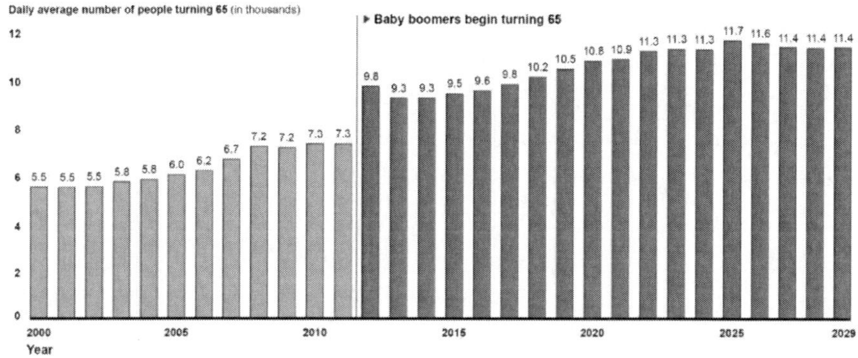

Source: GAO analysis of U.S. Census Bureau data. | GAO-18-111SP.

Note: Census data estimates of population are as of July 1 in each year. For baby boomers, born between 1946 and 1964, the age at which Social Security pays unreduced retirement benefits gradually increases from 66 to 67.

Figure 3.3. Large Numbers of Baby Boomers Nearing Eligibility to Retire.

Sustainable solvency: assurance that the projected balance between program assets and costs is positive throughout a 75-year period and is stable or rising at the end of the period.

Source: GAO (see glossary). | GAO-18-111SP.

In our previous work, we outlined a framework to evaluate proposals presented to address Social Security's challenges. This framework used three basic criteria: (1) the extent to which a proposal achieves sustainable solvency and how it would affect the national economy and the federal budget; (2) the relative balance struck between the goals of individual equity and income adequacy; and (3) how readily a proposal could be implemented, administered, and explained to the public.[173]

Long-term fiscal projections show that spending increases in Social Security's retirement program, together with the Social Security Disability Insurance program and Medicare, are key contributors to an unsustainable fiscal path for the federal government.[174] As with the Social Security

[173] GAO-16-75SP. We first identified sustainable solvency as a criterion for evaluating Social Security reforms in 1999. See GAO, *Social Security: Criteria for Evaluating Social Security Reform Proposals*, GAO/T-HEHS-99-94 (Washington, D.C. Mar. 25, 1999).

[174] For further discussion, see GAO-17-237SP.

retirement program, reserves had also built up over time in the trust fund for the Social Security Disability Insurance program, but in 2005, the program began paying out more than it was taking in. To avoid benefit reductions, which were expected to begin in 2016, Congress passed a law in late 2015 that temporarily reallocates some payroll tax revenue from the retirement trust fund to the disability trust fund.[175] Even with this added boost, reductions in disability benefits are projected to be needed beginning in 2028, according to SSA's most recent report.[176] It is difficult to predict exactly what would occur if this were to happen, because the Social Security Act does not provide for any procedure for paying less than full benefits. According to SSA, benefits could be reduced across the board by a set percentage, certain benefits could be prioritized, or benefits could be delayed.[177]

As with the Social Security Disability Insurance program, spending for Medicare is projected to outpace revenue over time, due to program and demographic changes. Medicare is funded by payroll taxes paid by most employees, employers, and people who are self-employed, by general revenue, and by other sources, such as a portion of taxes paid on Social Security benefits, interest earned on the trust fund investments, and premiums paid by Medicare beneficiaries. Over the years, Congress has made changes to Medicare so that more people have become eligible, such as those with end-stage renal disease, even if under age 65.[178] Also, Congress has added two more parts to Medicare: one part allowing insurance under private plans approved by Medicare (Medicare

---

[175] The Social Security Benefit Protection and Opportunity Enhancement Act of 2015, among other things, increased the proportion of the employer and employee tax contributions to the trust funds that specifically go to the DI trust fund from 1.8 percent to 2.37 percent starting in 2016 through the end of 2018. Pub. L. No. 114-74, tit. VIII, 129 Stat. 584, 601-20. The combined payroll tax remains at 12.4 percent of covered earnings.

[176] According to the 2017 Trustees' report, the favorable change in projected year of insolvency for the disability trust fund (which changed from 2023 in the preceding year's report to 2028 in this year's report), was largely due to the continuing decline in new disability applications and awards, which peaked in 2010. However, the ultimate disability incidence rate assumptions were unchanged.

[177] For further discussion, see GAO-16-75SP.

[178] In addition, Medicare beneficiaries also include individuals under age 65 who are receiving benefits from Social Security or the Railroad Retirement Board on the basis of a disability.

Advantage),[179] and another part providing prescription drug coverage. As of December 2016, about 58 million people were enrolled in one or more parts under Medicare. Projections indicate that in the coming decade, as more members of the baby-boom generation become eligible for benefits, the number of beneficiaries will rise to 75 million in 2026, and the trust fund for Medicare Part A (Hospital Insurance) may be unable to pay full benefits beginning in 2029.[180]

Employer-Sponsored Retirement Plans

The second pillar, employer-sponsored retirement plans, is also an important source of income for U.S. retirees. According to SSA data, private and public sector employer-sponsored plans and IRAs accounted for about 20 percent of income for households with a head of household age 65 or older in 2015, the most recent data available.[181] This includes traditional DB plans that typically provide benefits in the form of an annuity, as well as DC plans, such as 401(k) plans, that provide an account balance based on contributions and investment returns. Also, data indicate that the bulk of asset growth in IRAs is due to rollovers of funds from DC accounts or DB lump-sum payouts—approximately 92 percent in 2014.[182] DB and DC plans are key supports for retirement security, but over the last several decades, both types of plans have given rise to concerns in different ways.

---

[179] Medicare Advantage Plans (also known as Medicare Part C) are a type of Medicare health plan offered by a private company that contracts with Medicare to provide benefits for Part A (Hospital Insurance), Part B (Medical Insurance, for outpatient care and certain other medical supplies and services), and may also include Part D (prescription drug coverage). Medicare Advantage Plans include health maintenance organizations, preferred provider organizations, private fee-for-service plans, special needs plans, and Medicare medical savings account plans.

[180] The Boards of Trustees, *2017 Annual Report of the Boards of Trustees of the Federal Hospital Insurance and Federal Supplementary Medical Insurance Trust Funds* (Washington, D.C.: July 13, 2017). For further discussion, see GAO-17-237SP.

[181] Social Security Administration, *Fast Facts & Figures about Social Security, 2017.*

[182] As noted earlier in section 1, see ICI, "The Role of IRAs in US Households' Saving for Retirement, 2016," *ICI Research Perspective*, vol. 23, no. 1 (January 2017).

Declining DB Plans and PBGC Solvency Concerns

As described earlier in section 1, private sector DB plans that traditionally provide a lifetime annuity at retirement have been on the decline since 1975. This decline and shift to DC plans has meant a shift of responsibility for financing and managing retirement savings to individuals and the loss of certain protections, such as the benefit guarantees provided by PBGC. However, the benefit guarantees for those who still participate in private sector DB plans are also increasingly at risk, as PBGC's financial position deteriorates.

Although PBGC is one of the largest of any federal government corporations, with nearly $100 billion in assets, it faces serious fiscal risk due to its substantial liabilities. At the end of fiscal year 2016, PBGC's net accumulated financial deficit was over $79 billion—more than double what it was in 2013, largely due to the declining financial position of the multiemployer program (see Figure 3.4). PBGC also estimated that its exposure to potential future losses for underfunded retirement plans was nearly $243 billion.[183] As a result, PBGC's long-term financial stability remains uncertain, and the retirement benefits of millions of U.S. workers and retirees could be at risk of significant reductions.

In contrast to Social Security, PBGC is not funded by tax revenues, but by the premiums paid by plans or their sponsors, the assets acquired from terminated plans, and investment income earned on these funds. The primary drivers of the government's fiscal exposure related to PBGC's deficit are the collective financial risk of the many underfunded pension plans insured by PBGC and the long-term decline in the number of traditional DB plans. Since 1985, there has been a 79 percent decline in the number of plans insured by PBGC and more than 11 million fewer workers actively participating in PBGC-insured plans. In addition to having to contend with market uncertainty, some private sector DB plans, like Social Security, have had to adjust to shifting demographics, with a growing share of participants who are retirees and a shrinking share who are contributing to the plans.

---

[183] PBGC, *Annual Report 2016: Keeping Our Commitment to America's Workers* (Washington, D.C.: Nov. 15, 2016).

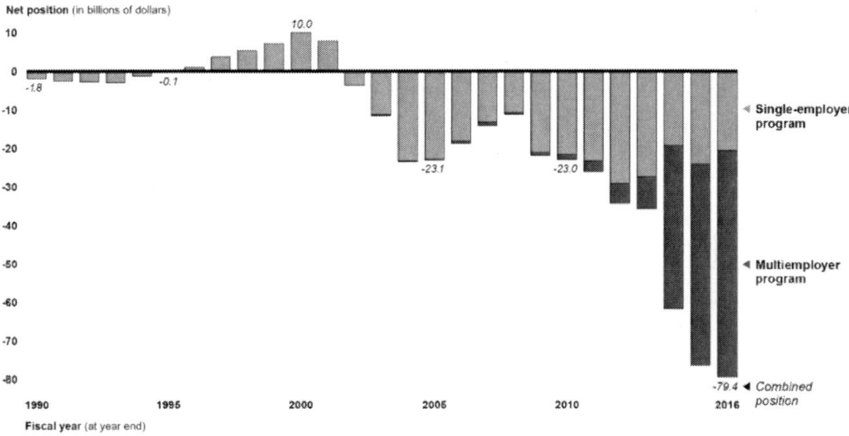

Source: GAO analysis of Pension Benefit Guaranty Corporation data. | GAO-18-111SP.

Figure 3.4. Pension Benefit Guaranty Corporation's Net Position Has Been Declining, Fiscal Years 1990-2016.

As a result, even though premium rates have increased significantly in recent years, PBGC's premium base has been eroding over time as fewer sponsors are paying premiums for fewer participants.[184]

Additionally, the structure of PBGC's premium rates—a key component of PBGC's funding—has long been an area of concern. For example, despite periodic increases in premium rates, which are set by law, the level of premiums has not kept pace with the risks that PBGC insures against. Moreover, plan underfunding is the only risk factor currently considered in determining a sponsor's premium rate. For example, premium rates do not consider the relative financial condition of sponsoring employers, nor the riskiness of their plans' asset allocation.

While the multiemployer program is much smaller than the single employer program, it accounted for about $59 billion of PBGC's financial deficit, compared to $20.6 billion for the single employer program.

[184] The decline in the number or participants in these plans is important because a portion of the premiums is based on the number of participants in a plan, and fewer participants mean less premium revenue. See GAO, *Pension Benefit Guaranty Corporation: Redesigned Premium Structure Could Better Align Rates with Risk from Plan Sponsors* GAO-13-58 (Washington, D.C.: Nov. 7, 2012).

According to PBGC, the dramatic increases in the multiemployer program deficit were attributable to broad economic factors and to the financial conditions of the plans PBGC insures. As noted earlier, PBGC estimates that plans covering 10 to 15 percent of the 10 million multiemployer participants are at risk of running out of money over the next 20 years.

Prompted by the large increase in PBGC's deficit, Congress passed the Multiemployer Pension Reform Act of 2014 (MPRA) in December 2014 with a number of provisions to promote the long-term viability of the multiemployer program.[185] Specifically, MPRA (1) provides severely underfunded plans, under certain conditions and with the approval of federal regulators, the option to reduce the retirement benefits of current retirees to avoid plan insolvency; (2) doubles the annual premium rates paid by multiemployer plans (from $13 to $26 per participant);[186] and (3) expands PBGC's ability to intervene when plans are in financial distress, under certain limited circumstances.

Prior to passage of MPRA, PBGC estimated that the multiemployer insurance fund would likely be exhausted by 2022 as a result of current and projected plan insolvencies. However, PBGC officials noted that the act did not fully address the crisis in the multiemployer program. In its 2016 annual report, PBGC stated that the agency believes there is a 50 percent chance that this program will be insolvent by the year 2025. More recently, in its FY16 Projections Report, PBGC notes that program risk continues to rise over time, and projects that the risk of insolvency in the multiemployer program will exceed 90 percent by 2029 and 99 percent by 2036.[187] Meanwhile, PBGC projected that the net financial position of the larger single-employer program is likely, but not guaranteed, to improve over the next decade, and that the single-employer program shows a surplus in 2025.

In light of concerns about the decline in the number of traditional DB plans and the collective financial risk of the many underfunded pension plans insured by PBGC, the agency's long-term financial stability remains

---

[185] Multiemployer Pension Reform Act of 2014, Pub. L. No. 113-235, div. O, 128 Stat. 2130, 2773-822.

[186] The premium rate is indexed for wage inflation and increased to $28 for 2017.

[187] PBGC, *FY 2016 PBGC Projections Report* (Washington, D.C.: Aug. 3, 2017).

uncertain, and the retirement benefits of millions of U.S. workers and retirees could be at risk of significant reductions in the future. We designated the single-employer program as high risk in July 2003 and added the multiemployer program to our high-risk list in January 2009, and both programs have remained on GAO's high-risk list, which is updated every 2 years. In our most recent high-risk update, we asked Congress to consider taking several actions to improve the long-term financial stability of both PBGC insurance programs, including:

- authorizing a redesign of PBGC's single employer program premium structure to better align rates with sponsor risk;
- adopting additional changes to PBGC's governance structure—in particular, expanding the composition of its board of directors;
- strengthening funding requirements for plan sponsors as appropriate given national economic conditions;
- working with PBGC to develop a strategy for funding PBGC claims over the long term, as the DB pension system continues to decline; and
- enacting additional structural reforms to reinforce and stabilize the multiemployer system that balance the needs and potential sacrifices of contributing employers, participants and the federal government.[188]

In the public sector, DB plans remain the predominant type of plan, available to about 93 percent of full-time state and local government workers (see Figure 3.5).[189] Following the 2007-2009 recession, we found that many state and local government pension plans had suffered significant investment losses, but were taking steps to move their plans to a more financially solvent position by reducing benefits and increasing

[188] GAO-17-317, pp. 609-618.

[189] As noted earlier in section 1, all federal workers also generally have access to a DB plan. As of fiscal year 2014, the primary plan for about 8 percent of federal workers (those hired before 1984) is a DB plan, and the primary plan for the remaining 92 percent (those hired in 1984 and after) includes both a smaller DB, with lower benefits, and a DC component.

employer and employee contributions.[190] Our more recent work has found that state and local pension asset balances have been increasing: Inflation-adjusted pension assets for 2015 exceeded the 2007 pre-recession historical high of $2.85 trillion.[191] However, our simulations suggest that state and local governments may still need to take steps to manage their pension obligations by reducing benefits or increasing contributions to maintain long-term fiscal balance.

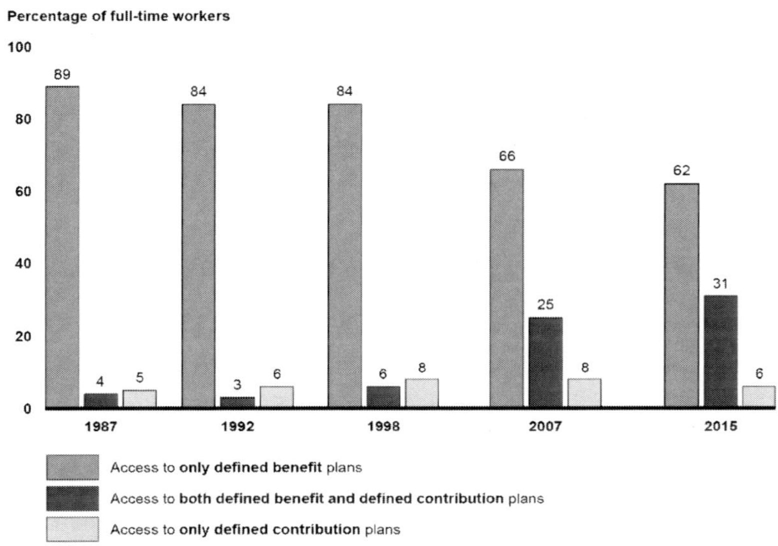

Source: Bureau of Labor Statistics data. | GAO-18-111SP.

Figure 3.5. State and Local Government Workers' Access to Retirement Plans, 1987-2015.

The risk of bankruptcy poses another potential threat to the retirement security of government workers with DB plans in some localities.[192]

---

[190] Reductions in benefits had mostly been for future employees due to legal provisions protecting benefits for current employees and retirees. See GAO, *State and Local Government Pension Plans: Economic Downturn Spurs Efforts to Address Costs and Sustainability*, GAO-12-322 (Washington, D.C.: Mar. 2, 2012).

[191] Dollar amounts are inflation-adjusted and expressed in 2009 dollars. See GAO, *State and Local Governments' Fiscal Outlook: 2016 Update,* GAO-17-213SP (Washington, D.C.: Dec. 8, 2016).

[192] States may authorize a municipality to file bankruptcy under Chapter 9 of the Bankruptcy Code, allowing the municipality to adjust its debts, subject to court approval.

Although there are far fewer bankruptcies in the public sector than in the private sector,[193] whenever the sponsors of employer-sponsored plans are facing bankruptcy—whether public or private—employees' retirement benefits can be at risk. A pension fund with a large unfunded liability can be a contributing cause for both types of bankruptcies, and this liability is often treated as an unsecured claim, only to receive funds once all secured claims have been paid in full.

However, there are some differences between public and private bankruptcies that add to the risks for government workers. In the private sector, most DB plans are insured by PBGC, but public sector DB plans are not insured by PBGC. In addition, in private sector bankruptcies, wage claims and contributions to employee benefit plans are afforded some special treatment among unsecured claims. In contrast, in municipal bankruptcies, wage claims and contributions to employee benefit plans generally do not receive any special treatment.[194] Bankruptcy filings by several cities around the country over the past 10 years, most notably by Detroit in 2013, have shed light on some of these issues.[195]

DC Plans on the Rise, but with Low Account Balances for Many

In recent decades, there has been a shift from DB to DC plans for a variety of reasons. As described earlier in section 1, DC plans allow employers to have more control over their costs, they were fostered by changes in the law with the creation of 401(k) plans, and according to some, their portability is better suited to meet the needs of a more mobile workforce. However, DC plans also place increasing risk and

---

[193] Since enactment of the 1937 amendments to the Municipal Bankruptcy Act of 1898, there have been fewer than 500 municipal bankruptcy petitions filed, compared with about 1.9 million business filings over this same period (based on U.S. Court data compiled by the American Bankruptcy Institute).

[194] For further discussion of the differences between bankruptcy in the private versus public sectors, see James E. Spiotto, *Primer on Municipal Debt Adjustment, Chapter 9: The Last Resort for Financially Distressed Municipalities* (Chicago, IL: Chapman and Cutler LLP, 2012).

[195] The financial crisis in Puerto Rico, with its main public pension systems headed toward insolvency, has also shed light on the difficulties of adjusting public debt to address funding shortfalls. See Steven Maguire, *Puerto Rico: CRS Experts* (Washington, D.C.. Congressional Research Service, June 5, 2017).

responsibility on individuals to plan and manage their retirement. DC plans are, essentially, employer-sponsored individual retirement savings accounts, distinguished from IRAs primarily by the contributions that employers provide. To the extent that employer contributions diminish in the future, the pillars of employer-sponsored plans and individual savings begin to merge. Meanwhile, even with employer contributions, many individuals are not saving enough in their DC plans to provide for an adequate retirement.

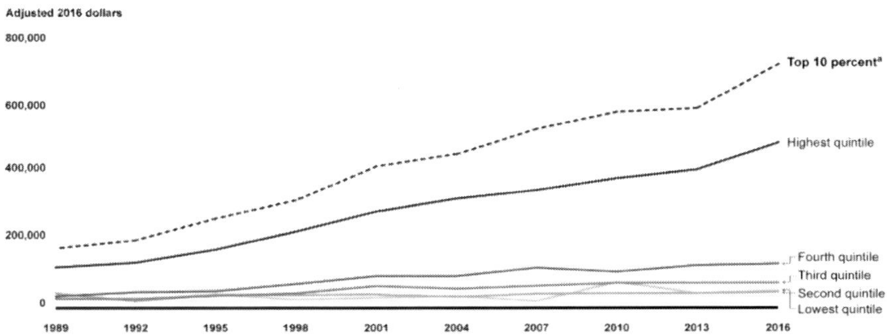

Source: GAO analysis of the Federal Reserve Board of Governor's 2016 Survey Consumer Finances Data. | GAO-18-111SP.

Note: The changes over time are cross-sectional comparisons, not longitudinal ones—that is, the households in a particular quintile in one year may not be the same households in that quintile in another year.

[a] The top 10 percent is also included in the highest quintile.

Figure 3.6. Households' Average Retirement Account Balances, by Income Quintiles, 1989-2016.

Our prior work analyzing 2013 SCF data found that among households with access to a DC plan, the amount of savings in those plans varied widely based on income, with the amounts saved by low-income households, in particular, least likely to be able to sustain an adequate retirement.[196] This is reflected in more recent 2016 SCF data, as well (see Figure 3.6). Households in the top 10 percent appear to be substantially better off than most others, with an average account balance of more than

[196] See GAO-16-408.

$720,000 in 2016. In contrast, among lower-income households, our prior work suggested that cashing out accounts when changing jobs may be a significant drain on retirement savings, along with shocks to their income that may also cause them to withdraw funds from their accounts pre-retirement.[197]

Little Progress from Federal Efforts to Increase Plan Formation

Despite substantial federal efforts to encourage increased plan formation by employers and increased participation in plans by workers through various tax incentives, there has been little progress in expanding coverage by either DB or DC employer-sponsored plans. To encourage saving for retirement, federal tax law allows favorable tax treatment for private sector employers to sponsor pension plans and retirement savings plans, and for workers to participate in those plans. For example, employers may deduct contributions to pension plans as a business expense at the time the contributions are made, rather than when the funds are distributed to employees after retirement. Current federal law also allows individuals with account based plans, like 401(k)s, to have the income taxes on their contributions and any market gains on their accounts deferred until the funds are distributed.[198] Yet, as noted earlier, despite these incentives, the total number of employer-sponsored private sector pension and retirement savings plans has declined since 2000. While tax incentives may have spurred some new plan formation, other events—such as company bankruptcies and consolidations—have caused some plans to terminate or merge together, so that the net number of plans has decreased.[199]

Meanwhile, these tax incentives come at a cost to the federal government (referred to as a tax expenditure), and the cost has grown considerably.

[197] For further discussion, see earlier section 2.

[198] For account based plans like 401(k) plans, the tax deferral for individuals applies to retirement savings from certain employer contributions to qualified employer-sponsored pension plans, contributions made at the election of employees from their salaries, and income earned on pension assets.

[199] For further discussion of tax incentives for retirement plans, see GAO-14-334R.

Tax expenditures: forgone revenue for the federal government due to preferential provisions in the tax code, such as exemptions and exclusions from taxation, deductions, credits, deferral of tax liability, and preferential tax rates.

Source: GAO (see glossary). | GAO-18-111SP.

In 1975, the tax incentives for employer-sponsored pension plans and retirement savings vehicles was estimated to cost the federal government about $5.6 billion, or about 0.33 percent of the nation's gross domestic product (GDP). By 2016, the estimated cost had grown to $177.9 billion, or about 0.96 percent of GDP, according to estimates from the Office of Management and Budget.[200] Tax incentives for retirement savings (DB and DC plans combined) are the second largest tax expenditure in the federal budget, following the exclusion of employer contributions for medical insurance premiums and medical care, which cost the federal government about $210.2 billion in foregone income tax revenues in 2016.

Individuals' Savings and Reliance on Safety Net Programs

The third pillar of the U.S. retirement system, individuals' savings outside of employer sponsored retirement plans, has also weakened. The personal saving rate in the United States trended steeply downward between 1975 and 2005 (see Figure 3.7). Since 2005, the rate has recovered somewhat, but has not yet reached its pre-1975 level. While the

---

[200] Office of Management and Budget, *Analytical Perspectives, Budget of the U.S. Government, Fiscal Year 2018* (Washington, D.C.: 2017).This total includes estimates for deferrals for contributions to DB plans, DC plans, and other plans covering partners and sole proprietors, IRAs, and certain retirement saving tax credits. This estimated total, which is based on provisions of federal tax law enacted through July 1, 2016, is measured as the tax revenue that the government does not currently collect on contributions and investment earnings, offset by the taxes paid by those who are currently receiving retirement benefits. Summing tax expenditure estimates is useful for gauging the general magnitude of revenue forgone through provisions of the tax code, but does not take into account interactions among individual provisions. Revenue loss estimates do not represent the amount of revenue that would be gained from repealing a tax expenditure, because repeal would probably change taxpayer behavior in some way that would affect revenue. A conceptually alternative way to consider the cost of the tax deferral is to estimate the impact of current year contributions on current and future tax revenue. This alternative methodology utilizes the concept of "present value," which reflects the fact that a dollar of revenue today is worth more than a dollar of revenue in the future because a dollar today can be invested.

U.S. saving rate is higher than in some countries, it generally has been lower than in several other countries over the last two decades—including, for example, in Germany and Italy. To the extent that individuals do not save enough to provide for a secure retirement, they may need to rely more heavily on safety net programs for various types of services, with fiscal implications for all levels of government.

The generally low saving rate in the United States has implications for individuals' retirement. A savings shortfall could mean a decline in standard of living in retirement—if not initially, over time. In our prior work, we found that in 2013, 25 percent of households age 65 through 74 had no retirement savings and had few other resources to draw on in retirement.[201] While those near the bottom of the income distribution may find that their Social Security benefit is sufficient,[202] others may find that their Social Security benefit alone will not sustain the quality of life they would like to maintain in retirement.

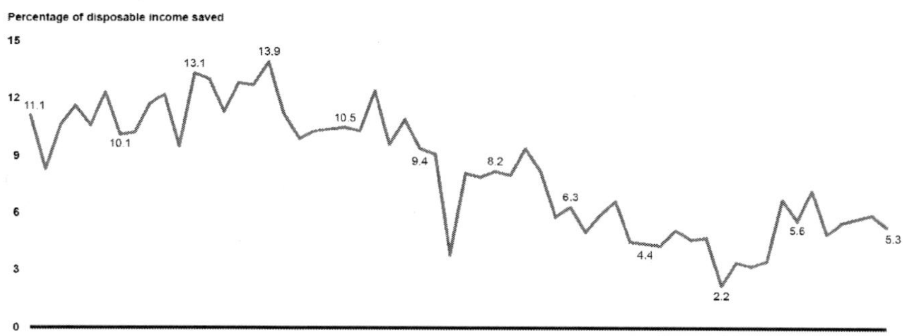

Sources: U.S. Bureau of Economic Analysis. | GAO-18-111SP.

Figure 3.7. Trend in U.S. Personal Saving Rate, 1959-2017.

Moreover, to the extent that individuals find that their savings are inadequate as a supplement to their retirement benefits from Social Security and any employer-sponsored plan, they may need to rely more heavily on various safety net programs for help, putting increasing pressure

---

[201] GAO-15-419.

[202] Andrew Biggs, "How Hard Should We Push the Poor to Save for Retirement?" *AEI Economics Working Paper 2017-13* (July 2017).

on the federal budget for these programs, and state and local governments' budgets, as well. The federal government provides state and local governments with funding for a broad array of home and community-based services for older adults through multiple federal agencies.[203] Our prior work has found that community-based organizations rely on funding from a mix of federal, state, and local programs, so when needs increase, the impact is felt at all levels of government.[204]

Our simulations of the state and local government sector illustrate the potential effects such fiscal pressures could have on future federal funding of intergovernmental programs and the potential capacity of state and local governments to help fund and implement these programs.[205] Absent any changes, state and local governments are facing—and will continue to face—a gap between receipts and expenditures in the coming years.

Researchers have found that about 70 percent of those age 65 or older are likely to need long-term services and supports at some point in their lives, for an average of 3 years; 20 percent will need that care for at least 5 years.[206] As the size of the older population grows, so will the number of older adults needing long-term services and supports, particularly those 85 or older. According to the Congressional Budget Office (CBO), expenditures on long-term services and supports for elderly individuals accounted for an estimated 1.3 percent of GDP in 2011, and CBO projected that the percentage would rise to between 1.9 and 3.3 percent of GDP by the year 2050.[207]

---

[203] These include the Administration on Aging and Centers for Medicare & Medicaid Services in the Department of Health and Human Services, and the Departments of Agriculture, Transportation, and Housing and Urban Development.

[204] GAO, *Older Adults: Federal Strategy Needed to Help Ensure Efficient and Effective Delivery of Home and Community-Based Services and Supports,* GAO-15-190 (Washington, D.C.: May 20, 2015).

[205] GAO-17-213SP.

[206] Peter Kemper, Harriet L. Komisar and Lisa Alecxih, "Long-Term Care Over an Uncertain Future: What Can Current Retirees Expect?" *Inquiry: The Journal of Health Care Organization, Provision, and Financing*, vol. 42 (Winter 2005/2006).

[207] CBO developed projections based on three alternative scenarios regarding the future prevalence of functional limitations among the elderly, holding constant other factors affecting those expenditures, such as growth in prices for long-term services and supports, changes in family structure that could affect the provision of informal care, and changes in how services and supports are delivered. See CBO, *The Rising Demand for Long-term Services and Supports for Elderly People* (June 2013).

Home and Community-Based Services

- Nutrition: The largest proportion of funding for major home and community-based services and related activities under the Older Americans Act of 1965 (OAA) goes to state units on aging for nutrition services—most of this amount for congregate or group meals provided at senior centers, churches, schools, or other sites. For example, in fiscal year 2016, of the more than $1.2 billion in OAA funding for health and independence for older adults, about 68 percent, or about $835 million, was for nutrition programs (not including the funding for Native American Nutrition & Support Services). In addition to OAA funding, four programs within the Department of Agriculture (USDA) provide nutrition assistance for older adults in a variety of forms, ranging from commodities, to prepared meals, to vouchers or other targeted benefits used in commercial food retail locations. For example, two of these USDA programs are exclusively for low-income older adults: the Commodity Supplemental Food Program and the Senior Farmers' Market Nutrition Program. In fiscal year 2016, these two programs received funding of over $240 million. The other two USDA programs—the Child and Adult Care Food Program and the Supplemental Nutrition Assistance Program—target food assistance, at least in part, to low-income older adults. In fiscal year 2016, expenditures for these two programs totaled $74.3 billion. Despite these programs, USDA reported that in 2015, about 8.3 percent of all households with adults age 65 or older were food insecure. Moreover, our prior analysis has found that among households with adults age 60 or older that are low-income, food insecurity was about 19 percent in 2009.
- Long-Term Care: Medicaid is the nation's primary payer for long-term services and supports, with $64.8 billion in federal longterm care expenditures in fiscal year 2015. The elderly and disabled are among the highest cost Medicaid beneficiaries. States are required by federal Medicaid law to cover certain mandatory home and community-based benefits, and may opt to cover additional services through a wide and complex range of options. Medicaid spending for home and community-based services has been steadily increasing as states invest more resources in alternatives to institutional care.
- Transportation: Funding under the OAA helps states to provide rides for older adults to doctor's offices, grocery stores, pharmacies, senior centers,

meal sites, and social events. In addition, the Department of Transportation's Enhanced Mobility of Seniors and Individuals with Disabilities program supports projects that improve access and alternatives to public transportation, such as volunteer driver programs. In fiscal year 2016, grants under this program totaled approximately $262 million.

- Housing: The Department of Housing and Urban Development administers the Supportive Housing for the Elderly (Section 202) program, which plays a critical role in addressing the demand for affordable, supportive housing for older adults in this country. The program maintains the supply of multi-family housing stock for low-income older adults through renewal of existing rental assistance contracts that cover the difference between a property owner's HUD-approved operating costs for a project and the tenants' payments. In addition, Section 202 supports independent living by funding the salaries of service coordinators nationwide to help residents in Section 202-funded properties find the home and community-based services and supports they need to continue living in their own homes. In fiscal year 2016, funding enacted for the Section 202 program totaled approximately $433 million.

Source: GAO and agency documents. | GAO-18-111SP.

Note: For more information on home and community-based services, see GAO-15-190 and GAO, *Nutrition Assistance: Additional Efficiencies Could Improve Services to Older Adults*, GAO-11-782T (Washington, D.C.: June 21, 2011).

Key federal programs intended to help meet this need include long-term care services funded by Medicaid,[208] and services funded under the

[208] Medicaid provides health care coverage and financing for millions of low-income individuals—including those age 65 or older. The federal government and states share in the financing of the Medicaid program, with the federal government matching most state expenditures for Medicaid services using a statutory formula. Estimated Medicaid outlays for fiscal year 2016 were $575.9 billion, of which $363.4 billion was financed by the federal government and $212.5 billion by the states. According to CMS, projected average annual growth in Medicaid spending for 2020 through 2025 is 5.8 percent, driven primarily by the changing profile of the program's population, as an increasingly higher share of beneficiaries is comprised of comparatively expensive aged and disabled individuals. The Medicaid program has been on GAO's high risk list since 2003 due to concerns about the adequacy of fiscal oversight. See GAO-17-317, pp. 560-578; and Centers for Medicare & Medicaid Services, Office of the Actuary, *2016 Actuarial Report on the Financial Outlook for Medicaid* (Baltimore, MD: 2017).

Older Americans Act of 1965,[209] which provides grants to states for such services as congregate and home-delivered meals, home-based care, transportation, and housing (see text box). However, our prior work has found that these services were not reaching many older adults who may need them, and that the funding for these programs had decreased, while the number of older adults had increased.[210] As the number of older adults needing assistance continues to grow, the gap in services can only be expected to widen, putting greater pressure on the federal government to increase funding.

Supplemental Security Income (SSI) is another safety net program that older adults may have to turn to should they find that their retirement income is inadequate. SSI is a federal income supplement program administered by SSA, but funded by general tax revenues (not Social Security taxes). It is designed to help people who are aged, blind, or have disabilities, and who have little or no income, by providing cash to meet basic needs for food, clothing, and shelter. To qualify for SSI, individuals must have little or no income and few resources. The value of resources owned must be less than $2,000 (less than $3,000 for married couples). Generally, the more a person's countable income, the less the SSI benefit will be, because countable income is subtracted from the SSI payment amount. The maximum federal SSI benefit generally changes yearly, based on changes in the Consumer Price Index. For 2017, the monthly federal payment amount is $735 for individuals ($1,103 for couples). In addition, all but four states supplement the federal SSI benefit with additional payments, making the total SSI benefit levels higher in those states.[211] Should the number of retirees eligible for SSI increase in the future, its effects will be felt on the governments' budgets both at the federal and state level.

---

[209] Pub. L. No. 89-73, 79 Stat. 218 (codified as amended at 42 U.S.C. §§ 3001-3058ff).

[210] See GAO, *Older Americans Act: Updated Information on Unmet Need for Services,* GAO-15-601R (Washington, D.C.: June 10, 2015).

[211] The four states that do not provide a supplemental benefit are: Arizona, Mississippi, North Dakota, and West Virginia.

Section 4. The Need to Re-Evaluate the Nation's Approach to Financing Retirement

Over the past 40 years, fundamental economic and societal changes have occurred in the United States, as well as a considerable transfer of risks and responsibilities from employers to individuals surrounding the planning and managing of retirement. Since the passage of ERISA, the nation has been taking a piecemeal approach to improving the U.S. retirement system. However, such an approach may not be able to effectively address the interrelated nature of the challenges facing the system today. A panel of retirement experts we convened in November 2016 agreed that there is a need for a comprehensive approach to financing retirement in the United States, and that the experiences of other countries can provide useful insights for ways to improve U.S. retirement programs and policies. In fact, international studies of retirement systems have found that the United States often ranks lower than many other countries with respect to the ability to ensure adequate retirement benefits and meet long-term obligations.

In Recent Decades, Retirement Issues Have Been Addressed with a Piecemeal Approach

Since 1974, Congress has generally attempted to address retirement-related issues and concerns one issue at a time. For example, in 1983, to address imminent funding shortages facing the Social Security retirement program, the Social Security Act was amended, in part, to gradually increase the retirement age from age 65 to age 67.[212] In 1984, to help address concerns that women were not receiving their fair share of private pension benefits, ERISA was amended, in part, to permit certain breaks in service without loss of pension credits, and to change treatment of pension benefits for widowed and divorced spouses.[213] In 1986, as part of a larger tax reform effort, the IRC was amended to include new nondiscrimination coverage rules and the minimum distribution requirement.[214]

Additional efforts to address issues in a piecemeal way followed. For example, in 1996, to help address concerns that smaller employers were not sponsoring plans, Congress created a simplified retirement savings

---

[212] Social Security Amendments of 1983, Pub. L. No. 98-21, 97 Stat. 65.
[213] Retirement Equity Act of 1984, Pub. L. No. 98-397, 98 Stat. 1426.
[214] Tax Reform Act of 1986, Pub. L. No. 99-514, 100 Stat. 2085.

vehicle for employers with 100 or fewer employees.[215] In 2001, to encourage more savings in employer-sponsored plans and IRAs, Congress increased the contribution limits for plan participants, among other things.[216] The Pension Protection Act of 2006 (PPA) amended ERISA in various ways, including revising the minimum funding requirements for DB plans, setting certain benefit limitations for underfunded DB plans, and facilitating the adoption of automatic enrollment and target date funds for DC plans.[217] These are just a few examples of the many laws that have been enacted over the past 40 years making changes to the retirement system in some way.[218]

In addition, three federal commissions have been established since 1974 that have examined various aspects of the U.S. retirement system (see Table 3). First, the 1979 President's Commission on Pension Policy, attempted to address retirement-related issues in a comprehensive way. This commission conducted a broad study of the nation's retirement-income policies and made a series of overarching recommendations addressing a wide range of retirement-related issues, including creation of a Minimum Universal Pension System (MUPS), federal protections for participants in state and local government plans, more consistent tax treatment of pension plans and retirement savings vehicles, provisions to strengthen Social Security, as well as proposals regarding employment of older workers and disability programs.[219] However, many of the commission's recommendations were not implemented.

Second, the 1981 National Commission on Social Security Reform (known as the Greenspan Commission) followed the 1979 commission. The final report from the Greenspan Commission provided the basis for the

---

[215] Small Business Job Protection Act of 1996, Pub. L. No.104-188, 110 Stat. 1755.

[216] Economic Growth and Tax Relief Reconciliation Act of 2001, Pub. L. No. 107-16, 115 Stat. 38.

[217] Pub. L. No. 109-280, 120 Stat. 78. Specifically, PPA placed limits on (1) plan amendments that would increase benefits, (2) benefit accruals, and (3) benefit distribution options (such as lump sums) in single-employer defined benefit plans that fail to meet specific funding thresholds.

[218] For brief descriptions of additional laws that were enacted during this time, see appendix I.

[219] For more details on the 1979 commission, see appendix V.

1983 Social Security Amendments, which made several changes to strengthen the program.

Table 3. Federal Commissions Addressing Retirement-Related Issues since 1974

Year	Commission
1979	President's Commission on Pension Policy: In 1978, President Carter signed an executive order authorizing this commission and it was established when committee members were appointed in 1979, 5 years after the enactment of the Employee Retirement Income Security Act of 1974 (ERISA). President Carter appointed all 11 commission members. The commission was called upon to conduct a 2-year study of the nation's pension systems and the future course of national retirement-income policies, and issue a series of reports on short-term and long-term issues with respect to retirement, survivor, and disability programs. The final report was issued in February 1981.
1981	National Commission on Social Security Reform (known as the Greenspan Commission): Appointed by the Congress and President Reagan in 1981, the commission was to conduct a study and make recommendations regarding the short-term financing crisis faced by Social Security at the time. The President, the Majority Leader of the Senate and the Speaker of the House of Representatives at the time were each responsible for selecting five members of the commission in a bipartisan way. The final report was issued in 1983 and was the basis for the Social Security Amendments of 1983, which addressed the long-term financing problem by gradually increasing the retirement age from 65 to 67, among other things; and made other significant changes to Social Security, such as expanding coverage.
2001	President's Commission to Strengthen Social Security: This bipartisan commission was established in May 2001 by President Bush to study and report, using six guiding principles, specific recommendations to preserve Social Security for seniors while building wealth for younger Americans. The final report, "Strengthening Social Security and Creating Personal Wealth for All Americans," was issued in December 2001.

Source: GAO. | GAO-18-111SP.

Third, in 2001, the President's Commission to Strengthen Social Security was formed. While the final report from the 2001 commission provided three reform plans for Social Security, all featuring voluntary personal retirement accounts as a central component, none of the plans were adopted.

It has been over 15 years since a federal commission has examined retirement issues, and nearly 40 years since a federal commission has examined retirement issues comprehensively.[220] Moreover, no one agency is responsible for overseeing the U.S. retirement system in its entirety. There are at least 10 agencies that have a role in some aspect of the system. For example, the DOL, PBGC, and IRS are generally responsible for administering ERISA; IRS also administers the IRC, which has provisions that affect pensions and retirement savings; SSA administers the Social Security program; the Department of Health and Human Services oversees CMS, which administers the health care programs for retirees; and the Administration on Aging, which encourages and assists state grantees that provide services for older adults. In addition, agencies such as the U.S. Department of Agriculture and the Department of Housing and Urban Development oversee food and housing programs for older adults.[221] Given the number of agencies that play roles in the current retirement system, there is no obvious federal agency leader for a comprehensive reform effort.

The issues identified nearly 40 years ago by the 1979 commission's comprehensive re-evaluation of the U.S. retirement system continue to be issues facing the nation today. In fact, these issues have only become more complex and more urgent due to fundamental changes that have occurred since, especially with the shift from DB to DC plans, and the associated increase in risks and responsibilities for individual workers. Taken together, these changes may make it harder for retirees to achieve financial security in retirement. Continuing to address retirement issues by using a

---

[220] However, during this time, entities outside of the federal government have convened various commissions and initiatives to examine issues related to the U.S. retirement system. For example, the Bipartisan Policy Center established a commission in 2014 to explore approaches for improving savings and strengthening retirement security. Also, the Society of Actuaries sponsored its Retirement 20/20 initiative from 2006-2010 and asked experts interested in and impacted by retirement issues to design new retirement systems that could better meet the economic and demographic needs for the 21st century in North America.

[221] As noted earlier in section 3, other agencies also have roles providing services and supports for older adults. For example, the Department of Transportation administers a program that improves access and alternatives to public transportation for seniors and individuals with disabilities, the Consumer Financial Protection Bureau, as part of its mandate to provide financial literacy education, helps consumers navigate financial choices related to retirement. The Federal Trade Commission can have consumer protection and investor oversight roles and responsibilities related to individuals borrowing against their pensions.

piecemeal approach may not be an effective strategy for tackling the interrelated nature of the challenges facing the retirement system today.

Experts Agree on the Need for a More Comprehensive Approach

To gain additional insights on the condition of retirement in the United States and various options for a new approach, we convened a panel of 15 retirement experts in November 2016.[222] There was agreement among many panelists that a retirement crisis may be looming and that a more comprehensive approach would be useful. They spoke of trends—including slow wage growth, rising health care costs, increasing life expectancy, and shrinking household size—that may be building to a situation in which future generations are less financially secure in retirement compared to prior generations. They noted weaknesses in the current system's ability to help ensure that all individuals can provide for a secure retirement and the burden that the current system's complexity places on individuals, employers, and government. Several panelists noted that the range of risks faced by individuals is especially worrisome. (For example, see text box.)

Panelist on the Lack of Tools to Address Risks

"...the shift of risk that we have put on the individual worker in the United States retirement system is a mess. It's the investment risk, it's the longevity risk, the health risk, the long-term care risk...ultimately we've put so much risk on individuals who don't really have the tools. And the tools that are out there to help them cost a lot of money."

Source: GAO expert panel. | GAO-18-111SP.

Panelists commented that, in their view, the general tendency among policymakers has been to continue to expand the scope and number of plans, programs, regulations, and policies, rather than seek to consolidate

---

[222] We conducted a content analysis of the transcript of the panelists' comments to identify key themes and shared the summary with several panelists to ensure that it reflected a balanced and fair characterization of the discussion. For more information about our methodology, see appendix III.

and modernize the government's efforts in support of a more efficient and effective approach to saving for retirement. As panelists discussed their vision of a new approach to providing for a secure retirement for future retirees, they noted that different strategies are needed for different income levels. For example, to help individuals with lower incomes, several panelists suggested that the focus should be on strengthening Social Security. But for individuals with middle to higher incomes—that is, those who have the capacity to save for retirement, but are not currently participating—several panelists agreed that the focus should be on expanding coverage and the need to provide better access to ways to save for retirement in addition to Social Security. Panelists also discussed the importance of taking steps to make the process of saving and managing retirement simpler, easier, and less risky for individuals, employers, and the federal government. One panelist noted that taking these steps would not only help make the system easier to navigate, but also help make the system fairer (see text box).

Panelist on the Importance of Simplicity

"All these resources that we're devoting to... optimizing Social Security claiming or any other kind of retirement decisions where there's unnecessary complexity... [they] create unfairness because... people who know the system can take advantage of it versus those who don't. So simplification, I think, is a big, big deal."

Source: GAO expert panel. | GAO-18-111SP.

In the discussion about how to increase access, panelists' comments focused primarily on the need for a new type of vehicle to save for retirement and the various ways it could be implemented. Some panelists suggested that a new government-sponsored savings vehicle should be created, while others supported modifying the existing employer-sponsored system to make any needed changes. For example, one panelist suggested that one way of providing a new savings vehicle, available to all, would be to attach a government-sponsored individual account component to Social

Security. Individuals and their employers could then contribute to these accounts over the course of an individual's working years. As an example of how a government-sponsored savings vehicle has worked elsewhere, some panelists described the approach being taken by the United Kingdom (UK). The UK approach expanded access to individuals by mandating that all employers automatically enroll employees in either their own or the government-sponsored retirement savings plan, the National Employment Savings Trust. (See text box).

United Kingdom's National Employment Savings Trust (NEST)

The UK Pensions Act of 2008 provided for the introduction of automatic enrollment into employment-based retirement savings plans. Automatic enrollment under the mandate has been gradually phased in since 2012, with the largest employers enrolling eligible employees into qualifying retirement plans in which employees will remain unless they actively opt out. NEST is one such qualifying retirement plan created by the UK government specifically for auto-enrollment as a low-cost, simple option that any employer can use to meet the auto-enrollment mandate. The rollout is scheduled to be completed by 2018, when it will cover employers of all sizes. The UK government expects 10 million workers to be enrolled by that date.

Once workers have been automatically enrolled they have 1 month to opt out, but employers are required to automatically re-enroll those workers every 3 years. For workers who do not opt out, the total minimum contribution from the employer, worker, and government will combine to gradually reach 8 percent by 2019—with 3 percent from employers, 4 percent from workers, and 1 percent from the government. Eligible workers are those between age 22 and State Pension Age (which varies based on factors such as age, gender, years of employment) and have earnings over 10,000 British pounds for the 2016-2017 tax year.

Source: Based on information from NEST Corporation documents. | GAO-18-111SP.

Notes: For further discussion of NEST, see GAO-15-556. Also, there are other non-governmental programs in the UK intended to expand access to employment-based retirement savings plans, such as The People's Pension and NOW: Pensions.

One panelist proposed a new retirement plan type that would allow workers to save for retirement in a DC-type individual account; but would accomplish this through a multiple employer approach that offered pooling of investments and a lifetime income option, more like a DB plan. The panelist also said such a plan could be government-sponsored and allow employers of all sizes who did not currently offer their own plan to join, as well as self-insured, self-employed individuals, and temporary and seasonal workers who did not otherwise have access to a plan. According to this panelist, such a plan could at least provide a vehicle for individuals to save for retirement with their own contributions, even if employer contributions were voluntary, making it similar to a DC plan; and would enable individuals to pool their investments and receive a benefit in a lifetime income stream at retirement, similar to a DB plan.

In the discussion about how to make the process of saving and managing retirement easier, there was widespread agreement on the importance of automatic mechanisms such as auto-enrollment and auto-escalation (i.e., increasing an employee's contribution rate to increase automatically at periodic intervals, such as annually). Several panelists commented that such mechanisms are key to making it easier for individuals to enroll and save for retirement without requiring them to become highly financially literate. (For example, see text box.)

Panelist on the Problem with Financial Literacy

"...we have a very, very acute problem with financial literacy. And I think it's actually gotten worse...as the financial instruments have gotten more complicated it makes it less likely that people can understand what they're doing."

Source: GAO expert panel. | GAO-18-111SP.

To simplify individuals' decision-making on how to spend down their savings through retirement, several panelists mentioned the potential value of encouraging employers to adopt some type of pooled-risk annuity option for their retirees. As noted by one panelist, under the current system, individuals can purchase an annuity with their DC account balances at retirement, but doing so on the retail market can be expensive and complicated. In contrast, as another panelist noted, with some type of pooled-risk annuity option, the costs and risks of choosing an annuity can be shared, as is done in DB plans.

With respect to employers, panelists discussed how the current private sector system poses financial and litigation risk for them, especially with respect to investment decisions, fiduciary duty, and fees. One panelist suggested that DC plan sponsors may welcome the federal government providing more guidance on the types of investments that would be regarded as prudent and safe as a way to reduce their litigation risk.

While panelists varied on the pros and cons of specific options and strategies for improving retirement security, there was general agreement that part of the problem confronting the nation today is the rigidity of the regulatory structure around retirement savings plans. For example, one panelist noted that the current regulatory structure for employer-sponsored plans poses barriers to innovation, inhibiting progress in adopting new types of plans. More generally, panelists urged that any new policies should allow for flexibility so that the system can adapt and evolve as conditions change, whatever approach is pursued at the national level going forward. In addition to creating a system with more flexibility, panelists also called for making the system simpler, easier, and less risky for all, noting that past reforms have tended to expand the scope of the system rather than consolidate or modernize existing programs. Overall, the issues identified by panelists underscored the complexity and the interrelationships within the current system as reasons why a piecemeal approach has not been effective.

International Comparisons Can Provide Insights for Re-Evaluating the U.S. Retirement System

International comparisons suggest that the United States could learn from other countries' experiences about possible ways to improve retirement policies with respect to the level of income or benefits provided (adequacy), the ability to finance the system over the long term (sustainability), and the strength of regulatory and administrative oversight of the system (integrity). Undertaking international comparisons is difficult because countries have widely varying retirement systems as well as social, political, and economic differences. Nonetheless, faced with the virtually worldwide trend of an aging population, policymakers in many countries have been grappling with the challenge of delivering adequate income in retirement while at the same time ensuring the financial sustainability of their systems. In this context, the experience of other countries may help inform U.S. policymakers in their efforts to balance these competing goals.[223]

The most comprehensive international study of retirement systems that we reviewed is the Melbourne Mercer study, which assessed the three dimensions of adequacy, sustainability, and integrity.[224] This study benchmarked 25 countries' retirement income systems using more than 40 indicators and found that, in 2015, the United States ranked lower than many other countries in some areas. Other international studies have been conducted in recent years by two other groups: the Center for Strategic and International Studies (CSIS)[225] and Allianz, an international financial services provider.[226] These studies each evaluated several countries' retirement systems in the areas of benefit adequacy and financial sustainability using different indicators, with different results, but generally ranking the United States somewhat higher than the Melbourne Mercer study. In addition, the Organisation for Economic Co-operation and Development (OECD) periodically gathers data and publishes reports on how pension systems across its 34 member countries are responding to the

---

223 For more information on the findings of the studies we reviewed, see appendix VI.

224 Mercer, *Melbourne Mercer Global Pension Index* (Melbourne, Australia: Australian Centre for Financial Studies, 2015). This index has been published every year since 2009.

225 R. Jackson, N. Howe, and T. Peter, *The Global Aging Preparedness Index, 2nd edition* (Washington, D.C.: Center for Strategic and International Studies, October 2013). This index was first published in 2010. The 2013 index is the second edition and covers a selection of developed and emerging economies. Indices are computed by taking the actual value of the underlying indicators in 2010 (with data in 2011 and 2012 added when available) and the projected value of these indicators in 2040.

226 Allianz, "2014 Pension Sustainability Index," *International Pension Papers 1/2014* (Munich, Germany: January 2014); and "Retirement Income Adequacy Indicator," *International Pension Papers 1/2015* (Munich, Germany: May 2015).

challenges they are facing. Although the OECD does not calculate indicators or indices to rank countries, its latest 2015 Pensions at a Glance report found mixed results for the United States on topics relevant to adequacy and sustainability, also suggesting that there may be opportunities for the United States to learn from other countries.[227]

Adequacy

The dimension of adequacy explores various aspects of the level of income or benefits provided to a nation's retirees. Recent studies looking at international comparisons of retirement income adequacy have found somewhat mixed results on where the United States ranks relative to other countries (see Table 4).

In the 2015 Melbourne Mercer study, the United States ranked #20 in terms of adequacy. This study assessed the adequacy of each country's retirement system based on such things as the level of minimum pension provided,[228] as well as the net replacement rate, for a median-income earner. It also considered the design features of the private pension system and savings from outside the formal pension programs.

For the United States to boost its adequacy rating, the Melbourne Mercer study recommended that it raise the minimum level of support provided for low-income retirees—which corresponds in the United States to increasing SSI benefits[229]—and boost individual contributions to Social Security to increase the net amount of income replaced for a median-income earner. In addition, the study suggested limiting early access to retirement savings, such as hardship withdrawals, and implementing a requirement that a portion of private pensions be taken as an income

---

[227] OECD, *Pensions at a Glance 2015: OECD and G20 Indicators (*Paris: 2015).

[228] In the Melbourne Mercer study, the level of minimum pension was expressed as a percentage of the average wage.

[229] In the Melbourne Mercer study, the minimum pension was defined as the minimum level of income provided to all aged citizens in a country, independent of contributions or work history. In the United States, this corresponds to SSI benefits. The study also stated that a minimum or basic pension below 30 percent of national average earnings scored less than their maximum score of 10. In addition, the basic pension received a score of zero if the minimum pension was 10 percent or less of average earnings.

stream at regular intervals over a certain period of time rather than as a lump sum.

Table 4. International Rankings of Retirement Systems on Adequacy of Income in Retirement

Melbourne Mercer study (included minimum pension, net replacement rate, and other savings)	CSIS Global Aging study (included living standard, poverty level, and informal family support)	Allianz study[a] (included pension coverage, replacement rate, and other assets and expenses)
#1 Australia	#1 The Netherlands	#1 The Netherlands
#2 The Netherlands	#2 United States	#2 Denmark
#3 Canada	#3 Brazil	#3 Norway
#4 Denmark #4 France (tied)	#4 Australia	#4 Switzerland
	#5 Germany	#5 Japan
#6 Ireland	#6 Sweden	#6 United States
#7 Germany	#7 United Kingdom	#7 Austria
#8 Switzerland	#8 Chile	#8 Sweden
#9 Sweden	#9 Canada	#9 Hungary
#10 Finland	#10 France	#10 New Zealand
#11 Italy	#11 Italy	#11 Finland
#12 Austria	#12 Spain	#12 Canada
#13 Brazil	#13 China	#13 Germany
#14 United Kingdom	#14 Japan	#14 United Kingdom
#15 Chile	#15 India	#15 Spain
#16 China	#16 Switzerland	#16 Brazil
#17 Poland	#17 Mexico	#17 Romania
#18 Mexico	#18 Russia	#18 Portugal
#19 Singapore	#19 South Korea	#19 Italy
#20 United States	#20 Poland	#20 France
#21 Japan		#21 Cyprus
#22 South Africa		#22 Belgium
#23 South Korea		#23 Bulgaria
#24 Indonesia		#24 Croatia
#25 India		#25 Czech Republic

Sources: GAO analysis of data from Mercer, *Melbourne Mercer Global Pension Index* (Melbourne, Australia: Australian Centre for Financial Studies, October 2015); R. Jackson, N. Howe, and T. Peter, *The Global Aging Preparedness Index, 2nd edition* (Washington, D.C.: Center for Strategic and International Studies, October 2013); and Allianz, "Retirement Income Adequacy Indicator," *International Pension Papers 1/2015* (Munich, Germany: May 2015). | GAO-18-111SP.

[a] The Allianz study ranked 49 countries. Only the top 25 countries are included here. (All rankings for the other two studies are shown: the Melbourne Mercer study ranked 25 countries; the Global Aging study ranked 20 countries.)

The study also identified overarching recommendations for all countries, such as raising the retirement age, to reflect increases in life expectancy and expanding private pension plan coverage.

> ***Net replacement rate*:** ratio of income received in retirement to income earned while working, taking into account deductions for taxes and Social Security contributions.
>
> Source: GAO (see glossary). | GAO-18-111SP.

In the 2013 CSIS Global Aging study, the United States ranked much higher, #2, on its benefit adequacy index.[230] In contrast with the Melbourne Mercer study, the CSIS study measured adequacy across 20 countries, based on indicators such as the living standard of the elderly (those age 60 or older) relative to that of the non-elderly, the poverty level (defined in the study as the percent of elderly with incomes below 50 percent of the median income for all persons), and informal family support networks. The CSIS study recommended that countries increase funded retirement savings and encourage longer working lives.

Allianz's 2015 Retirement Income Adequacy study ranked the United States #6 for its potential to provide adequate retirement income.[231] To compare income adequacy across the 49 countries it covers, the study took into account characteristics of public and private pensions, such as coverage and replacement rate, as well as other factors outside of pensions that affect the financial well-being of retirees, such as the value of housing, out-of-pocket health expenses, and time spent in retirement.

OECD's 2015 Pensions at a Glance included data on indicators similar to those used for these studies' adequacy rankings and found mixed results for the United States. For example, the OECD data (from 2012-13, the most recent available) showed that the income of those over age 65, relative to the income of the population as a whole, was higher in the United States (92.1 percent) compared to the OECD average (86.8

[230] *The Global Aging Preparedness Index.*

[231] *Retirement Income Adequacy Indicator.*

percent).[232] However, the more elderly within this group did not fare as well. The income of those older than 75 was lower in the United States (76.8 percent) compared to the OECD average (79.5 percent). In addition, minimum supports for low-income elderly individuals, corresponding to SSI, were relatively low in the United States compared to countries with equivalent per-capita income. Specifically, the value of the SSI benefit received by the aged with low or no income in the United States was about 19 percent of the economy-wide average earnings, while the comparable benefit across all OECD countries, on average, was 24 percent.

In addition, according to the OECD model, the net replacement rate from Social Security in the United States was lower than the rates from the mandatory national pensions in other OECD countries.[233] For example, the OECD model found that in the United States, individuals with lower earnings (i.e., those making half the U.S. average income) received Social Security benefits replacing about 54.3 percent of their pre-retirement earnings, while among individuals with similar lower earnings across all OECD countries, men received benefits replacing about 74.5 percent of pre-retirement earnings and women received benefits replacing about 74.1 percent, on average.[234] Similarly, the OECD model found that individuals in the United States with average earnings received Social Security benefits replacing about 44.8 percent of their pre-retirement earnings, while among individuals with average earnings across OECD member countries, men received benefits replacing about 63.0 percent of pre-retirement earnings and women received benefits replacing about 62.6 percent on average.[235] This reflects, in part, the different structure and intent of these programs in different countries.

---

[232] The OECD considered all sources of income for the elderly, including means-tested benefits, earnings-related pension benefits, income from work and from private pensions. It also adjusted incomes for household size.

[233] These rates are net replacement rates because they also take into account income taxes and Social Security contributions paid by workers and retirees. The OECD calculated net replacement rates for three different income levels: individuals having earned the economy-wide average income during their working years, those with half the average income, and those with 1.5 times the average income.

[234] These figures are average net replacement rates for all OECD member countries.

[235] The OECD model assumed that people enter the labor force at age 20 in 2014 and exit at the normal or full retirement age for all countries.

Sustainability

Table 5. International Rankings of Retirement Systems on Sustainability

Melbourne Mercer study	CSIS Global Aging study	Allianz study[a]
(included dependency ratio, benefits relative to the economy, and extent of private plan coverage)	**(included benefit dependence and benefits relative to the overall economy)**	**(included dependency ratio and benefits relative to the economy)**
#1 Denmark	#1 India	#1 Australia
#2 The Netherlands	#2 Mexico	#2 Sweden
#3 Sweden	#3 Chile	#3 New Zealand
#4 Australia	#4 China	#4 Norway
#5 Switzerland	#5 Russia	#5 The Netherlands
#6 Singapore	#6 Australia	#6 Denmark
#7 Chile	#7 Sweden	#7 Switzerland
#8 Finland	#8 Canada	#8 United States
#9 Canada	#9 Poland	#9 Latvia
#10 United States	#10 South Korea	#10 United Kingdom
#11 Mexico	#11 United States	#11 Estonia
#12 United Kingdom	#12 Switzerland	#12 Canada
#13 South Africa	#13 United Kingdom	#13 Finland
#14 South Korea	#14 Brazil	#14 Russian Federation
#15 Poland	#15 Japan	#15 Chile
#16 Indonesia	#16 France	#16 Hong Kong
#17 India	#17 The Netherlands	#17 Luxembourg
#18 Germany	#18 Germany	#18 Lithuania
#19 France	#19 Italy	#19 Singapore
#20 Ireland	#20 Spain	#20 Mexico
#21 China	#21 Czech Republic	
#22 Japan	#22 Poland	
#23 Brazil	#23 Ireland	
#24 Austria	#24 Romania	
#25 Italy	#25 Germany	

Sources: GAO analysis of data from Mercer, *Melbourne Mercer Global Pension Index* (Melbourne, Australia: Australian Centre for Financial Studies, October 2015); R. Jackson, N. Howe, and T. Peter, *The Global Aging Preparedness Index, 2nd edition* (Washington, D.C.: Center for Strategic and International Studies, October 2013); and Allianz, "2014 Pension Sustainability Index," *International Pension Papers 1/2014* (Munich, Germany: January 2014). | GAO-18-111SP.

[a] The Allianz study ranked 50 countries. Only the top 25 countries are included here. (All rankings for the other two studies are shown: The Melbourne Mercer study ranked 25 countries and the Global Aging study ranked 20 countries.).

The dimension of sustainability examines a country's ability to finance its retirement system over the long term. The aging of the population, primarily due to lower birth rates and increasing longevity, has been putting financial pressure on retirement income systems in many countries, raising concerns about the long-term sustainability of their systems.[236] Studies were more similar in their ranking of the United States on this aspect of retirement (see Table 5).

> ***Public debt***: the amount of debt owed by a government (or country) to its creditors. The value of assets owned by the government is subtracted from the gross debt amount to arrive at the net public debt.
>
> Source: GAO (see glossary). | GAO-18-111SP.

In the 2015 Melbourne Mercer study, the United States ranked #10 in terms of sustainability. The study considered several indicators to compute this index, including the projected old-age dependency ratio (i.e., the population age 65 or older divided by the working-age population, age 15 to 64) in 2035; the proportion of employees who are members of a private pension plan; the level of pension assets as a proportion of GDP; and public debt as a percentage of GDP, among others.

> ***Total government revenue***: the sources of revenue for governments include individual income tax, payroll taxes that fund social insurance programs, corporate income tax, excise taxes, value added tax, and others.
>
> Source: GAO (see glossary). | GAO-18-111SP.

According to the CSIS Global Aging study's fiscal sustainability index, the United States ranked #11 out of 20 countries.[237] The underlying indicators for this index included, among others, the projected total public benefits going to the elderly as a percentage of GDP in 2040, as well as the

[236] As discussed earlier in section 3, the primary drivers behind the Social Security program's financial difficulties are the aging of the population and the escalating retirement of the baby boomers.

[237] *The Global Aging Preparedness Index.*

projected total government revenue and net public debt as a percentage of GDP in 2040.

Allianz's 2014 Pension Sustainability Index ranked the United States #8 out of 50 countries.[238] The indicators used to develop the index included projections for 2050 of the old-age dependency ratio (calculated the same way as in the Melbourne Mercer study), and pension expenditures as a percentage of GDP.

Considering similar indicators of retirement system finances, the OECD also found that the old-age dependency ratio in the United States was low compared to the OECD average in 2015, and was projected to be lower in 2050, as well. This suggests that the United States, when compared to other OECD countries, has a relatively favorable ratio of older people to working age people.[239] The OECD also found that public expenditures on scheduled Social Security retirement benefits as a percentage of GDP in the United States have been below the OECD average for comparable benefits since 1990, and were projected to remain lower in 2050.[240] This suggests that, compared to other OECD countries, the strain that Social Security retirement benefits, place on society's economic resources in the United States is lower.[241]

Integrity

> ***Governance*:** determines who has power, who makes decisions, how other players make their voices heard, and how account is rendered.
>
> Source: GAO (see glossary). | GAO-18-111SP.

---

[238] *2014 Pension Sustainability Index.*

[239] The OECD dependency ratio was based on the number of people age 65 or older per 100 people of working age, defined as those between ages 20 and 64. The OECD dependency ratio in the United States in 2015 was 24.7; weighted and unweighted OECD average dependency ratios in the same year were 27.3 and 27.6, respectively. The projected figures for 2050 were 39.5 for the United States; for the OECD averages, they were 48.5 (weighted) and 51 (unweighted).

[240] OECD projections used scheduled Social Security benefits.

[241] The strain Social Security benefits place on society's resources in the United States reflects, in part, the long-term financial challenges facing Social Security and the projection that Social Security will be unable to pay full benefits promised to retirees beginning in 2035.

The dimension of integrity focuses on the strength of the regulatory and administrative oversight of a country's retirement system. According to Melbourne Mercer, integrity reflects factors that influence the overall governance and operations of retirement systems and affect the level of confidence that participants have in their systems. The Melbourne Mercer study was the only study among the international comparisons we reviewed that included an index of integrity of retirement systems.

The Melbourne Mercer integrity index focuses on three areas: regulation and governance, protection and communication for plan participants, and costs.[242] Also, the index focuses on private pensions because it expects private pensions to take on an increasingly important role in the provision of retirement income over time. In 2015, the Melbourne Mercer study ranked the United States #20 among 25 countries on this dimension. The underlying indicators used to compute the integrity index included, among others, whether private pensions were required to submit annual reports in a specific format to the regulator; the degree to which the regulator actively exercised its supervisory responsibilities; whether a private pension plan was required to be a separate legal entity from the employer; and the percentage of total pension assets held in various types of pension funds.

Potential Areas in Need of Comprehensive Reform for the U.S. Retirement System

Based on a distillation of the findings and recommendations from prior federal commissions, the input of our expert panel, various international studies, and an assessment of our prior work and the work of other researches and organizations, we identified five policy goals for a reformed U.S. retirement system. They are (1) promoting universal access to a retirement savings vehicle, (2) ensuring greater retirement income adequacy, (3) improving options for the spend down phase of retirement,

---

[242] While the Melbourne Mercer study applied its integrity criteria mainly to private pensions, a similar examination could be made with regard to state and local pension plans and to Social Security.

(4) reducing complexity and risk for both participants and employers, and (5) stabilizing fiscal exposure to the federal government (see Table 6).

Table 6. Policy Goals for Evaluating Potential Options for Reforming the U.S. Retirement System

Goals	Reasons for considering reform
Promote universal access to a retirement savings vehicle	About one-third of U.S. workers do not have access to an employer-sponsored retirement plan
Ensure greater retirement income adequacy	Many Americans are at risk of relying solely on Social Security in retirement
Improve options for the spend down phase of retirement	Plans may not provide sufficient tools to aid retirees in the spend down of their savings
Reduce complexity and risk for both plan participants and sponsors	Decisions related to managing retirement savings and plan sponsorship have reached a level of complexity that participants and plan sponsors, respectively, find difficult to navigate
Stabilize fiscal exposure to the federal government	As the number of retirees increases, so does the financial stress on government programs serving the aging population

Source: GAO analysis. | GAO-18-111SP.

Reforming the nation's retirement system to create a system that meets all of these goals will require a careful and deliberative approach. For example, some type of consensus about the goals would need to be established as a first step. Broad questions are likely to be raised about how each of the goals should be achieved. The examination of relevant issues by past federal commissions, the discussions at our November 2016 panel, as well as the experiences of other countries, further illustrate how complex any reform effort is likely to be.

Conclusions and Matter for Congressional Consideration

The U.S. retirement system is supported by three main pillars: Social Security, employer-sponsored pension or retirement savings plans, and individual savings. Currently, each of these pillars faces challenges. First,

Social Security is projected to be unable to pay full retirement benefits beginning in 2035, which could require future benefits to be reduced or delayed. Second, fewer employers offer DB pension plans, and the insurer of most of these plans, the PBGC, faced an accumulated deficit of more than $79 billion at the end of fiscal year 2016. Workers who participate in DC plans must often navigate complex financial decisions to plan for and manage their accounts, and many may be at risk of outliving their savings. Third, millions of workers do not have access to either a DB or a DC employer-sponsored plan, and their personal savings may not be enough to last through retirement. The personal saving rate in the United States, while improved since 2005, has not returned to its pre-1975 level. Should Social Security benefits and other income sources prove inadequate, federal safety net programs, such as those providing nutrition and housing assistance, may face additional budgetary pressure from retirees. Unless action is taken to address all these challenges, many older Americans could lack the means to have a secure and dignified retirement in the future.

The nation's retirement system has not been comprehensively examined by the federal government since the 1979 Commission on Pension Policy, established nearly 40 years ago. Issues identified by the 1979 commission not only continue to be relevant today, but have become more complex and more urgent with the shift from DB to DC plans, and the increasing risks and responsibilities workers face in planning and managing their retirement, as well as the increasing fiscal risks across the system. Retirement experts participating in the panel we convened agreed that a comprehensive solution needs to be found, and the experiences of other countries may provide useful insights for ways to improve the nation's approach to better promote retirement security.

The U.S. retirement system is complex, with many different federal agencies involved in various aspects of providing supports and services to older adults, and with no one agency responsible for overseeing the system in its entirety. Given this complexity and the interrelated nature of the challenges facing the retirement system today, a piecemeal approach without clear leadership will not be sufficient to address the policy goals of (1) promoting universal access to a retirement savings vehicle, (2) ensuring greater retirement income adequacy, (3) improving options for the spend down of savings in retirement, (4) reducing complexity and risk for both participants and employers, and (5) stabilizing fiscal exposure to the federal government. We recognize that some of these goals may compete with each other—in particular, ensuring greater retirement security and minimizing fiscal exposure to the federal government. Therefore, a balanced approach will be required, which can only result from a more holistic examination of the issues by those representing a broad range of perspectives.

Matter for Congressional Consideration

Congress should consider establishing an independent commission to comprehensively examine the U.S. retirement system and make recommendations to clarify key policy goals for the system and improve how the nation can promote more stable retirement security. We suggest that such a commission include representatives from government agencies, employers, the financial services industry, unions, participant advocates, and researchers, among others, to help inform policymakers on changes needed to improve the current U.S. retirement system.

Appendix I: Selected Federal Legislation and Other Milestones Shaping Retirement in the United States

The chronology below highlights selected federal legislation and other milestones to illustrate the evolution of retirement policies in the United States dating back to the beginning of the nation itself. It is not intended to be an exhaustive list of legislation and milestones that have impacted retirement in the United States, nor is it intended to include comprehensive descriptions of each law or milestone. Rather, our intention is merely to provide various glimpses into the evolution of retirement policies over time. Entries describing selected actions of the Continental Congress that pre-date the United States Constitution are based on the Journals of the Continental Congress. Entries describing selected provisions of federal legislation pertaining to retirement are based on a review of appropriate legal materials (rows highlighted in blue). Entries describing other selected milestones are based on agency documents and various secondary sources, listed below, following the chronology. Some of these entries in the chronology refer to state laws. In describing these state legislative actions, we relied entirely on secondary sources and did not conduct a separate legal analysis to confirm these facts, nor did we verify the legal accuracy of the other selected milestones. Entries are intended to convey what happened in the designated year or years noted; they are not intended to be statements about current provisions or conditions.

Chronology of Selected Federal Legislation and Other Milestones Shaping Retirement in the United States

1778	**Resolution establishing nation's first type of a service pension** Selected provisions: In response to an appeal from General George Washington at Valley Forge, the Continental Congress unanimously voted in favor of a pension of half pay for 7 years after the war's conclusion for all commissioned officers who continued in service to the end of the war. Soldiers were promised a gratuity of $80.
1780	**Resolution establishing nation's first type of survivors' pension benefits** Selected provisions: The Continental Congress resolved to provide benefits to the widows or orphan children of officers who were granted the 7-year service pension in May 1778, but who died before the 7 years had expired.
1780	**Resolution establishing nation's first type of a lifetime annuity pension** Selected provisions: Again in response to an appeal from General Washington, the Continental Congress resolved that all officers continuing in service to the end of the war should be entitled to half pay for life at retirement from service.
1783	**Resolution establishing nation's first type of lump-sum option** (commonly known as the Commutation Act) Selected provisions: Provided for commutation of the officers' half-pay-for-life pension to 5 years' full pay (in money, or in securities bearing interest at 6 percent per annum), in response to officers' fears that they would never get their due, instead allowing for full-pay during a term of years, or for a sum in gross.
1799	**Act for the Government of the Navy of the United States** Selected provisions: A navy pension fund was established for sailors disabled in the line of duty, with monies derived from the sale of captured prizes.[a]

(Continued)

1842 - 1867	The navy pension fund was exhausted following a history of overly-generous benefits after the War of 1812 that were granted (including to widows and orphans), and then repealed; fraud and mismanagement by pension officials; and losses due to the failure of Columbia Bank. Congress provided annual appropriations to fund navy pensions until the Civil War, when the fund began to accrue large sums from the sale of prizes taken at sea.
1857 - 1866	The earliest state law creating retirement benefits for public employees was passed in New York, providing a lump-sum payment to New York City police officers injured in the line of duty. This same coverage was afforded New York City's firefighters in 1866. (NCPERS)
1875	The American Express Company, a railroad freight forwarder, established the first private pension plan in the United States in an effort to create a stable, career-oriented workforce. It was a noncontributory plan—that is, employees were not required to contribute to the plan. (Latimer)
1878	The New York City police officers' retirement plan, initially only providing benefits to officers injured in the line of duty, was revised to provide a lifetime pension for police officers at age 55 after completing 21 years of service. (NCPERS)
1880	The Baltimore & Ohio Railroad established the second U.S. private pension plan, a contributory plan. (Latimer)
1886	The Pennsylvania Railroad established a pension plan that was considered innovative at the time in that it was administered by the firm itself, through an internal voluntary relief department, which was viewed as a vanguard of modern corporate personnel administration. (Sass)
1894	The earliest municipal pension plan for teachers was established in New York's borough of Manhattan. (NCPERS)
1901	The Chicago & North Western and the Illinois Central railroads adopted pension plans modeled after the Pennsylvania design, incorporating the principle of compulsory retirement. (Latimer)
1903	Standard Oil of New Jersey established a pension plan for its employees, with terms that serve as a model for many other plans to follow: eligibility for retirement is set at age 65, with 25 years of service, and a pension amount set at 25 percent of average pay over the preceding 10 years. (Latimer)
1905	A philanthropic gift from Andrew Carnegie provided the seed money for a prototype multiemployer plan in higher education, covering employees across nearly 100 different colleges and universities, and allowing them job mobility among these institutions without loos of their pension benefits. Although the plan was later phased out, the experiment eventually led to the establishment of the nonprofit Teachers Insurance and Annuity Association (TIAA) in 1918. (Greenough and King)
1909	**Corporate Income Tax Act of 1909** Selected provisions: Imposed an excise tax on corporations, joint stock companies, and associations organized for profit and having a capitol stock represented by shares, as well as certain insurance companies.

1911	Massachusetts established the first retirement pension plan for general state employees, but in general, states were slow to adopt these plans. (Clark, et al.)
1913	Wyoming became the 36th and last state needed to ratify the 16th Amendment into law, which stated: "Congress shall have power to lay and collect taxes on incomes, from whatever source derived, without apportionment among the several states, and without regard to any census or enumeration." (IRS)
1913	An Act to reduce tariff duties and to provide revenue for the Government, and for other purposes (commonly known as the Revenue Act of 1913 or the Tariff Act of 1913) Selected provision: Established an early framework for the current individual income tax.
1920	**An Act for the retirement of employees in the classified civil service, and for other purposes** (commonly known as the Civil Service Retirement Act of 1920) Selected provisions: Established a retirement system for certain federal employees. The Civil Service Retirement System (CSRS) was structured as a DB, contributory retirement system, with employees sharing in the expense of the annuities to which they would become entitled.
1921	**An act to reduce and equalize taxation, to provide revenue, and for other purposes** (commonly known the Revenue Act of 1921) Selected provisions: Exempted trust income from stock bonus or profit sharing plans (beyond an employee's contributions) from an employee's current taxable income; provided that trust income is taxed at the time it is distributed, to the extent the income exceeds the employee's own contributions; required that a profit-sharing or stock bonus plan be established for the exclusive benefit of "some or all" employees.
1923	The failure of the Morris Packing Company plan exposed weakness in the U.S. private pension system. After ceasing operations, Morris stopped making payments to its pension program, a contributory plan with 3,500 participants and 400 retirees drawing benefits. (Sass)
1926	**Revenue Act of 1926** Selected provisions: Exempted trust income from pension plans from an employee's current taxable income; in the same way provided to stock bonus or profit sharing plans in the Revenue Act of 1921.
1927-1932	As the Great Depression took hold during these years, nearly 10 percent of private pension plans were either discontinued or suspended. Yet over this same period, the number of private plans grew. Most of these new plans were contributory and contractual. By 1932, the unfunded liability of private pension plans across the entire corporate sector was estimated to be $2 billion, roughly 2 percent of the U.S. gross national product. (Sass)
1931-1934	The Railroad Employees' National Pension Association (RENPA) called on the government to protect the railroads' pension system, which was at risk of failing. (Sass)
1934	President Roosevelt's Committee on Economic Security—established by executive order and comprised of cabinet-level appointees—designed a social insurance program that was intended to resemble some of the soundest private plans, calling for it to be compulsory and contributory. The committee's report and the administration's legislative proposal served as a precursor to Social Security. (SSA)

(Continued)

1935	**Social Security Act of 1935** Selected provisions: Provided for the general welfare by, among other things, establishing a system of federal old-age benefits to begin at age 65 as the normal retirement age, and created the Social Security Board to administer the law. (The Board's functions were later transferred to the Federal Security Agency and the Social Security Administration.)c
1937	**Railroad Retirement and Carriers' Taxing Acts of 1937** Selected provisions: Established a national Railroad Retirement program, covering employees for retirement and disability. The program was financed with a tax, initially set at 2.75 percent, paid by both the employer and the employee on the first $300 of monthly income.[d]
1937	Following lower-than-expected tax receipts in 1936, the Joint Committee on Tax Evasion and Avoidance held hearings on the ways that taxpayers were using various schemes to defeat the intent of Congress to tax incomes in accordance with their ability to pay. For example, one of the areas of concern investigated by the committee included the tax treatment of pension trusts that were serving only small groups of officers and directors with high incomes within a corporation. (Report of the Joint Committee)
1942	**Revenue Act of 1942** Selected provisions: Added a numerical nondiscrimination coverage test and a general nondiscrimination test for benefits and contributions for a pension or retirement plan to be qualified under the tax code.
1942	**An Act to amend the Emergency Price Control Act of 1942, to aid in preventing inflation, and for other purposes** (commonly known as the Stabilization Act of 1942) Selected provision: Authorized the president to freeze wages in an attempt to contain wartime inflation.
1946	Union membership more than tripled in the decade leading up to and during World War II. In 1936, union members in the United States numbered just under 4 million; by 1946, membership had grown to nearly 14.5 million. (Mayer)
1947	**Labor-Management Relations Act of 1947** Selected provision: Provided fundamental guidelines for the establishment and operation of pension plans administered jointly by an employer and a union.
1950	The number of large public plans increased dramatically during the period starting from just prior to the enactment of Social Security legislation in 1935 up to when optional coverage was afforded state and local government employees in 1950. Specifically, between 1931 and 1950, nearly one-half of the largest state and local government pension plans in the country were established. (Pension Task Force Report)
1950	**Social Security Act Amendments of 1950** Selected provisions: Provided that state and local governments could elect coverage for most of their employees not covered by a retirement system.
1950	The Social Security Amendments of 1950 resulted in extending coverage to about 10 million employees of state and local governments. (SSA)

1951	**Railroad Retirement Act and Railroad Unemployment Insurance Act Amendments** Selected provisions: Established a financial interchange between the Railroad Retirement and Social Security programs to allow the Social Security Trust Funds to operate as if railroad employees were covered under Social Security rather than their own system.
1954	President Eisenhower issued a special message to Congress, noting that Social Security is the cornerstone of the federal government's programs to promote the economic security of the individual, and outlining various recommendations to correct "certain limitations and inequities in the law." For example, he recommended that coverage be broadened to include self-employed workers, more farmworkers and domestic workers, and various professional workers, among others. He also recommended that the level of benefits be increased, that the benefit formula be changed to fulfill its purpose of helping to combat destitution, and that people over age 65 be encouraged to take on part-time jobs without losing their benefits.[e]
1954	**Social Security Amendments of 1954** Selected provisions: Amended the Social Security Act and the Internal Revenue Code to extend coverage under Social Security and increase benefits, preserve the insurance rights of disabled individuals, and increase the amount of earnings permitted without loss of benefits, and for other purposes.
1956	**Social Security Amendments of 1956** Selected provision: Allowed women to elect early, reduced benefits at age 62, with full retirement benefits remaining available for those who retire at age 65.
1958	**Welfare and Pension Plans Disclosure Act** Selected provision: Provided for registration, reporting and disclosure of the financial operations of welfare and pension plans.
1961	**Social Security Amendments of 1961** Selected provision: Enacted a provision for men, comparable to the provision enacted for women in 1956, concerning early retirement at age 62.
1962	**Self-Employed Individuals Tax Retirement Act of 1962** Selections provision: Imposed minimum distribution requirements for self-employed participants in a qualified plan generally beginning at age 70½.
1963	Automobile manufacturer Studebaker-Packard Corp. shuttered its plant, leaving a poorly funded pension plan. Many retirees received a fraction of the pension benefits they had earned and thousands of others received nothing at all. This crisis drew national attention to the insecurity of pensions and was invoked in support of pension reform efforts that eventually led to the Employee Retirement Income Security Act of 1974. (Wooten)
1965	**Social Security Amendments of 1965** Selected provisions: Enacted new titles to the Social Security Act for Medicare and Medicaid. Medicare provided hospital, post-hospital extended care, and home health coverage to almost all Americans aged 65 or older; Medicaid provided states with the option of receiving federal funding for providing health care services to certain low income and medically needy individuals.

(Continued)

1967	**Age Discrimination in Employment Act of 1967** Selected provisions: Made it unlawful for an employer to discriminate against any individual with respect to compensation, terms, conditions, or privileges of employment because of age; and required the Secretary of Labor to carry on a continuing program of education and information, which could include research with a view to reducing barriers to the employment of older persons.
1974	**Employee Retirement Income Security Act of 1974** (ERISA) Selected provisions: Regulated private-sector employers who offer pension or welfare benefit plans for their employees. • Title I: Imposed reporting and disclosure requirements on plans; imposed certain responsibilities on plan fiduciaries. • Title II: Strengthened participation requirements for employees age 25 or older, establishes vesting rules, required that a joint and survivor annuity be provided, and establishes minimum funding standards. In addition, provided individual retirement accounts (IRAs) for persons not covered by pensions. • Title IV: Required certain employers and plan administrators to fund an insurance system to protect certain kinds of retirement benefits (i.e., to pay premiums to the federal government's Pension Benefit Guaranty Corporation (PBGC).
1978	**Revenue Act of 1978** Selected provisions: Established qualified deferred compensation plans called 401(k) plans after 26 U.S.C. § 401(k)), which allowed for pre-tax employee contributions to such plans (known as elective deferrals).
1978	President Carter signed an executive order calling for the establishment of the President's Commission on Pension Policy to conduct a 2-year study of the nation's pension systems and the future course of national retirement-income policies, and issue a series of reports on short-term and long-term issues with respect to retirement, survivor, and disability programs. The Commission was established in 1979 and issued its final report in February 1981.
1980	**Multiemployer Pension Plan Amendments Act of 1980** Selected provisions: Strengthened the funding requirements for multiemployer pension plans, authorized plan preservation measures for financially troubled multiemployer plans, and revised the manner in which insurance provisions applied to multiemployer plans.
1981	The Congress and President Reagan appointed a National Commission on Social Security Reform (known as the Greenspan Commission) to study and make recommendations regarding the short-term financing crisis that Social Security faced at the time. The report was issued in 1983 and was the basis for the Social Security Amendments of 1983.

1982	**Tax Equity and Fiscal Responsibility Act of 1982** Selected provisions: Reduced the maximum annual addition (employer contributions, employee contributions, and forfeitures) for each participant in a DC plan; reduced the maximum annual retirement benefit for each participant in a DB plan; introduced special rules for top heavy plans (i.e., plans in which more than 60 percent of the present value of the cumulative accrued benefits under the plan for all employees accrue to key employees, including certain owners and officers, and expanded minimum distribution requirements to all qualified plans.
1983	**Social Security Amendments of 1983** Selected provisions: Gradually raised the normal retirement age from 65 to 67, depending on an individuals' year of birth; expanded coverage, increased the self-employment tax for self-employed persons, subjected a portion of Social Security benefits to federal income tax for the first time, and changed how cost-of-living adjustments are calculated when trust funds are low.
1984	**Deficit Reduction Act of 1984** Selected provisions: Amended nondiscrimination testing requirements for 401(k) plans and required minimum distribution rules, and restricted prefunding of certain employee post-retirement welfare benefits (such as disability and medical benefits).
1984	**Retirement Equity Act of 1984** Selected provisions: Changed participation rules by lowering the minimum age that a plan may require for enrollment (from age 25 to 21), and permitted certain breaks in service without loss of pension credits. Also, strengthened treatment of pension benefits for widowed and divorced spouses.
1986	**Single-Employer Pension Plan Amendments Act of 1986** Selected provisions: Raised the per-participant PBGC premium from $2.60 to $8.50; established certain distress criteria that a contributing sponsor or substantial member of a contributing sponsor's controlled group must meet in order to terminate a single-employer plan under a distress termination; established certain criteria for PBGC to terminate a plan that does not have sufficient assets to pay benefits that are currently due (referred to as involuntary terminations; and created a new liability to plan participants for certain non-guaranteed benefits.
1986	**Federal Employees' Retirement System Act of 1986** Selected provisions: Established the Federal Employees' Retirement System (FERS). Unlike under CSRS, retirement and disability benefits under FERS were structured to be fully funded by employee and employer contributions and interest earned by the bonds in which the contributions were invested. The DB benefit under FERS was lower than under CSRS, but FERS also included a DC plan component: the Thrift Savings Plan.
1986	**Omnibus Budget Reconciliation Act of 1986** Selected provisions: Required employers that sponsor pension (DB plans) and retirement savings plans (DC plans such as 401(k)s) to provide benefit accruals or allocations for employees who work beyond their normal retirement age.

(Continued)

1986	**Tax Reform Act of 1986** Selected provisions: Established faster minimum vesting schedules; adjusted limitations on contributions and benefits for qualified plans; limited the exclusion for employee elective deferrals to $7,000; and amended nondiscrimination coverage rules. Also, restricted the allowable tax-deductible contributions to IRAs for individuals with incomes above a certain level and who participate in employer-sponsored pension plans, and imposed an additional 10 percent tax on early distributions (before age 59½) from a qualified retirement plan.
1987	**Omnibus Budget Reconciliation Act of 1987** Selected provisions: Strengthened funding rules for pension plans and the level and structure of PBGC premiums.
1993	**Omnibus Budget Reconciliation Act of 1993** Selected provision: Reduced compensation taken into account in determining contributions and benefits under qualified retirement plans. Expanded taxation of Social Security benefits.
1994	An Advisory Council on Social Security was established under Section 706 of the Social Security Act to consider financing issues, including the long-range financial status of the Social Security retirement and disability programs, as well as general Social Security issues, such as the relative equity and adequacy provided for persons at various income levels, in various family situations, and various age cohorts. The final report was issued in January 1997.
1994	**Retirement Protection Act of 1994** Selected provision: Strengthened funding rules for pension plans.
1996	**Small Business Job Protection Act of 1996** Selected provisions: Created a type of simplified retirement savings vehicle for small employers; added a nondiscrimination safe harbor for 401(k) plans; amended the definition of highly-compensated employee; and modified certain participation rules for DC plans.
1997	**Taxpayer Relief Act of 1997** Selected provisions: Established Roth IRAs, under which contributions are after-tax, but investment earnings and distributions after age 59½ are tax-free.
2000	**Senior Citizens' Freedom to Work Act of 2000** Selected provisions: Amended the Social Security Act to eliminate the earnings limit for individuals who have reached their normal retirement age.
2000	LTV Steel filed for Chapter 11 bankruptcy protection resulting in the largest termination and trusteeship in PBGC history. When PBGC assumed responsibility for the LTV plans in 2002, the plans had about 82,000 participants and were underfunded by about $2.2 billion.[f]
2001	President Bush established the President's Commission to Strengthen Social Security to conduct a bipartisan study and provide specific recommendations, using six guiding principles, to preserve Social Security for seniors while building wealth for younger Americans. The final report was issued December 2001.

2001	**Economic Growth and Tax Relief Reconciliation Act of 2001 (EGTRRA)** Selected provisions: Increased the individual elective deferrals that may be made to a 401(k) plan; added catch-up contributions that allow individuals age 50 or older to make additional contributions; increased the maximum annual contributions to DC plans and individual retirement accounts; increased the maximum annual benefits under a DB plan; increased the compensation limit for qualified trusts; reduced the minimum vesting requirements for matching contributions; changed the rules that permit plans to cash-out, without consent.
2002	Enron, a large energy company, went bankrupt after being plagued by financial fraud and insider trading, giving rise to the Sarbanes-Oxley Act of 2002. One aspect of this debacle involved Enron employees' retirement plan. Before the bankruptcy, when the value of Enron stock was plummeting, its rank and file DC plan participants were not permitted to sell their Enron shares and, therefore, suffered greater losses than they may have otherwise.
2002	**Sarbanes-Oxley Act of 2002** Selected provisions: Added a new requirement that individual account pension plans provide notice to participants and beneficiaries in advance of periods during which the ability of participants or participants or beneficiaries to take certain actions with respect to their accounts will be temporarily suspended, limited or restricted (referred to as blackout periods).
2006	**Pension Protection Act of 2006 (PPA)** Selected provisions: Strengthened the minimum funding requirements for DB plans; set certain benefit limitations for underfunded DB plans; enhanced the protections for spouses; amended plan asset diversification requirements; changed provisions concerning the portability of pension plans; allowed the adoption of automatic enrollment and target date funds for DC plans; and increased reporting and disclosure requirements for plan sponsors.
2007-2009	The nation suffered the worst recession since the 1930s. After adjusting for inflation, gross domestic product declined by 5.1 percent and the national unemployment rate peaked at 10.0 percent.
2008	**Worker, Retiree, and Employer Recovery Act of 2008** Selected provision: Modified PPA's funding requirements to grant relief for single-employer DB plans.
2010	President Obama established the National Commission on Fiscal Responsibility and Reform (known as the Simpson Bowles Commission), by executive order, to identifying policies to improve the fiscal situation of the federal government in the medium term and to achieve fiscal sustainability over the long run (including the lasting solvency of Social Security), and propose recommendations designed to balance the budget. The final report was issued in December 2010.
2012	**Moving Ahead for Progress in the 21st Century Act (MAP-21)** Selected provisions: Provided funding relief for single-employer DB plans by changing the interest rates used to reflect a 25-year historical average; increased premium rates for sponsors of single employer and multiemployer DB plans, and included other provisions intended to improve the governance of PBGC.

(Continued)

2012	**American Taxpayer Relief Act of 2012** Selected provisions: Extended the tax-free treatment of distributions from IRAs made for charitable purposes; allowed for certain in-plan transfers to a Roth account.
2014	The deficit in PBGC's Multiemployer Insurance Program was $42.4 billion at the end of fiscal year 2014, a five-fold increase from the program's $8.3 billion deficit at the end of fiscal year 2013.
2014	**Multiemployer Pension Reform Act of 2014 (MPRA)** Selected provisions: Allowed severely underfunded multiemployer plans, under certain conditions and with the approval of federal regulators, the option to reduce the retirement benefits of current retirees to avoid plan insolvency and expanded PBGC's ability to intervene when plans are in financial distress.

Source: GAO and various other sources, as cited. | GAO-18-111SP.

[a] Prior to passage of the Act for the Government of the Navy, both army and navy pensions were financed entirely on a pay-as-you-go basis from general revenues.

[b] For discussion of efforts to establish an income tax prior to ratification of the 16th amendment, dating back the 1862 and the Civil War, see IRS's *Historical Highlights of the IRS* (last reviewed or updated on July 6, 2016), accessed October 4, 2017, https://www.irs.gov/newsroom/historical-highlights-of-the-irs.

[c] According to the National Conference on Public Employee Retirement Systems, the Social Security Act excluded state and local government employees, due to concerns over constitutional issues related to the federal taxation of states and their political subdivisions.

[d] For discussion of the unsuccessful efforts to enact a railroad retirement act prior to 1937, see Kevin Whitman, "An Overview of the Railroad Retirement Program," *Social Security Bulletin*, vol. 68, no. 2 (2008).

[e] President Dwight D. Eisenhower, *Special Message to the Congress on Old Age and Survivors Insurance and on Federal Grants-in-Aid for Public Assistance Programs* (Jan.14, 1954).

[f] Pension Benefit Guaranty Corporation, "PBGC Protects Benefits of 82,000 LTV Workers in Largest-Ever Federal Pension Takeover," press release 02-16 (Mar. 29, 2002).

List of Sources

Centers for Medicare and Medicaid Services. *Medicare & Medicaid: Milestones 1937-2015*. Washington, D.C.: July 2015.

Clark, Robert L., Lee A. Craig, and Jack W. Wilson. *A History of Public Sector Pensions in the United States*. Philadelphia: Pension Research Council, University of Pennsylvania Press, 2003.

Clark, Robert L., Janemarie Mulvey, and Sylvester J. Schieber. "Effects of Nondiscrimination Rules on Pension Participation," in *Private*

Pensions and Public Policies, eds. William G. Gale, John B. Shoven, and Mark J. Warshawsky. Washington, D.C.: Brookings Institution Press, 2004.

Crane, Roderick B. "Chapter 6: Regulation and Taxation of Public Plans: A History of Increasing Federal Influence," in *Pensions in the Public Sector*, eds. Olivia S. Mitchell and Edwin C. Hustead. Philadelphia: Pension Research Council, University of Pennsylvania Press, 2001.

Employee Benefit Research Institute (EBRI). *History of Pension Plans*. Washington, D.C.: EBRI, March 1998.

Employee Benefit Research Institute (EBRI). *EBRI Databook on Employee Benefits Appendix E: Legislative History*. Washington, D.C.: EBRI, updated October 2015.

Glasson, William Henry. *History of Military Pension Legislation in the United States*. New York: Columbia University Press, 1900.

Georgetown University Law Center. *A Timeline of the Evolution of Retirement in the United States*. Washington, D.C.: Georgetown University, 2010.

Greenough, William C., and Francis P. King. *Pension Plans and Public Policy*. New York: Columbia University Press, 1976.

Internal Revenue Service. *Key Legislative History Affecting Retirement Plans*. Last reviewed or updated on September 29, 2017. Accessed October 4, 2017. https://www.irs.gov/Retirement-Plans/Key-LegislativeHistory-Affecting-Retirement-Plans.

Latimer, Murray Webb. *Industrial Pension Systems in the United States and Canada*. New York: Industrial Relations Counselors, Inc., 1932.

Library of Congress. *Journals of the Continental Congress,* 1774-1789, vol. XI, 1778, and vol. XXIV, 1783.

Mayer, Gerald. *Union Membership Trends in the United States*. Washington, D.C.: Congressional Research Service, Aug. 31, 2004.

Moore, Kathryn. "Raising the Social Security Retirement Ages: Weighing the Costs and Benefits." *33 Ariz. St. L.J.* 543 (Summer 2001).

National Conference on Public Employee Retirement Systems (NCPERS). *The Evolution of Public Pension Plans: Past, Present and Future*. Washington, D.C.: NCPERS, March 2008.

Pension Benefit Guaranty Corporation. *History of PBGC*. Accessed October 4, 2017. http://www.pbgc.gov/about/who-we-are/pg/history-ofpbgc.html.

Pension Task Force Report on Public Employee Retirement Systems. House Committee on Education and Labor. 95th Cong., 2d sess. Washington, D.C.: U.S. Government Printing Office, 1978.

Report of the Joint Committee on Tax Evasion and Avoidance of the Congress of the United States; pursuant to Public Resolution No. 40. 75th Cong., 1st sess. Washington, D.C.: U.S. Government Printing Office, 1937.

Sass, Steven A. *The Promise of Private Pensions: The First Hundred Years*. Cambridge, MA: Harvard University Press, 1997.

Social Security Administration. *Social Security History: Organizational History*. Accessed October 4, 2017. https://www.ssa.gov/history/orghist.html.

Social Security Administration. *Social Security In-Depth Research: Legislative History*. Accessed October 4, 2017. https://www.ssa.gov/history/law.html.

U.S. Congress. *The Public Statutes at Large of the United States of America, from the Organization of the Government in 1789, to March 3, 1845*. Vol. I. Boston: Charles C. Little and James Brown, 1848.

U.S. Department of Labor. *Summary of the Major Laws of the Department of Labor*. Accessed October 4, 2017. http://www.dol.gov/general/aboutdol/majorlaws.

Wooten, James A. "The Most Glorious Story of Failure in Business: The Studebaker–Packard Corporation and the Origins of ERISA." *Buffalo Law Review*, vol. 49 (2001)

APPENDIX II: OVERVIEW OF METHODS

In compiling the data for this chapter, we used a variety of methods to examine recent trends in retirement security and explore what these trends could mean for the nation. For all sections, we began with an examination of our recently published work (see Related GAO Products), and then supplemented our previous findings with additional information from various federal agencies, organizations, and institutions (see Table 7).

Table 7. Federal Agencies, Organizations, and Institutions Providing Data Cited in This Chapter

Federal agencies	Board of Governors of the Federal Reserve System Centers for Medicare & Medicaid Services Congressional Budget Office Pension Benefit Guaranty Corporation	Social Security Administration Bureau of Economic Analysis Census Bureau Department of Labor Department of the Treasury
Organizations and institutions	AARP Public Policy Institute Allianz American Enterprise Institute Center for Retirement Research at Boston College Center for Strategic and International Studies Employee Benefit Research Institute (EBRI)	Investment Company Institute Melbourne Mercer Organization for Economic Co-cooperation and Development (OECD) Plan Sponsor Council of America Pew Research Center Vanguard

Source: GAO. | GAO-18-111SP.

For example, in the first section, we supplemented our prior work on the fundamental changes that have occurred in the landscape of the U.S. retirement system by obtaining recent trend data from federal agencies such as the Social Security Administration, the Department of Labor, the Census Bureau, and the Centers for Medicare & Medicaid Services. In the second section, we relied primarily on our recently published work to summarize key challenges facing workers in their efforts to plan and manage a secure retirement, but added insights and examples from agency documents, organization reports, and studies from institutions such as the Center for Retirement Research at Boston College. In the third section, we examined the fiscal risks associated with the three pillars of the current U.S. retirement system based primarily on prior work such as our recent reports on the nation's fiscal health and high risk update, and an analysis of agency data on the financial status of certain programs, such as Social

Security, Medicare, and the Pension Benefit Guaranty Corporation's insurance programs.

Finally, in the fourth section, to evaluate the effectiveness of the nation's piecemeal approach to address retirement security challenges, we augmented an assessment of our prior work with insights from a panel of retirement experts convened in November 2016 (see appendix III) and the work and the work of other researches and organizations. We also analyzed the findings and recommendations from prior federal commissions and from studies conducted by various international organizations, such as Mercer, the Center for Strategic and International Studies, Allianz, and the OECD.

We received comments on the information contained in this chapter from the Department of the Treasury, the Internal Revenue Service, the Pension Benefit Guaranty Corporation, and the Social Security Administration, and incorporated the technical comments we received, as appropriate. We also received technical comments from four experts on the U.S. retirement system and also incorporated their comments, as appropriate.

We conducted this performance audit from February 2016 to October 2017 in accordance with generally accepted government auditing standards. Those standards require that we plan and perform the audit to obtain sufficient, appropriate evidence to provide a reasonable basis for our findings and conclusions based on our audit objectives. We believe that the evidence obtained provides a reasonable basis for our findings and conclusions based on our audit objectives.

APPENDIX III: GAO'S EXPERT PANEL ON THE STATE OF RETIREMENT

We convened a panel of retirement experts in November 2016 to obtain their insights on the condition of retirement in the United States and various options for a new approach to help ensure that all individuals can provide for a secure retirement. This appendix provides a description of our methodology for selecting the panel and analyzing their remarks, as well as a summary of the key themes discussed during the day-long session. (See text box for final list of 15 experts participating in our panel.)

State of Retirement Panel Participants	
William Bortz Michael S. Gordon Fellow Pension Rights Center	Regina Jefferson Professor of Law Columbus School of Law The Catholic University of America
Phyllis Borzi Assistant Secretary of Labor Employee Benefits Security Administration	David John Senior Strategic Policy Advisor AARP
Harry Conaway President & CEO Employee Benefit Research Institute	Melissa Kahn Managing Director, Retirement Policy Strategist State Street Global Advisors
Warren Cormier CEO and Founder Boston Research Technologies	Hank Kim Executive Director & Counsel The National Conference on Public Employee Retirement Systems
Teresa Ghilarducci Professor of Economics and Director of the Schwartz Center for Economic Policy Analysis The New School for Social Research	Diane Oakley Executive Director National Institute on Retirement Security
Bill Hallmark Vice President for Pensions American Academy of Actuaries	Virginia Reno Deputy Commissioner for Retirement and Disability Policy Social Security Administration
Will Hansen Senior Vice President for Retirement Policy ERISA Industry Committee	Sita Nataraj Slavov Professor of Public Policy, Schar School of Policy and Government George Mason University
Cindy Hounsell President Women's Institute for a Secure Retirement	

Source: GAO. | GAO-18-111SP.

Methodology for Selecting the Panel and Analyzing Their Remarks

To identify the experts to invite to this meeting, we compiled an initial list based on interviews with experts conducted during recent GAO retirement income security work and the organizations invited to participate in a 2005 GAO forum on the future of the defined benefit system and the Pension Benefit Guaranty Corporation.[243] Potential experts were identified based on the following criteria:

- Organizational type: To ensure that we considered the unique roles or situations of various entities involved in retirement income policy, we selected panelists from the federal government, state or local government, research institutes or universities, advocacy or membership organizations, and financial services firms.
- Organizational reputation: To ensure that our panelists spanned political perspectives, we selected panelists from organizations known to be conservative, moderate, and liberal (to the extent the reputation for the organization could be easily identified).
- Subject matter expertise: To ensure that the discussion considered as many aspects of retirement income security as possible, we selected panelists with expertise across a range of areas, including defined benefit (DB) plans, defined contribution (DC) plans, individual retirement accounts (IRA), demographic trends, vulnerable populations, actuarial science, income in retirement, financial literacy, and behavioral finance.
- Range of views: To ensure that our discussion was inclusive of different philosophies regarding the role of government with regard to the population and the economy, we selected panelists to represent the viewpoints of individuals and business.

---

[243] GAO, *Highlights of a GAO Forum: The Future of the Defined Benefit System and the Pension Benefit Guaranty Corporation*, GAO-05-578SP (Washington, D.C.: June 1, 2005).

- Representation of diverse groups: To ensure that the discussion benefitted from different viewpoints, we selected panelists to reflect gender, racial, and ethnic diversity.

An initial list of 41 potential experts was shared with GAO management officials with expertise in retirement issues, actuarial science, and strategic planning, as well as GAO methodologists, for their comments and suggestions. From this we developed a shorter list, eventually arriving at our final group of 15, listed above. These final 15 panelists were also evaluated for conflicts of interest. A conflict of interest was considered to be any current financial or other interest that might conflict with the service of an individual because it (1) could impair objectivity and (2) could create an unfair competitive advantage for any person or organization. All potential conflicts were discussed by GAO staff. The 15 experts were determined to be free of conflicts of interest, and the group as a whole was judged to have no inappropriate biases.

Panelists engaged in a day-long discussion about our nation's approach to retirement policy (see text box). The discussion was guided by a list of questions developed in advance, and the meeting was conducted by a GAO moderator to ensure that all panelists had an opportunity to participate and provide responses.

The meeting was recorded and transcribed to ensure that we accurately captured the experts' statements. Following the panel, to help ensure the quality and objectivity of our summarization of their remarks, we conducted a systematic content analysis of the panel transcript using NVivo, a software program designed for analyzing qualitative information. We used a multi-stage process in which themes were initially identified and then the transcript was coded to locate each time that theme was identified. A second analyst then reviewed the coding to ensure that all relevant comments were captured. Also, during the writing process, additional analysis was conducted by revisiting the underlying transcript to review discussion of specific topics and examine broader discussion of themes.

State of Retirement Expert Panel Agenda
Welcome and Opening Remarks **Session 1: How Well Is Our Current National Approach to Retirement Security Working?** Preamble: Retirement income sources in the United States have often been referred to as a three-legged stool – Social Security, employer-sponsored retirement plans, and personal savings. 1. Can the US retirement system today still be accurately described by these three retirement income sources? Why/why not? 2. Are there aspects of our nation's approach to retirement income security that are working well? If so, are these aspects functioning well for all, or only for particular populations? 3. Are there aspects of our nation's approach to retirement income security that are concerning? If so, what are your biggest concerns? 4. Are there any specific populations you are particularly concerned about? If so, which ones and why? **Session 2: Reevaluating the Roles of the Federal Government, Employers, and Individuals** Preamble: Key actors in assuring a secure retirement have traditionally included the federal government, employers, and individuals, but their roles have evolved over time. • Are there ways roles could or should be adapted or modified to address the strengths and weaknesses that have been identified for: • Federal government? • Employers? • Individuals? **Session 3: Reevaluating Our Nation's Approach to Retirement Policy** Preamble: Various proposals for a broader, more cohesive approach to retirement policy have been made over time. 1. Do you believe there is a need for some type of national retirement policy? 2. If such a policy were to be proposed— 2a. What could or should be the primary goals of such a policy? 2b. What could or should be the roles of key actors in achieving those goals? 3. What do you believe could be the greatest benefits of a national retirement policy? 4. What do you believe could be the greatest risks or potential downsides of a national retirement policy? 5. What barriers exist to creating a national retirement policy and how could the federal government best address these barriers?

Source: GAO | GAO-18-111SP.

We sent a draft of Section 4 of the report to eight GAO staff who had participated in the panel for their review and comment. We also sent a draft of this section to four experts participating in our panel to ensure that we provided a balanced and fair characterization of the meeting. We received replies from all four experts, who generally agreed with our summary. We made some additions and clarifications to our draft to incorporate their comments, as appropriate.

Summary of Panelists' Discussion

During the day-long session, the panel discussed a broad range of topics related to retirement, including the challenges and risks individuals face when planning and managing their retirement, and the ways in which the current system has become burdensome for employers. Panelists also shared their thoughts about how the system could be simplified in ways that could offer advantages to both individuals and employers, and to society as a whole.

Panelists' Concerns with Current Retirement Policies

There was agreement among many panelists that a retirement crisis may be looming, but there was not a universal description of what the crisis might look like. Many panelists spoke of trends—such as slow wage growth, rising health care costs, increasing life expectancy, and shrinking household size—that may be building to a situation in which future generations are less financially secure in retirement compared to prior generations. Panelists noted the importance of ensuring that the nation find a solution to Social Security's financial challenges, as it is the foundation of retirement security for a large segment of the population. Some panelists also mentioned concerns over the fiscal exposures and sustainability of PBGC's insurance of private sector DB plans, along with Social Security, as part of a broader concern about the nation's financial status. However, most of the discussion focused on the weaknesses of the current system from the perspectives of individuals trying to save for retirement, from employers wanting to help their employees save for and manage their retirement, and from government agencies trying to oversee and administer a very complex system designed to help individuals and employers accomplish these objectives.

Individuals

The panelists discussed the many challenges facing individuals as they have had to take on increasing risk and responsibility for saving for a secure retirement, often without a sufficiently effective means or tools to help them accomplish that task (for example, see text box). They noted that many individuals do not have employer-sponsored plans, are limited in their ability to save, and are likely to be heavily reliant on Social Security.

Panelist on the Lack of Tools to Address Risks

"...the shift of risk that we have put on the individual worker in the United States retirement system is a mess. It's the investment risk, it's the longevity risk, the health risk, the long-term care risk...ultimately we've put so much risk on individuals who don't really have the tools. And the tools that are out there to help them cost a lot of money."

Source: GAO expert panel. | GAO-18-111SP.

Panelists described various ways that the gap in private sector coverage—only about half of private sector workers participate in employer-sponsored plans at any one time—impacts not only lower-income workers, but also middle income workers, and those who work for small businesses or are engaged in a non-standard or alternative work arrangement (sometimes referred to as contingent employment). Having a low or middle income was cited by panelists as a major obstacle to accumulating and maintaining adequate retirement savings in three key ways: 1) diminished ability and motivation to contribute to a retirement savings plan consistently over time; 2) greater vulnerability to financial shocks and personal hardship, such as unemployment, divorce, or high medical expenses, that can create the need or desire to withdraw retirement funds early (for example, see text box); and 3) lack of resources to hire a financial advisor to help manage saving prior to and during retirement and avoid the pitfalls of limited financial literacy.

Panelist on How Life Events Can Impede Saving for Retirement

"...life events can overwhelm the best of financial education. Weeks unemployed, a dip in your income by 10 percent, a divorce... [If] the design of the plan isn't there, you're going to have life events overwhelm the best intentions."

Source: GAO expert panel. | GAO-18-111SP.

Current tax policies, for example, were described by several panelists as providing great financial incentives for higher-income individuals to save for retirement, but less effective in encouraging enrollment and the accumulation of retirement savings for lower- and middle-income individuals. One panelist commented that tax advantage policies mainly subsidize retirement saving that would have occurred regardless of the tax advantage, as opposed to encouraging new saving. More generally, some panelists said that current voluntary retirement policies are ineffective in offering greater retirement security for lower-income individuals who often lack the ability to save (for example, see text box).

Panelist on Disparity of Tax Benefits

"When we think about our tax code it does wonderful things to encourage savings by people who can afford to save. It doesn't do much for the people at the low end who [are] living just on Social Security...I don't want someone to take that Social Security check and go to a payday lender because they need to get their car replaced because that's how they get to the doctor."

Source: GAO expert panel. | GAO-18-111SP.

Several panelists also commented on the high-level of financial literacy and income required to manage one's account effectively and the growing complexity of the retirement system over time. One panelist described the system today as an "insider system," where some people know the system and can utilize a particular tax policy to their advantage, but others do not. They noted that the tools necessary to understand the current retirement system cost money, posing a further economic barrier. Panelists discussed how this results in greater disparities in retirement savings across groups, particularly across income levels, but also with regard to race and gender. At the same time, other panelists noted the various limitations of efforts to enhance financial literacy. One panelist noted that despite all the efforts to improve financial literacy over the years, little progress had been made (see text box). Another panelist commented on studies that have shown that enhanced financial literacy can lead to greater indecision. In addition, life events can overwhelm even the best financial literacy efforts.

Panelist on the Problem with Financial Literacy

"...we have a very, very acute problem with financial literacy. And I think it's actually gotten worse... [As] the financial instruments have gotten more complicated, it makes it less likely that people can understand what they're doing."

Source: GAO expert panel. | GAO-18-111SP.

Employers

Although acknowledging that employers have shifted increasing risk to participants with the growth of DC plans, panelists also discussed how the present private sector retirement system is too complex and burdensome for employers, posing too much financial and litigation risk to them. For example, some panelists said that, in their view, certain requirements on employers that sponsor retirement plans can detract from their core business interests and may make them less competitive (for example, see text box.) Some panelists also expressed concerns about the growing risk of litigation in recent years, especially with respect to investment decisions, fiduciary duty, and fees. Panelists said that some employers may see it in their best interest not to sponsor a plan in order to avoid encountering these potential risks and burdens.

Panelist on the Employer's Role in Promoting Retirement Savings

"...mandating employers to do things that [make them] noncompetitive is not a good thing for the country."

Source: GAO expert panel. | GAO-18-111SP.

In addition, several panelists commented on how the current system can be overly complex and confusing for employers as well as individuals (for example, see text box.) Some who had worked closely with employers or who were themselves in the private sector, reported that employers—especially smaller employers—are often confused by the system.

Panelist on Employers' Confusion with the System

"...especially with smaller employers...they're universally confused, and virtually all of them have some sort of a horror story that [they] went in to discover that whatever they had done was wrong or far too expensive..."

Source: GAO expert panel. | GAO-18-111SP.

One panelist noted that the complexity of the current system has driven many plan sponsors to take on a growing role in educating their employees on financial wellness. According to the panelist, employers have felt forced to take on this role to try to address their employees' stress levels about how best to save for retirement. The panelist also commented that this expectation that employers become the conduit for educating their employees about retirement has become burdensome.

Federal Government

Panelists observed that the federal government's role in administering and overseeing the current retirement system is overly complex and inefficient, and does not fit society's present-day needs. Specifically, they said that streamlining is needed to reduce the amount of regulations and requirements, including the number of plan types and roles of multiple agencies. Panelists commented that the general tendency among policymakers has been to continue to expand the scope and number of plans, programs, regulations, and policies, rather than seeking to consolidate and modernize the government's efforts in support of a more efficient and effective approach to retirement savings.

Panelists' Considerations for Envisioning a New Approach

As panelists discussed their vision for a new approach to providing for a secure retirement for future retirees, one key theme that emerged was the need to provide better access to ways to save for retirement in addition to Social Security. The other key theme that emerged was the importance of taking steps to make the process of saving and managing retirement simpler, easier, and less risky for everyone: individuals, employers, and government. One panelist noted the importance of taking these steps not just to help make the system easier to navigate, but to help make the system fairer.

Expanding Ways to Save for Retirement

In discussing the need to provide better access to ways to save for retirement, panelists noted that different strategies are needed for different income levels. For example, to help those with lower incomes, several panelists suggested that the focus should be on strengthening Social Security. But for those with middle to higher incomes—that is, those who have the capacity to save for retirement, but are not currently participating—the focus should be on expanding coverage.

Several panelists commented that Social Security is the foundation of retirement security for many people, especially those who are low income—people who do not have the means to participate in retirement savings programs. They noted that improving retirement security for these people means strengthening Social Security. For example, they spoke of the importance of ensuring that the nation finds a solution to Social Security's financial challenges, and they were generally optimistic that the nation will address this challenge. For the most part, they viewed Social

Security as working well, especially for low-income groups. At the same time, some panelists noted that Social Security could be strengthened with respect to particular groups, such as minorities and women. More specifically, some panelists commented that women are particularly underserved in the present system by virtue of pay equity issues, exiting the workforce to care for others during child-bearing years and later in life to care for other family members, and vulnerabilities related to marital status (e.g., divorced, widowed, or never married). One panelist noted the need to modernize Social Security and said that Social Security could offer caregiver tax credits as a potential means of improving retirement saving among individuals, particularly women, who take time out of the workforce to care for others (see text box.)

Panelist on the Need to Modernize Social Security

"...groups the system doesn't work so well for ...one big group is women. And part of that comes from the fact that Social Security was designed in the 1930s with the typical 1930s family in mind, [i.e.,] one-earner couples. And things have changed pretty dramatically. ... Can we modernize Social Security to...reflect the changing role of women?"

Source: GAO expert panel. | GAO-18-111SP.

While Social Security may provide a foundation, the panelists' discussion focused on the importance of ensuring that individuals have access to savings vehicles that would enable them to save enough to provide an adequate income in retirement, recognizing that adequacy is an ambiguous term. Some panelists stated that, at a minimum, individuals should not have to live in poverty during retirement. Others suggested a higher threshold, i.e., that individuals should have sufficient resources to maintain their standard of living, and to support a comfortable life, or a life with dignity, throughout retirement.

However, leaving aside the definition of adequacy, panelists generally agreed on the importance of providing better access to ways to save for retirement in addition to Social Security. One panelist noted that nearly half of private sector workers currently do not participate in employer-sponsored plans. Others commented that the current system—relying on tax incentives and voluntary employer sponsorship—has not accomplished much in terms of broadening coverage over the past 40 years. More generally, panelists agreed that structural changes may be needed if the nation is to make progress toward expanding coverage for those currently being left out of the system, such as minimum wage workers and middle-income workers who work for small businesses or have alternative work arrangements. (For example, see text box.)

Panelist on Efforts to Increase Access

"It's hard to imagine how you broaden the coverage in terms of retirement security without doing [something] more dramatic, more directive...I'm not saying it has to be a mandate...It could be stronger incentives, different types of matches."

Source: GAO expert panel. | GAO-18-111SP.

In the discussion about how to increase access, panelists' comments focused primarily on the need for a new type of savings vehicle and the various ways it could be implemented. Some panelists suggested that the new savings vehicle be government-sponsored, while others supported continuing to rely on the employer-sponsored system to make any needed changes.

For example, one panelist suggested that one way of providing a new savings vehicle, available to all, would be to attach a government-sponsored individual account component to Social Security to which individuals and their employers could contribute over the course of an individual's working years. Similarly, another panelist described a way of bolstering the retirement system by transferring savings from IRAs into Social Security. According to the panelist, such an approach would also allow individuals to annuitize and efficiently pool risk across a large group.

As one example of how a government-sponsored system has worked elsewhere, some panelists described the approach being taken by the United Kingdom (UK): expanding access to individuals by mandating that all employers automatically enroll employees in either their own or the government-sponsored retirement savings plan, the National Employment Savings Trust (NEST) (see text box). Panelists noted the positive effects that the UK system has had on employee participation, such as increased coverage, low opt-out rates, and high re-enrollment rates. At the same time, other panelists noted that to achieve increases in coverage, it is important not to exclude groups that are typically those without access to an employer-sponsored plan. For example, one panelist said that some of the systems established in other countries have recently considered not making those programs applicable to low-income and minimum wage workers because they are less likely to be able to afford to save for retirement, and noted that this approach would limit the system's ability to expand access.

Panelist on Efforts to Increase Coverage

"But when it comes to coverage, there's only one way to do it... It's a mandate. If you don't require that people have coverage, if they don't require that they have an account, whether that's employer-sponsored or employer-facilitated, it's not going to happen, period. And that's the experience in the UK."

Source: GAO expert panel. | GAO-18-111SP.

One panelist proposed a new retirement plan type that would allow workers to save for retirement in a DC-type individual account; but through a multiple employer approach that offered pooling of an investments and a lifetime income option more like a DB plan.[244] The panelist also said such a plan could be government-sponsored and allow employers of all sizes who did not currently offer their own plan to join, as

[244] Note that this is being described as a multiple employer approach, not a multiemployer plan. For a description of the difference, see section 2.

well as self-insured, self-employed individuals, and temporary and seasonal workers who did not otherwise have access to a plan. According to this panelist, such a plan could at least provide a vehicle for individuals to save for retirement with their own contributions, even if employer contributions were voluntary, making it similar to a DC plan; and would enable individuals to pool their investments and a receive a benefit in a lifetime income stream at retirement, similar to a DB plan. The panelist suggested that there could be one regional plan of this type in each of the Federal Reserve regions, run by an independent board, noting that this type of approach would lessen an employer's administrative costs, as well as their litigation risk. It could also move the United States towards something similar to the UK system, which provides nearly universal coverage whether or not employers contribute to the system.

To increase participation and savings in retirement savings plans, panelists also discussed the need to improve existing tax incentives—to make them fairer and more accessible to lower income workers. As noted by several panelists, the current structure of providing tax incentives for retirement savings—essentially though income tax deferral—does little for lower income households; instead, higher income households get most of the benefits. One panelist said current tax incentives reward employers equally, instead of providing increased incentives to those employers offering plans for which they bear more risk (i.e., DB plans).

Panelists also mentioned other actions that could be taken to increase savings in employer-sponsored retirement plans. They included providing an incentive to encourage employers to increase their matching contributions, and taking steps to encourage employees to work longer, such as by offering more flexible work arrangements to meet the needs of older workers, to help them avoid having to dip into their savings as soon or as much.

Making Saving for and Management of Retirement Simpler and Less Risky

Throughout the panelists' discussion of ways to improve how the nation provides for a secure retirement for future retirees, a persistent theme emerged concerning the importance of simplifying the present system. Several panelists commented that a simpler system is needed to make it easier for more individuals to save for and manage their retirement, and would require less financial expertise, similar to Social Security (see text box). Moreover, panelists commented that under the current system, individuals are being asked to take on increasing risk without a sufficiently effective means or tools to deal with it—both in the accumulation of savings and the management of their accounts after retiring. They also noted that adopting new, simpler approaches could have advantages for all concerned: individuals, employers, and government.

Panelist on the Simplicity of Social Security

"...You don't need financial literacy in order to get Social Security. You just need to pay your contributions in or have the employer do that for you...when compared with everything else, it's very, very simple..."

Source: GAO expert panel. | GAO-18-111SP.

One key way of simplifying saving for those participating in retirement savings plans mentioned by several panelists is through the use of automatic mechanisms such as auto-enrollment and auto-escalation. According to the panelists, such mechanisms make it easier for employees to enroll and save for retirement without requiring them to become more financially literate. While some panelists emphasized the importance of continued efforts to improve individuals' financial literacy, such as through online tools to help individuals navigate complex systems, others commented that such efforts had not been effective in the past, and said that encouraging employers to adopt more automatic mechanisms held more promise for increasing retirement savings.

To simplify the decision-making in determining how to spend down savings through retirement, several panelists mentioned the potential value of encouraging employers to adopt some type of pooled-risk annuity option for their retirees. As noted by one panelist, under the current system, individuals can purchase an annuity with their DC account balances at retirement, but doing this on the retail market can be expensive and complicated. Individuals would need to assess a variety of risks—investment risk, longevity risk, health risk, long-term care risk—and decide whether it would make sense to tie up their savings in a multiplicity of different annuity products. The panelist added that the current system essentially requires people to be their own investment advisor and actuary and that it is expensive and risky for people to purchase annuities on their own with their DC account balances. With some type of pooled-risk annuity option, another panelist noted, the costs and risks of choosing an annuity can be shared, as is done in DB plans. (For example, see text box.)

Panelist on the Importance of Simplicity

"All these resources that we're devoting to...optimizing Social Security claiming or any other kind of retirement decisions, where there's unnecessary complexity... [they] create unfairness because... people who know the system can take advantage of it versus those who don't. So simplification, I think, is a big, big deal."

Source: GAO expert panel. | GAO-18-111SP.

Another way to simplify the system and help increase retirement savings, mentioned by some panelists, is to encourage employers to change plan provisions that allow individuals to borrow against their DC accounts and to withdraw their accumulated DC account balances when they change employment. One panelist commented that some employers believe that fewer individuals would participate in their plans if they were not allowed to borrow from their accounts in emergencies or take hardship withdrawals. However, according to the panelist, this was not born out by the experience of at least one firm that took steps to prevent participants borrowing or withdrawing against their accounts.

Other panelists also mentioned that steps could be taken to simplify the Saver's Credit (a tax credit intended to encourage retirement savings among low- and middle-income individuals). According to one panelist, who has worked on projects studying the Saver's Credit over the past 15 years, low income people want to save and take advantage of the credit. But, another panelist commented that this has been made overly complicated. The credit uses a complex formula and requires individuals to file a long tax form (as opposed to a simple 1040-EZ, for example).

Although employers in recent decades have shifted risks increasingly to individuals, some panelists commented that under the current system, DC plan sponsorship has also become riskier due to an increase in litigation risk around investment advice, fees, and other issues. (For example, see text box.) More specifically, one panelist noted that DC plan sponsors currently are fearful of the litigation risk associated with being a plan's fiduciary, especially with respect to investment advice and fees. The panelist suggested that one way to reduce this litigation risk for employers would be for the federal government to provide more guidance on investments, noting that, unlike mandates in other areas, a mandate on the types of investments that would be regarded as prudent and safe would be welcomed by many DC plan sponsors.

Panelist on the Future Role for Employers

"It seems every week another employer is getting sued, and they're going to withdraw from what is a voluntary system. ... I see the future for employers as being funders and facilitators of benefits [rather than as plan sponsors]."

Source: GAO expert panel. | GAO-18-111SP.

Another panelist added that the current regulatory structure for employer-sponsored plans poses barriers to innovation, inhibiting progress in adopting new types of plans. More specifically, the panelist described a type of blended DB-DC plan design that could provide for greater shared risk between employers and employees by setting a hurdle rate of return, then adjusting the benefits that accrue each year based on actual earnings on the plan's assets. This would allow the cost to the employer to be relatively fixed, and the plan would be much more sustainable. Further, this risk sharing could be confined to active employees, so that retirees would still receive a fixed benefit. But despite the potential advantages of such a plan, and interest from plan sponsors, the panelist noted that progress in adopting such plans has been slow, mostly due to regulatory barriers. According to the panelist, during just one week, IRS had received more than 80 requests related to implementing some type of a blended plan that contained elements of DB and DC plans, but due to regulatory issues, IRS sent the requests out for technical advice. On the other hand, another panelist noted that the proliferation of different types of tax-advantaged retirement savings plans is not helpful either, and should be simplified.

Panelist also varied in their opinions about whether or not government-sponsored retirement savings programs, such as UK's NEST, were viewed favorably by employers as a possible alternative type of plan.

Some panelists noted that, based on their own direct interactions in the UK, employers there were pleased with the program due to its simplicity and minimal administrative burdens. However, another panelist said that, based on personal experience, the UK system has continued to place a heavy burden on employers because of the number of vendors they must employ, the amount of fees charged by those vendors, the advice they must provide to their employees about the system, and a myriad of administrative requirements.

While panelists varied on the pros and cons of specific options and strategies for improving retirement security, there was general agreement that allowing for flexibility in the policies would, in turn, allow the system to adapt and evolve (for example, see text box).

Panelist on the Need for Flexibility

"...the retirement plans of 40 years ago are not what we have today, and they're certainly not going to be what we have 40 years from now."

Source: GAO expert panel. | GAO-18-111SP.

APPENDIX IV: GAO RECOMMENDATIONS FROM PRIOR REPORTS

We have made numerous agency recommendations and matters for congressional consideration in prior reports to help address the challenges individuals face when trying to plan or manage their retirement to provide for a financially secure future. A description of some of our key recommendations, with the status of implementation as of the end of fiscal year 2017, is provided below, organized by section 2's three challenges: accessing employer-sponsored plans, accumulating sufficient retirement savings, and ensuring financial resources throughout retirement. For the most up-to-date status of these agency recommendations and matters for congressional consideration, see our website: http://www.gao.gov.

Expanding Access to Employer-Sponsored Retirement Plans

Table 8. Selected GAO Recommendations and Matters for Congress to Promote Greater Access to Retirement Savings Plans

GAO report	Agency recommendation or matter for Congress	Status (as of the end of fiscal year 2017)
Private Pensions: Better Agency Coordination Could Help Small Employers Address Challenges to Plan Sponsorship (GAO-12-326)	We recommended that the Department of Labor (DOL) convene an interagency task force with the Department of the Treasury (Treasury), the Internal Revenue Service (IRS), and the Small Business Administration to coordinate existing research, education, and outreach efforts to foster small employer plan sponsorship. We also recommended that IRS consider modifying tax forms to gather complete, reliable information about Simplified Employee Pension Individual Retirement Arrangements.	Not implemented The agencies generally agreed with our recommendations; except, DOL disagreed with our recommendation to create a single web portal for federal guidance. However, the recommendations were not implemented. Because federal resources are scattered across different sites, we continue to believe consolidating plan information onto one web portal could benefit small employers.

Table 8. (Continued)

GAO report	Agency recommendation or matter for Congress	Status (as of the end of fiscal year 2017)
Private Sector Pensions: Federal Agencies Should Collect Data and Coordinate Oversight of Multiple Employer Plans (GAO-12-665)	We recommended that DOL lead an effort to collect data on the employers that participate in Multiple Employer Plans. We also recommended that DOL and IRS formalize their coordination with regard to statutory interpretation efforts with respect to these plans, and jointly develop guidance on the plans' establishment and operation.	Partially implemented The agencies generally agreed with our recommendations. DOL implemented our data collection recommendation by requiring Multiple Employer Plans to submit additional information on Form 5500 beginning in plan year 2014. The recommendations to DOL and IRS on coordination were not implemented.
Retirement Security: Federal Action Could Help State Efforts to Expand Private Sector Coverage (GAO-15-556)	We suggested that Congress consider providing states limited flexibility regarding Employee Retirement Income Security Act preemption to expand private sector coverage. We recommended that DOL and Treasury take actions to address uncertainty created by existing regulations.	Open The agencies generally agreed with our recommendations.

Source: GAO. | GAO-18-111SP.

To promote greater access to retirement savings plans, our previous reports have focused on steps that federal agencies could take to support efforts by small businesses and the states. Selected recommendations from three past reports on this topic are summarized in Table 8.

Encouraging More Saving

To further encourage greater retirement savings, we have made a number of recommendations in our prior work on ways various aspects of DC plans could be improved. Selected recommendations from 10 past reports on this topic are summarized in Table 9.

Table 9. Selected GAO Recommendations and Matters for Congress to Improve Various Aspects of Defined Contribution Plans

GAO report	Agency recommendation or matter for Congress	Status (as of end of fiscal year 2017)
401(K) Plans: Increased Educational Outreach and Broader Oversight May Help Reduce Plan Fees (GAO-12-325)	We recommended that Department of Labor (DOL) develop and implement more proactive approaches to sponsor educational outreach, improve public access to annual Form 5500 data, and examine the definition of a fiduciary to determine if it captures the current relationship between sponsors and providers.	Implemented DOL generally agreed with our recommendations. DOL implemented outreach efforts including a newsletter, seminars, and webcasts, developed an "advanced" search tool to improve access to Form 5500 data, and finalized the conflict of interest rule that modified the definition of investment advice under which a provider would become a fiduciary.
Defined Contribution Plans: Approaches in Other Countries Offer Beneficial Strategies in Several Areas (GAO-12-328)	We recommended that DOL consider other countries' experiences as it continues to improve its (1) supervision and (2) requirements related to fee disclosures.	Implemented DOL generally agreed with our recommendations. DOL said it would monitor the risk-based pension oversight practices of other countries for applicability to the United States and participated in multinational research and discussions to inform policy efforts, including fee disclosures and conflict of interest.
401(K) Plans: Labor and IRS Could Improve the Rollover Process for Participants (GAO-13-30)	We recommended that DOL and the Internal Revenue Service (IRS) take certain steps to reduce obstacles and disincentives to plan-to-plan rollovers. We also recommended that DOL ensure that participants receive complete and timely information, including enhanced disclosures, about the distribution options for their 401(k) plan savings when separating from an employer.	Partially implemented DOL and the Department of the Treasury (Treasury) generally agreed with the recommendations. To help facilitate rollovers into 401(k) plans, Treasury issued guidance to plans. To reduce obstacles and disincentives to plan-to-plan rollovers, DOL has provided educational materials and seminars to help plan sponsors be aware of IRS guidance. To ensure that

Table 9. (Continued)

GAO report	Agency recommendation or matter for Congress	Status (as of end of fiscal year 2017)
		participants receive complete and timely information, DOL clarified its definition of fiduciary in its Conflict of Interest Rule. The other recommendation was not implemented.
Private Pensions: Revised Electronic Disclosure Rules Could Clarify Use and Better Protect Participant Choice (GAO-13-594)	We recommended that DOL and Treasury consider (1) clarifying regulatory requirements and (2) expanding participants' ability to opt out of electronic delivery.	Open DOL generally agreed with the recommendations. Treasury did not comment on the recommendations at the time the report was issued. Treasury decided not to implement the recommendations. DOL decided not to implement the recommendation to clarify regulatory requirements. DOL's recommendation to expand participants' ability to opt out of electronic delivery remains open.
Private Pensions: Targeted Revisions Could Improve Usefulness of Form 5500 Information (GAO-14-441)	We recommended that DOL, Treasury, and PBGC consider modifying Form 5500 plan investment and service provider fee information to address challenges identified by our panel. DOL, Treasury, and PBGC should look for options to conduct advance testing when making major revisions to the form. We suggested that Congress consider granting Treasury authority to require Form 5500 data be filed electronically.	Partially implemented PBGC agreed with the recommendations, while the other agencies did not state whether they agreed or disagreed. The agencies have implemented one recommendation, stating that they planned to work together to conduct advanced testing. The other recommendations and the matter are open.
401K Plans: Greater Protections Needed for Forced Transfers and Inactive Accounts (GAO-15-73)	We suggested that Congress consider (1) amending current law to permit alternative default destinations for plans to use when transferring participant accounts out of plans, and (2) repealing a provision that allows plans to disregard rollovers when	Open. DOL agreed with the recommendation.

GAO report	Agency recommendation or matter for Congress	Status (as of end of fiscal year 2017)
	identifying balances eligible for transfer to an IRA. We recommended that DOL convene a taskforce to explore the possibility of establishing a national pension registry.	
401(K) Plans: Clearer Regulations Could Help Plan Sponsors Choose Investments for Participants (GAO-15-578)	We recommended that DOL assess the challenges that plan sponsors and stakeholders reported, including the extent to which these challenges can be addressed, and implement corrective actions, as appropriate.	Open DOL generally agreed with our recommendation.
401(K) Plans: DOL Could Take Steps to Improve Retirement Income Options for Plan Participants (GAO-16-433)	We recommended DOL (1) clarify the criteria to be used by plan sponsors to select an annuity provider, (2) consider providing limited liability relief for offering an appropriate mix of lifetime income options, (3) issue guidance to encourage plan sponsors to select a record keeper that offers annuities from other providers, and (4) issue guidance to encourage plan sponsors to consider providing required minimum distribution-based default lifetime income-plan distributions as a default stream of lifetime income based on the required minimum distribution methodology.	Open DOL generally agreed with our recommendations.
Retirement Security: Improved Guidance Could Help Account Owners Understand the Risks of Investing in Unconventional Assets (GAO-17-102)	We recommended IRS (1) improve guidance for account owners with unconventional assets on monitoring for ongoing federal tax liability and (2) clarify how to determine the fair market value of hard-to-value unconventional assets.	Open IRS generally agreed with these recommendations.

Source: GAO. | GAO-18-111SP.

To further improve individuals' financial capabilities to plan for retirement, we have made a number of recommendations in our prior work on ways to provide clearer information to plan participants and improve federal efforts regarding financial literacy programs more generally.

Selected recommendations from four past reports on this topic are summarized in Table 10.

Table 10. Selected GAO Recommendations and Matters for Congress to Improve Financial Literacy

GAO report	Agency recommendation or matter for Congress	Status (as of end of fiscal year 2017)
Financial Literacy: Overlap of Programs Suggests There May Be Opportunities for Consolidation (GAO-12-588)	We recommended that the Consumer Financial Protection Bureau (CFPB) clearly delineate with other agencies respective roles and responsibilities, and that the Financial Literacy and Education Commission identify options for consolidating federal financial literacy efforts and address the allocation of federal resources in its national strategy.[a]	Partially implemented CFPB neither agreed nor disagreed with these recommendations and the Department of the Treasury (Treasury) agreed with the recommendations directed to the commission. CFPB implemented its recommendation by establishing regular communication with other agencies. The other recommendations are open.
Private Pensions: Clarity of Required Reports and Disclosures Could Be Improved (GAO-14-92)	We suggested that Congress consider shifting responsibility and necessary resources to the Department of Labor (DOL) for managing the pension benefit data that the Social Security Administration provides to retirees. We recommended that the agencies improve their online tools on reporting requirements and facilitate better readability of disclosures.	Partially implemented The agencies generally agreed with our recommendations. The matter is open. The recommendations are partially implemented. PBGC has made improvements to materials on its website and collaborated with DOL and the Internal Revenue Service to revise its guides for employee benefit plans reporting and disclosure requirements.
Retirement Security: Better Information on Income Replacement Rates Needed to Help Workers Plan for Retirement (GAO-16-242)	We recommended that DOL provide additional examples and guidance on using a replacement rate for estimating retirement savings needs in its planning tools, and modify the planning tools so the rate can be adjusted.	Partially implemented DOL generally agreed with our recommendations. DOL added additional examples for estimating retirement savings needed in its planning tools. The other recommendation is open.

GAO report	Agency recommendation or matter for Congress	Status (as of end of fiscal year 2017)
401(K) Plans: Effects of Eligibility and Vesting Policies on Workers' Retirement Savings (GAO-17-69)	We suggested Congress consider a number of changes to ERISA, including changes to the minimum age for plan eligibility and plans' use of a last-day policy. We recommended that Treasury evaluate existing vesting policies to assess if current policies are appropriate for today's mobile workforce and seek legislative action to revise vesting schedules, if deemed necessary.	Open Treasury had no comment on the recommendation. We believe that such an evaluation would be beneficial, given the potential for vesting policies to reduce retirement savings.

Source: GAO. | GAO-18-111SP.

[a] The Secretary of the Treasury chairs the Financial Literacy and Education Commission.

Helping Individuals Manage Their Finances through Retirement

Table 11. Selected GAO Recommendations and Matters for Congress to Protect and Promote Consideration of Various Spend-down Options for Retirees

GAO report	Agency recommendation or matter for Congress	Status (as of end of fiscal year 2017)
Private Pensions: Timely Action Needed to Address Impending Multiemployer Plan Insolvencies (GAO-13-240)	We suggested that Congress consider comprehensive and balanced structural reforms to reinforce and stabilize the multiemployer system.	Implemented The Pension Benefit Guaranty Corporation (PBGC) generally agreed with our findings and analysis. In December 2014, Congress enacted the Multiemployer Pension Reform Act of 2014, which substantially established in law actions described in our report.

Table 11. (Continued)

GAO report	Agency recommendation or matter for Congress	Status (as of end of fiscal year 2017)
401(K) Plans: Other Countries' Experiences Offer Lessons in Policies and Oversight of Spend-down Options (GAO-14-9)	We recommended that the Department of Labor (DOL) and the Department of the Treasury (Treasury), as part of their ongoing efforts, consider other countries' approaches in helping 401(k) plan sponsors expand access to a mix of spend-down options for participants. We also recommended that DOL consider other countries' approaches in providing information about options and regulating the selection of annuities within defined contribution plans.	Partially implemented DOL generally agreed with our recommendations. Treasury issued a final rule making it easier for 401(k) plan participants to purchase deeply deferred annuities, also known as qualified longevity annuity contracts. Treasury officials told us they considered the experiences of other countries when finalizing the rule. The recommendations for DOL are open.
401(K) Plans: Improvements Can Be Made to Better Protect Participants in Managed Accounts (GAO-14-310)	We recommended that DOL consider provider fiduciary roles, require disclosure of performance and benchmarking information to plan sponsors and participants, and provide guidance to help sponsors better select and oversee managed account providers.	Open DOL agreed with our recommendations.
Pension Advance Transactions: Questionable Business Practices Identified (GAO-14-420)	We recommended that the Consumer Financial Protection Bureau (CFPB) and the Federal Trade Commission (FTC) review the pension advance practices identified in this chapter and exercise oversight or enforcement as appropriate. We recommended that CFPB coordinate with relevant agencies to increase consumer education about pension advances.	Implemented CFPB and FTC agreed with our recommendations. CFPB and FTC took steps to increase oversight and enforcement of pension advance practices. In addition, CFPB released a consumer advisory regarding pension advances.

GAO report	Agency recommendation or matter for Congress	Status (as of end of fiscal year 2017)
Private Pensions: Participants Need Better Information When Offered Lump Sums That Replace Their Lifetime Benefits (GAO-15-74)	We recommended that DOL improve oversight by requiring plan sponsors to notify the agency when they implement lump-sum windows, and coordinate with Treasury to clarify guidance on the information sponsors provide to participants. Further, Treasury should reassess regulations governing relative value statements, as well as the interest rates and mortality tables used in calculating lump sums.	Open The agencies generally agreed with our recommendations.

Source: GAO. | GAO-18-111SP.

To improve income security in retirement, we have made a number of recommendations in our prior work to protect and promote consideration of various options for spending down retirement savings. Selected recommendations from five past reports on this topic are summarized in Table 11.

APPENDIX V: TWO PAST FEDERAL COMMISSIONS ON RETIREMENT ISSUES

We examined two federal commissions focused on issues related to the U.S. retirement system to gain insights on how such commissions can be used to address such issues. This appendix provides a brief overview of the scope and structure of these two commissions: the 1979 President's Commission on Pension Policy (Carter Commission) and the 1981 National Commission on Social Security Reform (known as the Greenspan Commission). We selected these two commissions to illustrate possible structures for federal commissions, the scope of work these commissions can take on, and the types of recommendations they can make.

Carter Commission (1979-1981)

In 1978, President Carter signed an executive order authorizing the Carter Commission, which was established when committee members were appointed in 1979. The commission was to conduct a 2-year sturdy of the nation's pension systems and the future course of national retirement income policies. President Carter appointed all 11 commission members. The commission also had an executive director and 37 staffers. Its final report, *Coming of Age: Toward a National Retirement Income Policy*, was released in February 1981.[245]

Charge to the Carter Commission

The commission was ordered to:

- Conduct a comprehensive review of retirement, survivor, and disability programs existing in the United States, including private, federal, state, and local programs.
- Develop national policies for retirement, survivor, and disability programs that can be used as a guide by public and private programs. The policies were to be designed to ensure that the nation had effective and equitable retirement, survivor, and disability programs that took into account available resources and demographic changes expected into the middle of the next century.
- Submit to the president a series of reports, including the commission's findings and recommendations on short-term and long-term issues with respect to retirement, survivor, and disability programs. The commission was charged with covering the following issues in its findings and recommendations:
- overlaps and gaps among the private, state, and local sectors in providing income to retired, surviving, and disabled persons;

[245] President's Commission on Pension Policy, *Coming of Age: Toward a National Retirement Income Policy* (Feb. 26, 1981).

- the financial ability of private, federal, state, and local retirement, survivor, and disability systems to meet their future obligations;
- appropriate retirement ages, the relationship of annuity levels to past earnings and contributions, and the role of retirement, survivor, and disability programs in private capital formation and economic growth;
- the implications of the recommended national policies for the financing and benefit structures of the retirement, survivor, and disability programs in the public and private sectors; and
- specific reforms and organizational changes in the present systems that may be required to meet the goals of the national policies.

Carter Commission's Recommendations

In its final report, the Carter Commission prescribed a goal for retirement income policy and made numerous recommendations. According to the report, a desirable retirement income goal is the replacement of pre-retirement income from all sources. Recommendations focused on strengthening four areas: employer pensions, Social Security, individual efforts (personal savings, employment of older workers, and disability), and public assistance. Recommendations were also made regarding the administration of the U.S. retirement system. Examples of ways to strengthen each area follow:

- Strengthening Employer Pensions. The commission recommended establishing a Minimum Universal Pension System (MUPS) for all workers. MUPS was intended to provide a portable benefit that was supplemental to Social Security. It would have built upon existing employer plans and existing plans that did not meet the requirements would have needed to be amended. Another recommendation was to establish a Public Employee Retirement Income Security Act (i.e., a public sector version of ERISA) so that public and private sector employees would receive similar protections.

- Strengthening Social Security. The commission recommended mandatory universal coverage, raising the retirement age for workers who were not approaching retirement, re-examining or making adjustments to the special minimum benefit as well as the spousal benefit and other miscellaneous benefits.
- Strengthening Individual Efforts. The commission recommended that contribution and benefit limitations for all individuals should be treated more consistently for all types of retirement savings. The commission also recommended a refundable tax credit for low- and moderate-income individuals to encourage saving for retirement. For older workers, recommendations included improving unemployment benefits to provide short-term income maintenance and keep them in the labor force. The commission also recommended further in-depth study of the Disability Insurance program.
- Strengthening Public Assistance. The commission made recommendations to address inflation protection for retirement income and setting Social Security's Supplemental Security Income at the poverty line level and eliminating its assets test.
- Administration. The commission recommended consolidating the administration of all federal retirement systems as well as consolidating ERISA administrative functions under one entity. It also recommended an interdepartmental task force to coordinate executive branch agencies dealing with retirement income.

Greenspan Commission (1981-1983)

In 1981, President Reagan signed an executive order establishing the Greenspan Commission. The President asked the commission to conduct a 1-year study and propose realistic, long-term reforms to put Social Security on sound financial footing and to reach bipartisan consensus so these reforms could be passed into law. The President, the Senate Majority Leader, and the Speaker of the House of Representatives each made five appointments, with no more than three of the five appointments coming from one political party to ensure a bipartisan commission. The President was responsible for appointing the commission's chair. The commission had a staff of 23. The final report, *Report of the National Commission on Social Security Reform*, was issued in January 1983.[246]

Charge to the Greenspan Commission

The commission was ordered to:

- Review relevant analyses of the current and long-term financial condition of the Social Security Trust Funds.
- Identify problems that could threaten the long-term solvency of such funds.
- Analyze potential solutions to such problems that would both assure the financial integrity of the Social Security system and appropriate benefits.
- Provide appropriate recommendations to the Secretary of Health and Human Services, the President, and Congress.

Greenspan Commission's Recommendations

In its final report, the Greenspan Commission found both short and longterm financing problems and recommended that action should be taken to strengthen the financial status of the Social Security program. Twelve commission members voted in favor of a consensus package with 13 recommendations to address Social Security's short-term deficit, including, for example:

- Expand Social Security to include coverage for nonprofit and civilian federal employees hired after January 1, 1984, as well as prohibit the withdrawal of state and local employees.
- Shift cost-of-living adjustments to an annual basis.

---

[246] National Commission on Social Security Reform, *Report of the National Commission on Social Security Reform* (Washington. D.C.: Jan. 20, 1983).

- Make the Social Security Administration its own separate, independent agency.
- Make adjustments to spousal and survivor benefits.
- Revise the schedule for Social Security payroll taxes.
- Establish the taxation of benefits for higher-income persons.

In addition, these 12 commission members agreed that the long-range deficit should be reduced to approximately zero, and their recommendations were projected to meet about two-thirds of the long-range financial deficit. Seven of the 12 members agreed that the remaining one-third of the long-range financial deficit should be met by a deferred, gradual increase in the normal retirement age, while the other 5 members agreed that it should be met by an increase in future contribution rates starting in 2010.

After the Greenspan Commission's final report was issued, Congress enacted the Social Security Amendments of 1983. The amendments incorporated many of the Greenspan Commission's recommendations and made comprehensive changes to Social Security coverage, financing, and benefit structure. These changes included addressing Social Security's long-term financing problems by gradually increasing the retirement age from 65 to 67, among other things.

APPENDIX VI: RETIREMENT SYSTEMS IN SELECTED COUNTRIES

International comparisons of retirement systems may help inform policymakers who face the challenge of delivering adequate retirement income while ensuring the financial sustainability of their systems. In this appendix, we provide a series of text boxes with brief snapshots of the systems in other countries that ranked high in three of the international studies we reviewed: the 2015 Melbourne Mercer study,[247] the 2013 Center for Strategic and International Studies (CSIS) Global Aging study,[248] and Allianz's 2015 Retirement Income Adequacy study.[249] We did not conduct an independent legal analysis to verify the information provided about the laws, regulations, or policies of the countries selected for these snapshots. Instead, we relied on appropriate secondary sources, interviews, and other sources to support our work.

Australia's Retirement System, Ranked High in Adequacy

The most comprehensive of the three studies, the 2015 Melbourne Mercer study, ranked Australia #1 in retirement income adequacy, based on various factors such as the level of income or benefits provided. Australia's retirement system has three components: (1) a means-tested public pension, the Age Pension, financed by general revenues; (2) mandatory employer contributions into occupational superannuation funds (mostly defined contribution-type retirement saving plans); and (3) additional voluntary contributions from employers, employees or the self-employed into these superannuation funds. Thus, like the United States, Australia has an account-based system on top of a basic public system—with a key difference that the account-based system is universal and mandatory. The mandatory employer contribution is currently set at 9.5 percent of earnings but scheduled to increase by 0.5 percentage point each year starting in 2021 until it reaches 12 percent of earnings in 2025. The net replacement rate in Australia for a worker earning the median income from the mandatory components of the retirement system was over 70 percent in the 2015 Melbourne Mercer study. The study gave the largest weight to this indicator when computing the adequacy index, which partly explains Australia's #1 ranking.

Source: Australian government documents and GAO analysis of Pensions at A Glance 2015 and Melbourne Mercer Global Pension Index. | GAO-18-111SP.

---

247 Mercer, *Melbourne Mercer Global Pension Index* (Melbourne, Australia: Australian Centre for Financial Studies, October 2015).

248 R. Jackson, N. Howe, and T. Peter, *The Global Aging Preparedness Index, 2nd edition* (Washington, D.C. Center for Strategic and International Studies: October 2013).

249 Allianz, "Retirement Income Adequacy Indicator," *International Pension Papers 1/2015* (Munich, Germany: May 2015).

The Netherlands' Retirement System, Ranked High in Adequacy

The Allianz and CSIS Global Aging studies both ranked the Netherlands #1 in adequacy (the Melbourne Mercer study ranked the Netherlands #2). The Netherlands' retirement system has three components: (1) a flat rate public pension that is based on the minimum wage (hence independent of income and past contributions) and financed by payroll taxes; (2) occupational mostly defined benefit-type pensions, which are quasi-mandatory insofar as they are negotiated through collective agreements between employer and employees and cover over 90 percent of workers; and (3) individual saving plans. The net replacement rate for a median earner, which is the most important indicator of adequacy in the Melbourne Mercer study, was over 100 percent for the Netherlands, contributing to its high ranking. In the 2013 CSIS Global Aging study, the Netherlands ranked high in the indicator that measures the living standard of the old relative to the young.

Source: Dutch Ministry of Social Affairs and Employment, *The Old Age Pension System in the Netherlands*; and GAO analysis of *Melbourne Mercer Global Pension Index*, "Retirement Income Adequacy Indicator," and *The Global Aging Preparedness Index*. | GAO-18-111SP.

Denmark's Retirement System, Ranked High in Sustainability

The Melbourne Mercer study ranked Denmark #1 in sustainability—that is, the ability to finance the system over the long term. Denmark's retirement system consists has three components: (1) minimum benefits comprised of a basic old-age pension that is tax-financed and a pension that is a defined contribution-type plan (Arbejdsmarkedets Tillægspension, or ATP), funded by employer and employee contributions based on hours worked; (2) quasi-mandatory defined contribution-type occupational plans negotiated through collective agreements between employers and employees, covering about 85 percent of employees; and (3) voluntary individual pensions. Denmark earned the maximum score in the Melbourne Mercer study for the private pension coverage indicator, which signals a sustainable retirement income system with reduced pressure on government expenditures. It also received a high score for the indicator measuring pension assets relative to gross domestic product, which indicates that the Danish economy has the ability to meet its pension payments in the future.

Source: ATP, The Interaction of Public and Private Pensions, The Danish Case (October 2015); and GAO analysis of Pensions at A Glance 2015; The World Bank, The Payout Phase of Pension Systems (April 2010); and Melbourne Mercer Global Pension Index. | GAO-18-111SP.

Finland's Retirement System, Ranked High in Integrity

The Melbourne Mercer study ranked Finland #1 in integrity. Finland's retirement system has three components: 1) a basic national pension that supplements a low earnings-related occupational pension and a guarantee pension that ensures a minimum income for the elderly with no occupational pension, both of which are tax-financed; 2) mandatory occupational pensions that are financed by employer and employee contributions and the state, computed based on annual salary and an accrual rate of 1.5 percent (1.7 percent for those age 53 to 62 until 2025) and adjusted for increases in life expectancy; 3) other, such as voluntary supplemental pensions. In the Melbourne Mercer study, Finland received the maximum score of 10 in 6 of the 13 indicators used in the integrity index. Finland scored 9 or above in another 4 indicators, including in the areas of the largest weight: supervision and the involvement of the regulator, and the requirements for trustees and fiduciaries.

Source: Finnish Centre for Pensions, 2017 Your Guide to Earnings-related Pensions; and GAO analysis of Melbourne Mercer Global Pension Index. | GAO-18-111SP.

Glossary of Terms

The definitions of terms in this appendix are based on their use in our previous work, and supplemented by other relevant sources as appropriate, including federal law and regulations, agency documents, and retirement industry, public policy, and economic organization publications. More specifically, we referred to sources from the following federal agencies: Department of Labor; Pension Benefit Guaranty Corporation, and Consumer Financial Protection Bureau. In addition, we referred to the work of the Financial Industry Regulatory Authority, an independent not-for-profit regulator that monitors financial and exchange markets.

Retirement industry firms we referred to included TIAA, a large retirement services provider, and Mercer, a consulting firm which annually publishes the Melbourne Mercer Global Pension Index, in collaboration with Australian Centre for Financial Studies. We also reviewed the work of the Tax Policy Center, a public policy think tank. Also, we reviewed the work of the Organisation for Economic Co-operation and Development, an intergovernmental economic organization which issues the OECD Pensions at a Glance and the OECD Pensions Outlook, both of which are published on a biennial basis. We do not intend for these definitions to be definitive statements on the legal or other official meanings of the respective terms, but rather offer them to help clarify how we are using these terms in this chapter.

- **Annuity:** provides a payment for life; with payments distributed at a determined and fixed interval, such as monthly.
- **Auto-enrollment:** plan feature whereby eligible workers are enrolled into a plan automatically, or by default, unless they explicitly choose to opt out.
- **Auto-escalation:** plan feature that increases employee contributions automatically on a predetermined schedule, such as annually, up to a pre-set maximum.
- **Cliff vesting:** no employer contributions and no investment returns based on those contributions are vested until the full vesting period is satisfied, whereupon 100 percent is vested all at once (after no more than 3 years of service).
- **Compounding interest:** interest credited on both the principal and previously credited interest.
- **Defined benefit (DB) plan:** an employer-sponsored retirement plan that traditionally promises to provide a benefit for the life of the participant, based on a formula specified in the plan that typically takes into account factors such as an employee's salary, years of service, and age at retirement.
- **Defined contribution (DC) plan:** an employer-sponsored account based retirement plan, such as a 401(k) plan, that allows

individuals to accumulate tax-advantaged retirement savings in an individual account based on employee and/or employer contributions, and the investment returns (gains and losses) earned on the account.

- **Employer match:** when an employee contributes to an employer-sponsored retirement savings account, an employer may make a matching contribution, which is typically a percentage of the employee's contributions, up to a certain limit.
- **Financial literacy:** the ability to make informed judgments and take effective actions to improve one's present and long-term financial wellbeing.
- **Fiscal exposures:** responsibilities, programs, and activities that may legally commit or create expectations for future federal spending based on current policy, past practices, or other factors.
- **Governance:** determines who has power, who makes decisions, how other players make their voices heard, and how account is rendered.
- **Graduated vesting:** an increasing percentage of employer contributions and the investment returns on those contributions are credited to an individual account over time: at least 20 percent after 2 years of service, with the percentage increasing at least by 20 percent for each additional year of employment thereafter, reaching 100 percent vested after no more than 6 years.
- **Immediate vesting:** employer contributions and the investment returns based on those contributions are credited to an individual account without having to work for a minimum length of time.
- **Lifetime income options:** products or services that can turn participant savings into a retirement income stream for the rest of the participant's life.
- **Longevity risk:** the risk that individuals may outlive their retirement savings.
- **Lump sum:** one immediate payment based on the estimated present value of the participant's lifetime benefit.

- **Managed account:** services under which providers manage participants' 401(k) savings over time by making investment and portfolio decisions for them.
- **Net replacement rate:** ratio of income received in retirement to income earned while working, taking into account deductions for taxes and Social Security contributions.
- **Nondiscrimination rules:** rules that generally require contributions or benefits provided under a pension or retirement savings plan not to discriminate in favor of highly-compensated employees in order for the plan to qualify for preferential tax treatment.
- **Portability of defined contribution (DC) account balances:** in a DC plan, portability is a plan feature that allows participants to take their account contributions and any account earnings when changing jobs, and move the funds to a new employer's DC plan or to an individual retirement account (generally with no tax penalty), or take as a cash lump sum (which would be taxed as income with a corresponding early withdrawal penalty, if before age 59%).
- **Public debt**: the amount of debt owed by a government (or country) to its creditors. The value of assets owned by the government is subtracted from the gross debt amount to arrive at the net public debt.
- **Required minimum distribution:** participants age 70% or older who have defined contribution plans or individual retirement accounts must receive minimum annual payments from their plan savings based on their account balance and remaining life expectancy.
- **Rollover:** plan savings that are moved to a new qualified employer plan or an individual retirement account when a plan participant is separating from an employer.
- **Safe harbor 401(k) plan:** a safe harbor 401(k) is similar to a traditional 401(k) plan, but the employer is required to make contributions for each employee. The safe harbor 401(k) eases

administrative burdens on employers by eliminating some of the rules ordinarily applied to traditional 401(k) plans.

- **Sustainable solvency:** assurance that the projected balance between program assets and costs is positive throughout a 75-year period and is stable or rising at the end of the period.
- **Target date funds:** investment option whereby funds are allocated into investments among various asset classes and automatically shifted to lower-risk, income-producing investments as a "target" retirement date approaches.
- **Target replacement rate:** the percentage of pre-retirement income needed to maintain a certain standard of living in retirement.
- **Tax-advantaged:** able to defer the payment of taxes on income earned now until some point in the future, such as when funds are withdrawn from a qualified retirement savings account.
- **Tax expenditures:** forgone revenue for the federal government due to preferential provisions in the tax code, such as exemptions and exclusions from taxation, deductions, credits, deferral of tax liability, and preferential tax rates.
- **Total government revenue:** the sources of revenue for governments include individual income tax, payroll taxes that fund social insurance programs, corporate income tax, excise taxes, value added tax, and others.
- **Vesting of defined contribution (DC) account balances:** in a DC plan, vesting is a plan feature that determines when participants can keep the employer contributions to their accounts (and the investment returns based on those contributions) if they leave a job. (Note: Different criteria apply for vesting in a defined benefit (DB) plan.)

In: Retirement Savings and Security
Editor: Trevor Barton
ISBN: 978-1-53615-647-8

Chapter 2

WORKPLACE RETIREMENT ACCOUNTS: BETTER GUIDANCE AND INFORMATION COULD HELP PLAN PARTICIPANTS AT HOME AND ABROAD MANAGE THEIR RETIREMENT SAVINGS*

United States Government Accountability Office

ABBREVIATIONS

ATO	Australian Taxation Office
DB	defined benefit
DC	defined contribution
DOL	Department of Labor
EBSA	Employee Benefits Security Administration

* This is an edited, reformatted and augmented version of United States Government Accountability Office; Report to the Ranking Member, Committee on Finance; United States Senate, Publication No. GAO-18-19, dated January 2018.

ERISA	Employee Retirement Income Security Act of 1974
FATCA	Foreign Account Tax Compliance Act
FBAR	Report of Foreign Bank and Financial Accounts
IGA	Intergovernmental Agreement
IRA	individual retirement account
IRC	Internal Revenue Code
IRS	Internal Revenue Service
MOU	memorandum of understanding
MPF	Mandatory Provident Fund
MPFA	Mandatory Provident Fund Schemes Authority
PBGC	Pension Benefit Guaranty Corporation
PFIC	Passive Foreign Investment Company
PLR	private letter ruling
PTIN	preparer tax identification number
SSA	Social Security Administration
Social Security	Old Age and Survivors' Insurance program
State	U.S. Department of State
TBOR	Taxpayer Bill of Rights
TPA	third-party administrator
Treasury	Department of the Treasury

WHY GAO DID THIS STUDY

Saving for retirement can be difficult. However, when participants lose their workplace retirement accounts when they change employers or participate in a workplace retirement plan abroad they can encounter additional challenges in securing adequate retirement savings. GAO was asked to review steps federal agencies might take to assist participants with these challenges.

This chapter examines key challenges U.S. participants face with: (1) unclaimed retirement accounts in the United States, and (2) complying with U.S. tax reporting requirements on their foreign retirement savings.

GAO reviewed relevant federal laws and regulations, and reviewed selected tax treaties. GAO interviewed stakeholders in the United States and in Australia, Canada, Hong Kong, Switzerland, and the United Kingdom—chosen because these locations host relatively large populations of U.S. individuals and have well-developed workplace retirement systems.

WHAT GAO RECOMMENDS

GAO recommends Congress consider addressing taxation issues affecting the transfer of retirement assets between plans within the same foreign country. GAO is making seven recommendations, including that DOL issue guidance to help ongoing plan sponsors search for separated participants, and that IRS issue guidance to clarify how U.S. individuals should report foreign retirement savings to the IRS. The agencies generally agreed with GAO's recommendations. IRS disagreed with two of GAO's recommendations.

WHAT GAO FOUND

Plan participants in the United States face challenges after they change jobs, including not receiving communications from their plan sponsor and being vulnerable to unforeseen tax consequences that can result in a loss of retirement savings. GAO previously reported that when participants leave savings in a plan after separating from a job, the onus is on them to update former employers with their new address and to respond to their former employer's communications. GAO found that although an employer may incur costs searching for separated participants, there are no standard practices for the frequency or method of conducting searches. GAO reported that from 2004 through 2013, over 25 million participants in workplace plans separated from an employer and left at least one retirement account behind, despite efforts of sponsors and regulators to help participants manage their accounts. Department of Labor (DOL) officials told GAO that some sponsors do not search for participants when disclosures are returned as undeliverable. DOL has issued guidance on searching for missing participants for some plans that are terminating, but guidance does not exist on what actions DOL expects ongoing plan sponsors to take to keep track of separated participants. A key element of DOL's mission is to protect the benefits of workers and families. However, without guidance on how to search for separated participants who leave behind retirement accounts, sponsors may choose to do little more than remove unclaimed accounts from the plan when possible, and workers may never recover these savings.

Stakeholders told GAO that U.S. individuals who participate in foreign workplace retirement plans face challenges reporting their retirement savings for tax purposes because of complex federal requirements governing the taxation of foreign retirement accounts and a lack of clear guidance on how to report these savings. For example, stakeholders told GAO it is not always clear to U.S individuals or their tax preparers how foreign workplace retirement plans should be reported to the Internal Revenue Service (IRS) and the process for determining this can be complex, time-consuming, and costly. In the absence of clear guidance on how to correctly report these savings, U.S. individuals who participate in these plans may continue to run the risk of filing incorrect returns. Further, U.S. individuals in foreign retirement plans also face problems transferring retirement savings when they switch jobs. In the United States, transfers of retirement savings from one qualified plan to another are exempt from U.S. tax. However, foreign plans are generally not tax-qualified under the Internal Revenue Code, according to IRS officials, and such transfers could have tax consequences for U.S. individuals participating in foreign retirement plans. Officials from the Department of the Treasury (Treasury) told GAO that a change to the U.S. tax code could improve the tax treatment of transfers between foreign retirement plans that Treasury has already examined. Without action to address this issue, U.S. individuals may not consolidate their foreign retirement accounts or may have to pay higher U.S. taxes on transfers than taxpayers participating in qualified plans in the United States, threatening the ability of U.S. individuals to save for retirement abroad.

January 31, 2018

The Honorable Ron Wyden
Ranking Member
Committee on Finance
United States Senate

Dear Senator Wyden:

Saving for retirement through workplace plans can be difficult for U.S. citizens, whether they are participants in U.S workplace plans or participants in foreign workplace plans.[1] Regardless of whether the plan is a U.S. or a foreign workplace retirement plan, participants encounter challenges that go beyond finding ways to save enough for retirement. For example, workers can accumulate multiple workplace retirement accounts as they change jobs over the course of their careers. Former employers may merge causing the retirement plan to change names and administrators, making it more difficult for plan participants to locate their original plan accounts.[2] In the United States, plan participants are

[1] The term "U.S. individuals," as used in this report, refers to (a) U.S. citizens and (b) U.S. resident aliens. According to IRS, section 7701(b) of the Internal Revenue Code provides that U.S. resident aliens generally include U.S. lawful permanent residents (also known as Green Card holders) and individuals (who are not U.S. citizens or U.S. lawful permanent residents) who are present in the United States for a certain number of days over a specified testing period. IRS officials told us U.S. citizens and U.S. resident aliens are generally subject to the same U.S. income tax and information reporting rules with respect to their U.S. or foreign workplace retirement accounts. This report focuses on (a) U.S. individuals participating in plans sponsored by private-sector U.S. employers for work generally performed in the United States (U.S. workplace retirement plans); and (b) U.S. individuals participating in plans sponsored by private-sector foreign employers for work generally performed abroad (foreign workplace retirement plans).

[2] In the United States, employers choosing to offer plans generally sponsor two broad types of workplace retirement plans: (1) defined contribution (DC) plans, in which benefits are based on contributions and the performance of the investments in participants' individual accounts; and (2) defined benefit (DB) plans, generally funded by the employer, which promise participants a specified monthly benefit in retirement generally based on factors such as an

responsible for keeping track of their unclaimed accounts[3] by continuing to communicate with their previous employers by updating contact details to receive important information about their accounts. In addition, plan sponsors also generally have a responsibility to act solely in the interest of the participants, which includes an obligation to attempt to locate separated participants in some circumstances. Despite the efforts of plan participants, plan sponsors, and regulators to manage unclaimed accounts in the U.S. workplace retirement plan system, accounts can remain unclaimed for multiple reasons, which may eventually affect the retirement security of plan participants.[4]

As we previously reported, other countries have made it easier for U.S. individuals who work abroad and save for retirement through workplace retirement plans to manage their accounts by providing mechanisms to track and consolidate them.[5] However, U.S. individuals who participate in foreign workplace plans face different challenges than their counterparts in U.S. workplace retirement plans. For example, foreign plans may not be eligible for preferential tax treatment under U.S. law, and U.S. participants in those plans may be subject to additional reporting requirements. As of April 2015, the U.S. Department of State (State) estimated that 8.7 million U.S. citizens lived abroad, more than the populations of 39 individual U.S.

---

employee's years of service and salary, regardless of the performance of the plans' investments. In this report, unless otherwise clear from context, we use the term workplace retirement accounts, or simply retirement accounts to refer to both DC accounts and DB benefits within workplace retirement plans (i.e., private-sector single-employer plans), even though DB plans do not typically have individualized accounts. These are accounts that private-sector employers provide to employees in the workplace as a vehicle for saving for retirement. For the purpose of this report, workplace retirement accounts do not include individual retirement accounts (IRA), benefits under the Social Security Old-Age and Survivors' and Disability Insurance program (Social Security) in the United States, or government programs in foreign countries that may be similar to Social Security. We also excluded retirement savings vehicles that are not employer-sponsored.

[3] For this report we define unclaimed retirement accounts as accounts belonging to separated participants with deferred vested benefits left in a previous employer's retirement plan. The definition includes accounts of separated participants for whom the plan has an incorrect mailing address, and accounts of separated participants for whom the plan has an accurate address but the participant is unresponsive.

[4] From 2004 through 2013, separated employees left more than 16 million accounts of $5,000 or less in workplace plans, with an aggregate value of $8.5 billion. See GAO, *401(k) Plans: Greater Protections Needed for Forced Transfers and Inactive Accounts*, GAO-15-73 (Washington, D.C.: Nov. 21, 2014).

[5] See GAO-15-73.

states. Given the issues facing participants managing workplace retirement accounts in the United States and abroad, you asked us to review steps federal agencies might take to assist them. This chapter examines key challenges U.S. participants face

1) with unclaimed workplace retirement accounts in the United States, and
2) complying with U.S. tax reporting requirements on their foreign workplace retirement savings.

To understand the key challenges U.S. participants face with unclaimed workplace retirement accounts in the United States, we interviewed officials from the Department of Labor (DOL), the Pension Benefit Guaranty Corporation (PBGC), the Internal Revenue Service (IRS), and record keepers and third-party administrators (TPA) that provide search and other services to plan sponsors. We also reviewed relevant federal laws and regulations, as well as guidance and other related documents from DOL and IRS. We also reviewed reports from the 2013 ERISA Advisory Council on Missing or Lost Participants.

To understand the challenges faced by U.S. individuals who participate in foreign workplace retirement plans to comply with U.S. tax reporting requirements on their foreign workplace retirement savings,[6] we selected five international case study locations with well-developed workplace retirement systems to examine. Each of the case study locations have relatively large populations of U.S. workers and high total amounts of foreign earned income reported by U.S. taxpayers living in that location.[7] We deliberately included case study locations with and without a bilateral

[6] For purposes of this report, we focused on applicable U.S. income tax requirements for U.S. individuals. Unless otherwise indicated, we excluded issues such as: taxation of employers or plan sponsors; other types of U.S. taxes participants may be subject to, such as Social Security or unemployment taxes; U.S. taxation of plan participants who are not U.S. citizens; and any taxes imposed by a foreign country.

[7] We reviewed data on foreign earned income reported by the IRS Statistics of Income Division. Foreign earned income is generally income received, such as wages, salaries or professional fees, for personal services a taxpayer performs in a foreign country during a period the taxpayer's tax home is in a foreign country.

tax treaty with the United States, based on Department of the Treasury (Treasury) information.[8] Our case study locations were Australia, Canada, Hong Kong, Switzerland, and the United Kingdom. For each case study we reviewed documentation related to the tax treatment of workplace retirement accounts accumulated in that location by U.S. individuals, such as tax treaties and Intergovernmental Agreements (IGAs) related to the Foreign Account Tax Compliance Act (FATCA).[9] We also reviewed publicly available research and reports about each case study location's retirement system, and interviewed relevant stakeholders. For each case study we interviewed government officials, plan sponsors, and service providers. Where available, we reviewed relevant data provided to us by relevant government officials. We did not conduct an independent legal analysis to verify the information provided about the laws or regulations in the locations we selected for this study. Instead, we relied on appropriate secondary sources and interviews with relevant officials to support our work. We also interviewed IRS and Treasury officials, including those in the Office of Chief Counsel, the Office of Tax Policy, the Tax Exempt and Government Entities Division, and the Taxpayer Advocate Service. We

---

[8] The United States has income tax treaties with a number of foreign countries. As described on IRS' website, under these treaties, residents (not necessarily citizens) of foreign countries are taxed at a reduced rate, or are exempt from U.S. income taxes on certain items of income they receive from sources within the United States. According to IRS, these reduced rates and exemptions vary among countries and specific items of income and treaty provisions generally are reciprocal (i.e., apply to both treaty countries).

[9] According to IRS, FATCA is a colloquial term commonly used to refer to certain provisions of Subtitle A of Title V of the Hiring Incentives to Restore Employment Act, Pub. L. No. 111-147, §§ 501-541, 124 Stat. 71, 97-117 (2010). Specifically, IRS told us that FATCA is commonly used to refer to section 501 of that law (Reporting on certain foreign accounts), which added chapter 4 to the Internal Revenue Code (IRC) (codified at 26 U.S.C. §§1471-1474), and section 511 (Disclosure of information with respect to foreign financial assets), which added section 6038D to the IRC (codified at 26 U.S.C. § 6038D). According to IRS, chapter 4 and section 6038D are separate and distinct reporting regimes. Chapter 4 generally requires foreign financial institutions and certain other foreign entities to report to the IRS on foreign financial accounts held by U.S. taxpayers. IRS has entered into Intergovernmental Agreements (IGAs) with foreign countries to implement these requirements. Section 6038D of the IRC requires individual U.S. taxpayers to report foreign financial assets that exceed a certain threshold amount. For the remainder of this report, we generally use "IRC section 6038D" to refer to this provision, and "FATCA" to refer to Chapter 4. However, in describing stakeholder discussions, we use the term "FATCA" when stakeholders used this term but did not specify which provisions were being referred to.

also spoke with organizations representing U.S. expatriates, foreign and domestic retirement experts, tax advisors, and tax preparers who specialize in assisting individuals with foreign income and assets when filing their U.S. tax returns. We also reviewed transcripts of testimonies the National Taxpayer Advocate gave before Congress pertaining to international tax issues and FATCA, as well as IRS and Treasury documentation on foreign workplace retirement plans and reporting foreign income and assets.

GAO conducted this performance audit from July 2015 to October 2017 in accordance with generally accepted government auditing standards. Those standards require that GAO plan and perform the audit to obtain sufficient, appropriate evidence to provide a reasonable basis for our findings and conclusions based on our audit objectives. GAO believes that the evidence obtained provides a reasonable basis for the report's findings and conclusions based on the report's audit objectives.

BACKGROUND

Employee Retirement Income Security Act of 1974 (ERISA) and the Internal Revenue Code (IRC)

The Employee Retirement Income Security Act of 1974 (ERISA) contains various provisions intended to protect the interests of plan participants and beneficiaries in workplace retirement plans.[10] These protections include requirements related to reporting and disclosure, participation, vesting, and benefit accrual, as well as plan funding.

---

[10] Pub. L. No. 93-406, 88 Stat. 832 (codified as amended in scattered sections of 26 and 29 U.S.C.). Title I of ERISA, including the reporting and disclosure and fiduciary responsibility requirements, does not generally cover plans sponsored by government entities or plans "maintained outside of the United States primarily for the benefit of persons substantially all of whom are nonresident aliens," among others. 29 U.S.C. § 1003.

For example, ERISA requires plans to provide plan participants with a summary plan description, including information on their rights under ERISA, periodic benefit statements, and upon request, a copy of the annual report including a financial statement, according to DOL. ERISA sets fiduciary standards that generally require workplace retirement plan funds to be handled prudently and in the sole interest of participants.[11] ERISA also establishes certain requirements related to plan termination.[12] ERISA does not require employers to provide workplace retirement plans, but those that do must comply with applicable requirements and standards.

The Internal Revenue Code (IRC) provides favorable tax treatment for workplace retirement plans that meet certain qualification requirements set out in the IRC.[13] For example, employees are generally not taxed on contributions made on their behalf but instead are taxed on benefits received.

Federal Agencies' Roles with Respect to U.S. Workplace Retirement Plans

Several federal agencies play a role with respect to U.S. workplace retirement plans. Responsibility for enforcing ERISA is shared by DOL, Treasury, and PBGC. Treasury, through IRS, is primarily responsible for enforcing the IRC.

---

[11] Under ERISA, a fiduciary is any person, to the extent they (1) exercise any discretionary authority or control over plan management or any authority or control over the management or disposition of plan assets, (2) render investment advice with respect to plan money or property for a fee or other compensation, or (3) have any discretionary authority or responsibility for plan administration. 29 U.S.C. § 1002(21)(A). Plan fiduciaries are required to act prudently, solely in the interest of plan participants and beneficiaries, and for the exclusive purpose of providing benefits and defraying reasonable expenses of administering the plan. Fiduciaries are also required to diversify the investments and act in accordance with plan documents, which set the terms of the retirement plan, insofar as such documents are consistent with ERISA. 29 U.S.C. § 1104(a).

[12] See Congressional Research Service: *Summary of the Employee Retirement Income Security Act (ERISA)*, (Washington, D.C., April 10, 2008).

[13] The IRC is codified in Title 26 of the U.S. Code.

Department of Labor's Employee Benefits Security Administration (EBSA)

The mission of DOL's Employee Benefits Security Administration (EBSA) is to assure the security of retirement, health, and other workplace-related benefits of U.S. workers and their families. DOL administers Title I of ERISA, which includes the fiduciary standards and disclosure and reporting requirements. To carry out its responsibilities, EBSA issues regulations in these and other areas, and conducts programs and initiatives to assist and educate workers, plan sponsors, fiduciaries, and service providers on their rights and obligations under ERISA. EBSA also issues guidance and field assistance bulletins to assist plan sponsors and plan fiduciaries with managing retirement plans. For instance, in 2014, EBSA issued Field Assistance Bulletin (FAB) 2014-01 to assist fiduciaries of terminating DC plans in fulfilling their obligations under ERISA to locate missing participants[14] and properly distribute their account balances.[15] EBSA also maintains an outreach program employing approximately 100 benefits advisors throughout the country in 13 field offices. The program offers services to educate U.S. workers, beneficiaries, and plan sponsors about their rights and obligations under federal employee benefit laws, and helps individuals obtain retirement benefits that have been improperly denied.[16]

---

[14] According to the bulletin, under the IRC, plan administrators are required to distribute all plan assets as soon as administratively feasible after plan termination, and before making a distribution, the plan administrator has a responsibility to contact the plan's participants for directions on how to distribute their account balances. See 26 U.S.C. § 402(f). In the bulletin, DOL used the term "missing participants" to refer broadly to those participants who fail to respond to these notices or for whom mail is returned. The bulletin provided guidance on what steps plan fiduciaries should take to search for these unresponsive participants. See DOL Field Assistance Bulletin 2014-01. With respect to DB plans, the Pension Benefit Guaranty Corporation has a Missing Participants Program for searching for and distributing benefits on behalf of missing participants of terminating DB plans covered by Title IV of ERISA. Under ERISA, the term "missing participant" is defined as a participant or beneficiary under a terminating plan whom the plan administrator cannot locate after a diligent search. See 29 U.S.C. § 1350.

[15] We previously recommended that DOL convene a taskforce to consider establishing a national pension registry to assist participants with locating unclaimed retirement accounts; DOL agreed to evaluate the possibility of doing so. See GAO-15-73.

[16] According to EBSA, in fiscal year 2016, the benefits advisors closed 193,669 inquiries/complaints and recovered just over $394 million in benefits for participants who had been improperly denied through an informal negotiation process with the employer.

Internal Revenue Service (IRS)

Under Title II of ERISA and subsequent amendments to the IRC, IRS issues and enforces rules that plans must meet to be qualified for preferential tax treatment. IRS also enforces certain provisions in Title I of ERISA regarding participation, vesting, benefit accrual, and minimum funding. IRS' mission is to help U.S. taxpayers understand and meet their tax responsibilities and to enforce the law with integrity and fairness. To help achieve its mission, IRS issues tax regulations and other guidance to help taxpayers comply with the IRC.[17] IRS guidance provides detailed and technical explanations of tax laws for professional tax preparers as well as taxpayers.[18] IRS also manages a number of initiatives, programs, and systems to enforce federal tax law and assist taxpayers that are related to our review of unclaimed retirement accounts.[19] For example, to assist taxpayers, IRS adopted a Taxpayer Bill of Rights in 2014 to provide a better understanding of taxpayers' rights under the IRC. IRS also periodically publishes a strategic plan for a given period that outlines how it will improve service to taxpayers and enforce the law. To help ensure that taxpayers are paying the correct amount of tax due and to identify discrepancies, IRS' Automated Under reporter Program matches taxpayer income and deductions submitted on information returns by third parties against amounts reported by taxpayers on their individual income tax returns. IRS also assists taxpayers and payers with information about federal tax withholding obligations. To assist taxpayers with foreign accounts, since 2003 IRS has offered an Offshore Voluntary Disclosure Program. This program provides a way for taxpayers with previously

---

[17] Treasury also participates in the formulation of certain forms of guidance.

[18] Other IRS sources of information include forms, instructions, and publications for taxpayers to use in preparing their returns; news releases, fact sheets, and tax tips to the news media; online interactive tools in which taxpayers can receive answers after asking general or taxpayer-specific questions; and instructional audio and video presentations. These various communication tools are intended to help taxpayers understand tax laws, improve voluntary compliance with the IRC, and control IRS' administrative costs.

[19] In addition to the IRS, other entities within Treasury are responsible for various aspects of tax law administration. For instance, Treasury's Office of Tax Policy develops and implements tax policies and programs and reviews regulations and rulings to administer the IRC. Treasury's Office of International Tax Counsel is responsible for negotiating and reviewing income tax and estate and gift tax treaties with foreign countries, and for coordinating tax treaty matters with the U.S. Department of State and Congress.

undisclosed income and undisclosed offshore accounts that need to be reported to contact IRS and resolve their tax matters.

IRS also assists sponsors that administer qualified retirement plans through a number of systems and programs. For example, IRS offers assistance to plan sponsors through the Employee Plans Compliance Resolution System, which helps sponsors of qualified plans remedy operational and form mistakes made in the course of administering a retirement plan and avoid plan disqualification. IRS also forwards letters to missing individuals on behalf of private individuals or government agencies for a "humane purpose" when there is no other way to relay the information to the individual.[20] Between 1994 and 2012, IRS forwarded letters through a letter forwarding program on behalf of entities that control assets that may be due a taxpayer, such as from sponsors of qualified plans that are attempting to locate missing participants.

Pension Benefit Guaranty Corporation (PBGC)

Title IV of ERISA created PBGC as a U.S. government corporation to provide plan termination insurance for certain DB plans that are unable to pay promised benefits. For example, when a PBGC-insured single-employer DB plan fails, PBGC trustees the plan and pays benefits up to statutory limits. PBGC also oversees the voluntary ("standard") termination of fully funded PBGC-insured single-employer DB plans to ensure participants will receive the benefits to which they are entitled. As part of the standard termination process, PBGC's Missing Participants Program connects participants—missing when the plan closes out—to their retirement benefits, in part by maintaining a centralized, online database the public can use to find lost retirement benefits.[21]

---

[20] A "humane purpose" is one in which a person is seeking to find a missing person to convey a message of an urgent or compelling nature, or is seeking to find a missing person because of an emergency situation. For example, these would include letters to notify a person of a serious illness, imminent death, or the death of a close relative, to locate a missing relative to convey an urgent or compelling message, or to help locate persons being sought for a medical study to detect and treat medical defects or diseases.

[21] PBGC recently issued a final rule that expanded the Missing Participants Program to DC plans. Missing Participants, 82 Fed. Reg. 60,800 (Dec. 22, 2017). According to PBGC officials, although current statute gives PBGC the authority to compel plans to provide information to

Social Security Administration (SSA)

SSA provides retirement benefits to eligible individuals under the federal Social Security Old Age and Survivors' Insurance program (Social Security). Although SSA does not oversee workplace retirement plans, SSA maintains data that are reported to IRS by plans using Form 8955-SSA on separated participants with vested but undistributed benefits.[22] When individuals claim Social Security benefits, SSA may provide them with a "Potential Private Pension Benefit Information" notice that indicates they may be entitled to a retirement benefit through a past employer.

Ongoing and Terminated Workplace Retirement Plans

DOL reported that in 2014 there were just over 639,000 DC plans and nearly 43,500 DB plans in the United States. These plans were sponsored by individual employers (i.e., private single-employer plans) and provided benefits to nearly 118 million participants.[23] When a qualified plan terminates[24]—whether it is a DB or DC plan—federal law requires plan participants to immediately be 100 percent vested in all accrued benefits (to the extent funded in the case of a DB plan)[25] regardless of the vesting schedule in the plan document, according to IRS. A plan sponsor is required to distribute assets from a terminated plan as soon as

---

the agency on the disposition of participant retirement accounts, PBGC made this optional in the final rule. In other words, with respect to missing participants, a DC plan choosing to participate can choose to transfer account balances directly to PBGC or to provide PBGC with information about where the account balances were transferred. Either way, according to officials, the agency will try to find the missing participant and when located, will provide either benefits or information (depending on which approach the plan used). With both approaches, PBGC will add the missing participants to its public online database, according to PBGC officials.

[22] Plan administrators must complete IRS Form 8955-SSA to satisfy the reporting requirements of section 6057(a) of the IRC (which requires plan administrators of plans subject to the vesting standards of ERISA to report certain information about separated participants with deferred vested benefits under the plan.)

[23] See Employee Benefits Security Administration, United States Department of Labor, Private Pension Plan Bulletin Historical Tables and Graphs, 1975-2014. Washington, D.C., Sept. 2016.

[24] In this report, we refer to DC and DB plans that have not been terminated as "ongoing plans."

[25] 26 U.S.C. § 411(d)(3); 26 C.F.R. § 1.411(d)-2(a)(1).

administratively feasible, but generally within 1 year after plan termination.[26] For terminated DC plans, such as 401(k) plans, participants generally receive the full amount of their vested account balance upon plan termination, according to IRS.

Transferring Savings of Missing Participants in U.S. Defined Contribution Retirement Plans

When an employee separates from an employer but still has vested savings in a qualified defined contribution retirement plan, the plan can, under certain conditions and without the participant's consent, transfer accounts out of the plan—commonly referred to as a "forced transfer."[27] Before the Economic Growth and Tax Relief Reconciliation Act of 2001[28] was enacted, ongoing DC plans could, in the absence of participant instructions, distribute balances of $5,000 or less by paying them directly to the participant, referred to as a "cash-out." This law sought to protect participants' retirement savings by requiring ongoing plans that have a cash-out limit that exceeds $1,000 (up to $5,000), in the absence of participant instructions and subject to certain notice requirements, to transfer balances that exceed $1,000 (up to $5,000) to an individual retirement account (IRA), preserving their tax-preferred status.[29]

[26] Rev. Rul. 89-87, 1989-2 C.B. 81. In an involuntary termination, if a terminated DB plan that is covered by Title IV of ERISA has insufficient funds to pay all of the benefits, the PBGC will become the plan's trustee and will guarantee the payment of vested pension benefits up to limits set by law. In fiscal year 2017, PBGC paid retirement benefits to nearly 840,000 retirees in more than 4,800 plans totaling over $5.7 billion.

[27] See 26 U.S.C. § 401(a)(11), (a)(31)(B) and 26 U.S.C. § 417(e). We have reported on forced transfers in GAO-15-73.

[28] Pub. L. No. 107-16, 115 Stat. 38.

[29] In these circumstances, the plan may transfer eligible account balances to an IRA. IRAs are a type of retirement savings vehicle–different from workplace retirement plans–that generally allow eligible individuals to save for retirement on a tax-deferred basis. See 26 U.S.C. § 408. After the account is transferred into an IRA, it is generally subject to the rules governing IRAs and no longer subject to ERISA. Ongoing plans generally may not distribute vested accounts of more than $5,000 without the consent of the participant. 26 U.S.C. § 411(a)(11).

Terminating plans are subject to different requirements. Fiduciaries of terminating plans are obligated to search for missing participants, to notify them of the termination and pending distribution of benefits before transferring participants' unclaimed accounts to an IRA or elsewhere, according to DOL guidance.[30] The guidance further provides that fiduciaries of terminating plans who are unable to locate missing participants may also be permitted to transfer accounts belonging to missing participants, without consent, to a federally-insured bank account or to a state's unclaimed property fund. This occurs if the plan fiduciary cannot find an IRA provider to accept a direct rollover distribution for a missing participant or otherwise determines not to roll over the distribution to an IRA, for some other compelling reason. For tax reporting purposes, transfers made to a bank or a state unclaimed property fund are generally subject to income taxation, according to the guidance. This contrasts with rollovers to IRAs in which transferred retirement savings remain tax-favored. Plan sponsors are generally required to withhold 20 percent of the account balance on transfers to a bank or state unclaimed property fund and will send the withheld amount to Treasury to be used toward any potential taxes due on the distribution.[31]

Tax Treatment of U.S. and Foreign Workplace Retirement Plans in which U.S. Individuals Participate

In the United States, employee and employer contributions and investment earnings in a qualified retirement plan are generally not taxed as income until the employee receives the benefit. For example, employees

---

[30] DOL FAB 2014-01. According to this guidance, if a plan follows certain required search steps, but does not find the missing participant, the duties of prudence and loyalty require the fiduciary to consider if additional search steps are appropriate. A plan fiduciary should consider the size of a participant's account balance and the cost of further search efforts in deciding if any additional search steps are appropriate. See GAO-15-73 for additional information on specific requirements for forced transfers and the differences between terminating plans and ongoing plans.

[31] Sponsors will also generate a form 1099-R to report the income and tax withholding to both the IRS and the participant.

participating in a 401(k) plan can generally elect to have their employer contribute a portion of their compensation to their account on a pretax basis. This deferred compensation (commonly referred to as a pretax elective contribution by IRS) is not subject to income tax withholding, and employees are not required to report it as wages on their individual U.S. tax returns at the time of the contribution. In addition, employers can provide matching or non-elective contributions to an employee's 401(k) account; these matching or non-elective contributions are generally tax-deductible by the employer and employees also are not required to report these contributions as wages on their U.S. tax returns or pay income tax on these contributions at the time the contributions are made. Distributions from a qualified DC plan in the United States made to participants, including those who have separated from their employer, may be treated differently for tax purposes, depending on the nature and timing of the distribution. For example, a direct rollover, in which money is transferred directly from one qualified workplace retirement plan or IRA to another eligible retirement plan or IRA, is not taxable at the time of the rollover but should be reported on the participant's federal tax return. By contrast, a distribution that is not rolled over[32] is generally taxable income in the year in which it is received by the participant, according to IRS.

Foreign workplace retirement plans are generally not tax-qualified under the IRC or covered by ERISA, according to IRS officials and tax experts with whom we spoke. They are, however, generally subject to the regulatory structure in place in the country where the retirement plan exists.[33] Foreign workplace retirement plans that cover U.S. individuals may be subject to certain provisions of the IRC and other federal laws governing reporting and taxation of these retirement assets, as well as any

[32] Participants may be able to defer tax on all or part of an eligible rollover distribution by requesting the payor to directly roll over the taxable portion into an IRA or to an eligible retirement plan. If the distribution is made before the occurrence of certain events (and not timely rolled over), such as before the participant reaches age 591/2, it may also be subject to a 10 percent additional tax on early withdrawals. See 26 U.S.C. § 72(t).

[33] In addition, in two of our case study locations, participation by workers in a workplace retirement plan is mandatory under certain conditions, according to government officials with whom we spoke. For this report, we did not conduct a legal review of the regulations or laws in the case study locations that pertain to workplace retirement plans.

applicable income tax treaties between the United States and the foreign country (see more about these treaties below). The extent to which U.S. individuals are subject to U.S. income tax on the contributions and earnings accruing in their foreign workplace retirement account depends on the specific characteristics of the plan.[34] For example, according to tax experts with whom we spoke, many foreign workplace retirement plans qualify as employees' trusts, and the taxation of contributions and earnings from these plans are governed by section 402(b) of the IRC.[35] According to IRS, as long as the foreign retirement plan is determined to be an employees' trust, the U.S. individual must include on their U.S. tax return contributions to the trust if the contributions are not subject to a substantial risk of forfeiture (vested). In addition, IRS officials said contributions that become vested after the year of contribution are taxable in the year of vesting, and earnings are taxable when distributed.[36] Some foreign workplace retirement plans may include investments in a Passive Foreign Investment Company (PFIC),[37] which, according to one tax preparer with whom we spoke, are investments in foreign mutual funds, hedge funds, or other kinds of pooled investments not incorporated in the United States.

---

[34] Contributions may include employee contributions and employer contributions.

[35] According to international tax publications we reviewed, section 402(b) governs the taxation of funded employee benefit trusts that are not qualified plans. Whether and when contributions and generated income from a section 402(b) trust are taxable as income to the participant depends on various factors, including whether the contributions are "substantially vested" and whether the participant is a highly compensated employee. See 26 U.S.C. §§ 402(b), 83(a).

[36] However, according to IRS, if the foreign retirement plan is not an employees' trust, then the contributions and realized earnings are required to be reported on the U.S. individual's U.S. tax return.

[37] A Passive Foreign Investment Company (PFIC) is generally defined as a foreign corporation for which (a) 75 percent or more of its gross income for the taxable year is passive income, or (b) at least 50 percent of the average percentage of assets held by the corporation during the taxable year produce passive income, or are held for the production of, passive income. 26 U.S.C. § 1297(a). According to IRS, passive income includes items such as dividends, interest, rents, royalties, and other items that are not generally derived from the active conduct of business.

A U.S. individual who is a shareholder of a PFIC may be subject to annual reporting requirements and a high income tax rate on certain distributions.[38]

U.S. individuals who participate in a foreign workplace retirement plan also may be subject to income tax on any distribution they receive from their plan during the current tax year. Depending on the circumstances, U.S. individuals also may be subject to income tax on certain distributions they have not actually received, such as transfers of assets between or within foreign workplace retirement plans, if they are in "constructive receipt" of (or otherwise have income inclusion with respect to) the funds.[39] In addition, U.S. individuals who pay foreign income taxes on distributions from their foreign workplace retirement plans may be eligible to claim a foreign tax credit on their U.S. tax return.[40]

Income Tax Treaties

As of October 2017, the United States had a network of 57 comprehensive income tax treaties covering 66 countries, according to Treasury. U.S. individuals are subject to U.S. income tax on their worldwide income, and this could include contributions and earnings within and distributions from a foreign workplace retirement plan. However, tax treaty provisions may reduce foreign income taxes owed by

---

[38] See generally 26 U.S.C. §§ 1291-1298. Treasury regulations generally exempt from the annual reporting requirements participants in a "foreign pension fund" if there is an applicable income tax treaty that provides that the income earned by the foreign pension fund may be taxed as the income of the participant only when, and to the extent the income is paid to, the participant. 26 C.F.R. § 1.1298-1(c)(4).

[39] In general, gains, profits, and income are to be included in gross income for the taxable year in which they are actually or constructively received by the taxpayer. 26 C.F.R. § 1.451-1(a). Under Treasury regulations, "income, although not actually reduced to a taxpayer's possession, is constructively received by him in the taxable year during which it is credited to his account, set apart for him, or otherwise made available so that the he may draw upon it at any time, or so that he could have drawn upon it during the taxable year if notice of intention to withdraw had been given." However, income is not constructively received if the taxpayer's control of its receipt is subject to substantial limitations or restrictions. See 26 C.F.R. § 1.451-2.

[40] Such credits may be available under applicable tax treaties or the U.S. tax code; *see, e.g.,* 26 U.S.C. §§ 901-909.

U.S. individuals who receive income sourced from a treaty country; for example, through the use of credits, deductions, exemptions, or tax rate reductions.[41] (See appendix I for more information on how IRS recommends taxpayers review tax treaties.)

U.S. Income Tax Treaties with Other Countries

One objective of tax treaties is to provide taxpayers some relief from having to pay taxes in both the United States and a foreign country on the same income—referred to as "double taxation"—without creating opportunities for tax evasion or avoidance. Treaty provisions generally apply to both countries that have signed the treaty. A U.S. resident who receives income from a treaty country may be entitled to certain treaty benefits—credits, deductions, exemptions, or reductions in the rate of tax—on the taxes owed to that foreign country. Similarly, residents of the foreign country may be entitled to treaty benefits on their U.S. taxes on income from U.S. sources. However, with certain exceptions, tax treaties generally do not reduce the U.S. tax liability of U.S. residents.

Source: Department of the Treasury and the Internal Revenue Service. | GAO-18-19.

According to IRS and Treasury, almost all U.S. tax treaties also contain what is known as a "saving clause," which IRS describes as a way to preserve or "save" the right of each country to tax its own residents (and in the case of the United States, its citizens) as if no tax treaty were in effect.[42] As a result, these treaties do not generally reduce the U.S. income tax for U.S. individuals, unless an exception applies.

---

[41] For example, tax treaties may provide for how each country will tax pension contributions, earnings, and distributions. Since the treaties are bilateral, these treaties may also reduce the U.S. income tax imposed on residents of foreign countries on their income from U.S. sources. The 2016 U.S. Model Income Tax Convention (i.e., model treaty) developed by Treasury uses the term "resident" and includes a definition of that term for purposes of the model treaty. Similarly, tax treaties with other countries may establish their own definitions of who is covered by the treaty.

[42] See IRS Publication 519, U.S. Tax Guide For Aliens, For Use In Preparing 2016 Returns, p. 47.

In February 2016, Treasury issued a revised U.S. Model Income Tax Convention (i.e., model treaty), which is the baseline text the agency uses when it negotiates tax treaties.[43] Depending on the outcome of the treaty negotiations, the final treaty with a particular foreign country may or may not include language from the model treaty.

Reporting Foreign Accounts and Foreign Financial Assets

According to IRS, the Foreign Account Tax Compliance Act (FATCA) and IRC section 6038D are important developments in U.S. efforts to combat tax evasion by U.S. individuals holding accounts and other financial assets offshore,[44] which may have implications for U.S. individuals who have foreign retirement accounts. FATCA generally requires foreign financial institutions to provide information to IRS regarding foreign financial accounts held by U.S. taxpayers.[45] IRC section 6038D generally requires U.S. individuals to report to IRS their foreign financial assets that exceed a certain threshold. Beginning in July 2014, U.S. entities were required to withhold 30 percent on certain payments to a foreign financial institution unless the institution has entered into an agreement with IRS regarding FATCA reporting or is in a jurisdiction that is treated as having an Intergovernmental Agreement (IGA) in effect.[46]

---

[43] For example, Article 17 of the 2016 U.S. Model Income Tax Convention ("Pensions, Social Security, Annuities, Alimony, and Child Support") includes proposed language describing how pension distributions and earnings are to be taxed in each country and how transfers of funds between pensions may be exempt from taxation under certain circumstances. Article 18 ("Pension Funds") includes proposed language describing the tax treatment in each country of pension fund contributions.

[44] According to IRS, FATCA is commonly used to refer to sections 501 and 511 of the Hiring Incentives to Restore Employment Act (codified at 26 U.S.C. §§ 1471-1474 and 26 U.S.C. § 6038D, respectively). Section 511 establishes reporting requirements for individuals, while section 501 (generally referred to in this report as FATCA) establishes reporting requirements for foreign financial institutions and certain other foreign entities. However, in describing our discussions with stakeholders, we use the term "FATCA" if stakeholders used this term but did not specify which provisions were being referred to.

[45] See 26 U.S.C. §§ 1471-1474.

[46] However, IRS Notice 2014-33 established calendar years 2014 and 2015 as a transition period for purposes of IRS enforcement and administration of the FATCA withholding requirements, among other things. The notice stated that during this period, IRS will take

However, FATCA regulations exempt foreign financial institutions from reporting on retirement accounts that meet certain requirements. Treasury has entered into IGAs with other countries to assist with implementing FATCA that may also provide an exemption for foreign financial institutions reporting of certain retirement accounts. This exemption does not exist under IRC section 6038D, which requires individuals, including U.S. citizens, to report their foreign retirement accounts on IRS Form 8938 if they meet certain regulatory thresholds. For example, unmarried U.S. individuals living abroad must file if the total value of their specified foreign financial assets is more than $200,000 on the last day of the tax year or more than $300,000 at any time during the tax year.[47]

Estimated Number and Financial Profile of U.S. Citizens Living and Working Abroad

The U.S. Department of State (State) estimates that as of April 2015, 8.7 million U.S. citizens lived abroad. (See appendix II for other estimates.)

---

into account the extent to which the foreign financial institution has made good faith efforts to comply with the requirements.

[47] See 26 C.F.R. § 1.6038D-2(a). An unmarried taxpayer living in the United States or married taxpayers filing separate income tax returns living in the United States must file if the total value of his or her specified foreign financial assets is more than $50,000 on the last day of the tax year or more than $75,000 at any time during the tax year. Married taxpayers filing a joint income tax return and living in the United States must file if the total value of their specified foreign financial assets is more than $100,000 on the last day of the year or more than $150,000 at any time during the tax year. Unmarried taxpayers living abroad must file if the total value of their specified foreign financial assets is more than $200,000 on the last day of the tax year or more than $300,000 at any time during the year. Married taxpayers filing a joint income tax return living abroad must file if the total value of their specified foreign financial assets is more than $400,000 on the last day of the tax year or more than $600,000 at any time during the year. Specified foreign financial assets include, among other things, savings, deposit, checking, brokerage accounts, stocks, bonds, retirement accounts, annuities, and other investment accounts. Real estate and physical assets are excluded from IRC section 6038D reporting.

Income data published by IRS for 2011[48] suggest that a majority of U.S. taxpayers who earned income from foreign sources likely owed little federal income tax because their reported adjusted gross income[49] was relatively low due to tax credits and exemptions available to taxpayers on foreign-earned income.[50] IRS estimated that in 2011 over 449,000 returns were filed by taxpayers reporting foreign-earned income and just over 445,000 of these returns reported using the foreign-earned income exclusion. We previously reported that for tax year 2011, taxpayers claiming the foreign-earned income exclusion had higher average income ($163,450) than the average Form 1040 filer ($58,706), and about 45 percent of those taxpayers had an adjusted gross income of less than $10,000.[51] These data reflect that some taxpayers were able to exclude all or most of their foreign-earned income in calculating their adjusted gross income. We also reported that taxpayers claiming the foreign-earned income exclusion had lower average U.S. tax rates than all Form 1040 filers.[52]

---

[48] IRS compiles and reports data describing foreign income earned by U.S. individuals abroad for use in its publicly available Statistics of Income Bulletin. We reviewed data reported by IRS for tax year 2011. See Internal Revenue Service, Statistics of Income Bulletin, Spring 2014, Washington, D.C.

[49] The IRC defines adjusted gross income as gross income minus adjustments to income. These adjustments can include items such as moving expenses, contributions to IRAs or other qualified retirement plans or health savings accounts, alimony payments, and student loan interest payments, among others. See 26 U.S.C. § 62.

[50] U.S. individuals who live and work abroad may be eligible for a credit or deduction against U.S. tax for foreign income taxes paid to other counties (the foreign tax credit). 26 U.S.C. § 901. Under section 911 of the tax code, U.S. individuals who live and work abroad may also be eligible for an exclusion of foreign-earned income (up to $101,300 in 2016) and an exclusion or deduction of certain foreign housing costs. The income that U.S. citizens and resident aliens may exclude under section 911 is generally limited to amounts earned for services performed abroad, including salaries and wages. It does not include income derived from capital, such as interest, dividends, capital gains, or retirement distributions.

[51] See GAO, *Tax Policy: Economic Benefits of Income Exclusion for U.S. Citizens Working Abroad Are Uncertain,* GAO-14-387 (Washington, D.C.: May 20, 2014).

[52] A majority of the returns reporting use of the foreign-earned income exclusion in 2011 (just over 84 percent) reported adjusted gross income from foreign sources as under $100,000 and 71 percent reported adjusted gross income under $50,000. Nearly a quarter of the returns reported no adjusted gross income for tax year 2011 from foreign sources due to allowable deductions and adjustments to income, including the foreign-earned income exclusion. Although these taxpayers reported no adjusted gross income for 2011, their average foreign earned-income was just above $49,000, according to GAO analysis of IRS data.

PARTICIPANTS FACE CHALLENGES MANAGING UNCLAIMED RETIREMENT ACCOUNTS AND AGENCIES HAVE NOT PROVIDED SUFFICIENT GUIDANCE AND INFORMATION TO ASSIST THEM OR PLAN SPONSORS

Participants Have Challenges Managing Unclaimed Retirement Accounts

Participants in U.S. workplace retirement plans face challenges managing unclaimed accounts accumulated over the course of their careers. We previously reported that some 401(k) plan participants find it difficult to keep track of their savings, particularly when they change jobs, because of challenges with consolidation, communication, and information.[53] First, we found that individuals who accrue multiple accounts over the course of a career may be unable to consolidate their accounts by rolling over savings from one employer's plan to the next.[54] Second, maintaining communication with a former employer's plan can be challenging if companies are restructured and plans are terminated or merged and renamed. Third, key information on lost accounts may be held by different plans, service providers, or government agencies, and participants may not know where to turn for assistance. As one witness testified to the ERISA Advisory Council in 2013, it is not uncommon for former employees to have difficulty locating a previous employer.

---

[53] See GAO-15-73. We reported that when participants leave their savings in a plan after leaving a job, the onus is on them to update former employers with address and name changes, and to respond to their former plan sponsor's communications. We also reported that although an employer may incur costs searching for separated participants, there are no standard practices for the frequency or method of conducting searches. GAO reported that from 2004 through 2013, over 25 million participants in workplace plans separated from an employer and left at least one retirement account behind.

[54] We previously reported that 401(k) plan processes for handling separating participants' accounts create barriers for participants to roll their savings to a new plan, making IRA rollovers an easier and faster choice for those who want to consolidate their savings. However, we also reported that the plan environment generally has lower fees, better comparative information, and ERISA plan fiduciaries are required to select and monitor reasonable investment options. See GAO, *401(k) Plans: Labor and IRS Could Improve the Rollover Process for Participants,* GAO-13-30 (Washington, D.C.; Mar. 7, 2013).

Existing reporting and disclosure requirements directed at plan sponsors can provide participants who separate from their employer information about their accounts via multiple disclosures. However, plan sponsors have no automatic way to keep participants' contact information up to date, nor do they have ways to ensure that separated participants will respond to their communications. Many participants rarely read the notices they receive. We conducted a review of private sector pension plan notices in 2013, and found that participants were interested in information about their individual benefits, which could reasonably include information about a pending distribution of their unclaimed account.[55] Due to the large number of participant notices, we found participants struggled with what they must or should read.

When participant notices are ineffective, accounts can become lost or unclaimed and eventually shrink or disappear entirely, diminishing a source of income in retirement. For example, accounts with a balance of $1,000 or less can be cashed out of a plan without participant consent; account balances can be reduced by tax withholding and early distribution taxes, or conditionally forfeited by the plan sponsor until the participant emerges to make a claim.[56] Accounts with balances under $5,000, and sometimes those with larger balances, can be forcibly transferred to an IRA, where the account balances may decrease over time as the fees outpace low investment returns, as we reported in our prior work. In 13 of the 19 forced-transfer IRA scenarios we considered in 2014, a $1,000 account balance was reduced to zero within 30 years.[57] DOL has also uncovered tens of thousands of participants of retirement age with

---

[55] GAO, *Private Pensions: Clarity of Required Reports and Disclosures Could Be Improved*, GAO-14-92, (Washington, D.C., Nov. 21, 2013).

[56] IRS regulations allow a qualified plan to provide that a benefit is forfeitable "on account of the inability to find the participant or beneficiary to whom payment is due, provided that the plan provides for reinstatement of the benefit if a claim is made by the participant or beneficiary for the forfeited benefit." 26 C.F.R. § 1.411(a)-4(b)(6). IRS officials told us the language "inability to find the participant or beneficiary" implies a requirement to make reasonable efforts to find the participant or beneficiary. Executives at one record keeper told us that when DC accounts are conditionally forfeited, there should still be a record of that asset amount, but that great diligence is required to maintain the record through mergers and acquisitions.

[57] See GAO-15-73.

unclaimed accounts that remained in their plans who were not receiving the retirement income they were due.

DOL Has Not Provided Guidance to Ongoing Plan Sponsors for Locating Missing Participants

Although DOL has provided guidance to plan sponsors of terminated DC plans about locating missing participants and unclaimed accounts, DOL has not provided similar guidance to ongoing plans.[58] DOL officials told us that they are conducting investigations of steps taken by ongoing plans to find missing participants under their authority to oversee compliance with ERISA's fiduciary requirement that plans be administered for the exclusive purpose of providing benefits.[59] Plan sponsors are required to send notices to participants in a variety of circumstances, such as to obtain direction before making a distribution.[60] However, the communication is not always successful, and may result in a mailing to an out-of-date address.

With the absence of guidance, it is not clear to sponsors of ongoing DC plans how they should satisfy requirements to notify participants when participant addresses are out of date. Undeliverable mail is the main indicator for identifying a participant as missing, according to third-party administrators (TPA), who help manage missing participant issues for plan sponsors. However, DOL officials told us a recent pilot investigation found that some ongoing plans send notices that were returned undeliverable but then fail to follow-up with any search process.[61] In contrast, if participants

---

[58] See Field Assistance Bulletin No. 2014-01.

[59] Among other requirements, a plan fiduciary is required to discharge his duties with respect to a plan solely in the interest of the participants and beneficiaries, for the exclusive purpose of providing benefits to participants and beneficiaries and defraying reasonable expenses of administering the plan, and with the care, skill, prudence and diligence under the circumstances then prevailing that a prudent man acting in like capacity and familiar with such matters in the conduct of an enterprise of a like character and with like aims. 29 U.S.C. § 1104(a)(1).

[60] *See*, e.g., 26 C.F.R. § 1.411(a)-11(c).

[61] Two third party administrators and one record keeper told us they would not send personal financial information to an address known to be incorrect.

in a terminated plan do not respond to a notice, plan sponsors need to take certain steps, at a minimum, to locate the participant or a beneficiary. According to our analysis of stakeholder interviews, in some circumstances plan sponsors may be considering a participant to have been "notified," even when the mail used to notify them was returned undeliverable. Executives at one firm that conducts missing participant searches told us that for an average client, 7 to 10 percent of mail will be returned undeliverable, which means communication was unsuccessful, potentially leaving participants without notification of changes to the plan or potential distributions or transfers.

It also is not clear how ongoing plan sponsors should arrange for paying to obtain updated addresses of participants with unclaimed accounts. Because search costs are not all paid from plan assets, finding missing participants can be an additional business expense for plan sponsors. Once an account is force-transferred out of the plan to an IRA, the account may be charged a $65 annual search fee by the IRA provider, as we reported one provider did in 2014.[62] Plan sponsors are permitted to pay only reasonable plan administration expenses, although they may charge expenses associated with a specific participant to that participant's account.[63] To reduce costs for its plan sponsor clients, representatives at one TPA told us that it will generally try to cash out accounts in ongoing plans under $1,000 immediately, before an address becomes obsolete.[64]

DOL audit findings also show that ongoing plans have challenges staying in touch with missing participants and paying them their benefits when due. DOL officials told us that in a recent DOL pilot investigation of 50 large DB plans, they found tens of thousands of separated participants who were entitled to benefits but were not receiving them. They told us that between 1 and 7 percent of all participants could be missing and not receiving letters from the plan, depending on the industry. They said their investigations found databases with missing names, addresses, and Social

---

[62] See GAO-15-73.

[63] See FAB 2003-03.

[64] Representatives of the third-party administrator noted they send notice of the impending cash-out 30 days ahead of time.

Security Numbers, and data they suspected were unreliable, such as participants named "Jane Doe" or with birth dates listed as "1/1/1900."

DOL enforces the fiduciary standards of ERISA, which require plan fiduciaries to act solely in the interest of plan participants and their beneficiaries, for the exclusive purpose of providing benefits to them, among other things. After plan termination, plan fiduciaries must distribute all plan assets as soon as administratively feasible, which could create an urgent need for plan sponsors to find participants. DOL officials said that part of their enforcement role is examining how plans are maintaining good records and what plans are doing to find and communicate with participants—officials are aware that additional guidance indicating what is expected of plan fiduciaries would be helpful.

PBGC has recently published a final rule which expands its Missing Participants Program to cover most terminated DC plans, and DOL intends to revisit its guidance within that context.[65] At that time, DOL will have an opportunity to also provide guidance to ongoing DC plan sponsors on their obligations under ERISA to prevent, search for, and pay costs associated with missing participants. By doing so, DOL can provide plan sponsors with better tools to manage unclaimed accounts and help ensure that future DOL investigations do not also uncover ongoing DC plans with substantial numbers of participants not receiving benefits to which they are entitled.

IRS Has Not Issued Guidance Clarifying Tax Withholding Requirements for Cashed-Out Unclaimed Retirement Accounts

Based in part on our discussions with IRS and our review of ERISA Advisory Council documentation, when a plan sponsor cashes out an

---

[65] Under section 4050 of ERISA, PBGC operates a Missing Participants Program, which establishes certain requirements for terminating DB plans with respect to locating missing participants and dealing with their benefits. The Pension Protection Act of 2006 amended ERISA to require PBGC to expand its Missing Participants Program to include most DC plans, among others. On December 22, 2017, PBGC finalized a rule expanding the program. PBGC will charge a one-time fee of $35 per missing participant or beneficiary when their assets are transferred to PBGC by a DC plan choosing to use the program, and will accept amounts under $250 for free. Fees were set in consideration of guidance from GAO and OMB. See Missing Participants, 82 Fed. Reg. 60,800 (Dec. 22, 2017).

unclaimed account and sends the money to the participant address it has on file, the address may be obsolete. As a result, the participant may not include the distribution in his or her taxable income for the year because the participant may not have received the payment from the plan sponsor or be aware of the transfer. According to an IRS publication on tax withholding for plan sponsors, a 20 percent income tax withholding generally is mandatory on amounts distributed from the plan that are not rolled over directly into another qualified plan or an IRA.[66] However, our findings that some participants may not actually receive these distributions raise questions about whether withholding should be required in situations when it is reasonable to believe distributions will not be received by the participants.

Misconceptions exist regarding how and when IRS will credit tax withholding toward a taxpayer's tax liability. For example, two TPAs told us they believed that IRS will credit tax withholding on cashed-out accounts to the tax liabilities of missing participants.[67] One industry representative we interviewed in 2013 told us that he withheld taxes when he could not find a participant because he believed the withholding would cause IRS to make the participant aware of the account. According to DOL bulletins issued in 2004 and 2014, some plan sponsors were using 100 percent withholding—in effect transferring the entire account to IRS—under the assumption that the withheld amounts would be matched and applied to a participant's tax liabilities.[68] DOL bulletins clarified it was not

---

[66] According to IRS Publication 15-A, Employer's Supplemental Tax Guide, account balances that are eligible to be rolled over tax free to an IRA or another eligible retirement plan are subject to a flat 20 percent withholding rate if they are distributed rather than rolled over directly into one of those vehicles. The publication further provides that distributions that are (a) required by law, (b) one of a specified series of equal payments, or (c) qualifying "hardship" distributions are not subject to the mandatory 20 percent federal income tax withholding.

[67] Tax withholding occurs when accounts of $1,000 or less are cashed out, with a check mailed to an address on file for the participant, and for terminated plans, with accounts transferred to a federally-insured bank account or state unclaimed property fund. As previously discussed, workplace retirement accounts may be cashed out without the consent of a participant only if certain conditions are met.

[68] In DOL Field Assistance Bulletin 2004-02, DOL prohibited the practice, citing its discussions with IRS staff and its understanding of IRS data processing at the time. DOL updated that guidance in 2014 with FAB 2014-01, noting again that some plan fiduciaries were using 100 percent withholding, and stating that it did not believe that 100 percent withholding

an appropriate distribution option for plan sponsors. Table 1 shows a variety of approaches to tax withholding. However, according to IRS, none of the tax withholding strategies automatically reduces the tax liability of the account holder. IRS officials told us that the agency does not routinely credit federal tax withholding to a taxpayer's current federal tax liability unless the taxpayer has made a claim.[69]

Table 1. A Variety of Approaches to Tax Withholding for Distributions from Workplace Retirement Plans

No tax withholding	Ensures that income withheld does not exceed the income received by plan participant.
20 percent withholding	Amount commonly withheld from cash-outs from plans.
100 percent tax withholding	Used in the past by plan sponsors in an attempt to reduce participants' tax liability.

Source: GAO analysis of Department of Labor and Internal Revenue Service documentation. | GAO-18-19.

Retirement accounts with small balances are most vulnerable to the tax consequences of tax withholding by plan sponsors. We previously reported that in the absence of participant instructions, accounts with a balance of $1,000 or less can be cashed out of the tax-deferred plan environment by plan fiduciaries without the separated participant's consent.[70] From 2004 to 2013, separated participants left more than 13 million accounts of $1,000 or less in workplace retirement plans with an aggregate value of $1.2 billion, according to SSA.[71]

---

would necessarily result in a crediting of the withheld amount against the missing participant's income tax liabilities (for example, the amount withheld may exceed a missing participant's income tax liabilities). As a result, DOL stated, missing participants might not receive the full benefit to which they are entitled. In both the 2004 and 2014 guidance documents, DOL concluded that 100 percent withholding is not in the best interest of participants and would violate ERISA's fiduciary requirements.

[69] According to the IRS, in the United States, taxes are paid through a system based on self-reporting. Tax withholding generally must be claimed by the taxpayer for it to be credited toward the taxpayer's tax liability.

[70] See GAO-15-73.

[71] This analysis was conducted by SSA of data submitted to plan sponsors on Form 8955- SSA.

Taxpayer Bill of Rights (TBOR)

Internal Revenue Code section 7803(a)(3) requires the IRS Commissioner to ensure that IRS employees are familiar with and act in accordance with the 10 fundamental rights that make up the TBOR. Among others, these rights include:

Right to Be Informed

Taxpayers have the right to know what they need to do to comply with the tax laws. They are entitled to clear explanations of the laws and IRS procedures in all tax forms, instructions, publications, notices, and correspondence. They have the right to be informed of IRS decisions about their tax accounts and to receive clear explanations of the outcomes.

Right to Quality Service

Taxpayers have the right to receive prompt, courteous, and professional assistance in their dealings with the IRS, to be spoken to in a way they can easily understand, to receive clear and easily understandable communications from the IRS, and to speak to a supervisor about inadequate service.

Right to Pay No More than the Correct Amount of Tax

Taxpayers have the right to pay only the amount of tax legally due, including interest and penalties, and to have the IRS apply all tax payments properly.

Right to a Fair and Just Tax System

Taxpayers have the right to expect the tax system to consider facts and circumstances that might affect their underlying liabilities, ability to pay, or ability to provide information timely. Taxpayers have the right to receive assistance from the Taxpayer Advocate Service if they are experiencing financial difficulty or if IRS has not resolved their tax issues properly and timely through its normal channels.

Source: Internal Revenue Service. | GAO-18-19.

Withholding taxes on balances of $1,000 or less at the time of distribution may result in participants paying taxes twice on the account. IRS told us that missing participants generally have up to 3 years to become aware of and claim the withheld amounts for them to be credited towards their tax liability. However, missing participants who claim their account after 3 years may again pay federal income tax on the account balance, although IRS officials said they thought such a scenario would be rare. (See Figure 1).

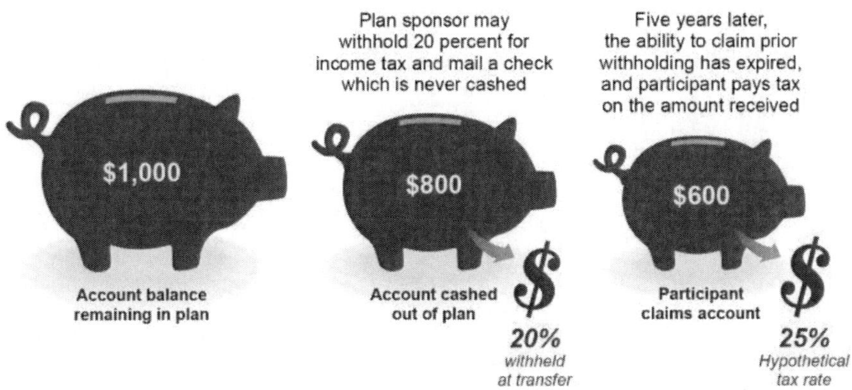

Source: GAO analysis of Internal Revenue Service (IRS) documentation. | GAO-18-19.

Note: This figure depicts a situation in which the plan sponsor cashes out a workplace retirement account without the consent of the participant, which can happen for accounts of $1,000 or less, absent participant instructions. Such cash-outs can result in an uncashed check sent to an old address. According to IRS, tax withholding on unclaimed accounts is not automatically credited to the account owner's tax liability by IRS. Instead, taxpayers generally must be aware of the withholding and claim it on their tax return for it to be credited. Taxpayers may not be aware of either the withholding or the income if the plan sponsor does not have their current address, according to IRS documentation and industry representatives with whom we spoke.

Figure 1. Illustrating Possible Double Taxation of a Small Unclaimed Workplace Retirement Account Involuntarily Cashed Out and Later Claimed.

IRS has not issued specific guidance clarifying the withholding requirements that apply to distributions from unclaimed accounts in situations in which the participant may be unlikely to receive the distribution. By reviewing the issue of distributions to participants with unclaimed accounts, including reviewing the IRC in this context, IRS may be able to issue guidance on applicable tax withholding and other tax requirements with respect to such accounts.[72] The Taxpayer Bill of Rights states that taxpayers are entitled to clear explanations of the tax laws in IRS publications and notices, and federal internal control standards require agencies to communicate effectively with external stakeholders to help achieve agency goals.[73] U.S. participants already facing the challenge of finding a small account transferred without their consent may discover, when the account is located, 20 percent of their account eliminated by taxes.[74] Without an IRS review of this issue and subsequent guidance, questions may remain about withholding from distributions in situations where the participant may be missing.

Plan Sponsors Can No Longer Use IRS' Letter Forwarding Program to Locate Missing Participants

Under IRS' letter forwarding program, between 1994 and 2012 plan sponsors could ask IRS to use IRS' most current address on file to forward

---

[72] In October 2017, Treasury released its 2017-18 Priority Guidance Plan, which indicated Treasury intends to provide "guidance on missing participants" in the future. IRS officials told us in November 2017 information about its content or form was not yet available.

[73] See GAO, *Standards for Internal Control in the Federal Government*, GAO-14-704G (Washington, D.C.: September 2014). IRS' Taxpayer Bill of Rights states that taxpayers have the right to know what they need to do to comply with tax laws. In addition, IRS' strategic plan states that IRS guidance should help taxpayers understand their tax responsibilities through targeted outreach, communications, and education. See IRS Strategic Plan, Fiscal Years 2014-2017, Objective 2: Develop clear and focused outreach, communications, and education programs to assist taxpayer understanding of tax responsibilities and awareness of emerging tax laws.

[74] In addition to the 20 percent tax withholding, depending on the circumstances an unclaimed retirement account may also be subject to a 10 percent additional early distribution tax if the distribution is made before certain events, such as the participant turning age 591/2. 26 U.S.C. § 72(t).

a letter with information about an account to a missing plan participant. However, in 2012 IRS modified the service and no longer forwards letters on behalf of qualified retirement plan sponsors attempting to locate plan participants.[75] According to the 2013 Report of the ERISA Advisory Council on Locating Missing and Lost Participants, the letter forwarding program was a popular alternative for plan sponsors when email and U.S. mail proved ineffective at contacting separated participants. Executives at one large record keeper told us the letter forwarding program provided very important assistance for locating missing participants, noting that few individuals are going to ignore correspondence from IRS. Although the letter forwarding program never notified the plan sponsor as to whether or not the letter reached the intended recipient, executives at one TPA characterized the program as effective. In addition, they said the fact that it was sponsored by IRS and sanctioned by DOL gave plan fiduciaries confidence that they were acting prudently.

Missing participant search services and their value vary widely today, based on industry representatives we interviewed. For example, representatives of one search firm told us they charged $1.25 for a search. However, an executive at a TPA firm told us another firm charged $35 for a Social Security Number-based search, which reliably connected with participants. PBGC estimates the cost of a commercial locator service to be $40 per search.[76]

---

[75] Revenue Procedure 2012-35 modified Revenue Procedure 94-22 to no longer provide services to locate taxpayers who may be owed assets, citing the Internet as a missing participant locator resource that had been unavailable in 1994. The letter forwarding program continues today, limited to humane purposes, such as notifying close relatives of an illness in the family and emergency situations.

[76] An executive at another TPA told us their contract offered unlimited searches for $25 per month, and said it can be helpful sometimes but not always. Searching by Social Security Number, while more expensive, is more effective than other methods, according to representatives from two TPAs with whom we spoke. One TPA told us that a Social Security Number-based search costs $20-$25. However, a plan sponsor may spend multiple times that amount and still not find a missing participant. For example, one TPA told us that in some cases it can cost as much as $150 to find a participant. An attorney in Canada told us that one of her plan sponsor clients paid $500 Canadian per person to search for four lost DB plan participants, and still only found three.

Industry stakeholders told us that the steps currently required by existing guidance do not provide a straightforward way to send a letter about an unclaimed account to a missing plan participant.[77] They described benefits that only IRS can provide through this service, such as the likelihood recipients will open a letter from IRS and the confidence fiduciaries have using an IRS-sponsored program. We discussed with IRS officials the commensurate fees charged in the private sector for missing participant searches and we discussed the variety of services and associated costs currently available.

According to OMB Circular A-123, agencies and individual federal managers must take systematic and proactive measures to develop and implement appropriate, cost-effective management controls for results-oriented management. IRS has always charged a user fee for the letter forwarding program, and the fee has not changed since 1994.[78] IRS officials told us resource constraints led them to revise the letter forwarding program. While IRS management controls will need to ensure that a program expansion is cost-effective, by reinstating the letter forwarding program for plan participants in a cost-effective manner, IRS can help support the retirement security of separated plan participants and plan sponsor efforts to meet their obligations under the IRC and ERISA.

---

[77] Representatives of two TPAs told us they turned to commercial locator services for a more reliable way to find participants after the free Internet searches required under DOL FAB 2014-01 were unproductive. DOL guidance for terminated plans is sometimes used by ongoing plans to make decisions in the absence of other guidance, according to an industry association with whom we spoke. DOL Field Assistance Bulletin 2004-02 included discussion of the letter forwarding programs. IRS also issued a memorandum to its employee plan examiners regarding required minimum distributions and missing participants on October 19, 2017. The memorandum directs examiners not to challenge a qualified plan for failure to commence or make a distribution to a participant or beneficiary to whom a payment is due, if the plan has taken certain steps. These steps include searching plan, sponsor, and publicly-available records; using a commercial locator service, a credit reporting agency, or a proprietary Internet search tool; and attempting contact participants via United States Postal Service certified mail to their last known mailing address and other appropriate means.

[78] The fee is only on bulk requests of 50 or more letters. Forwarding letters to fewer than 50 missing participants was free. Furthermore, according to one service provider, plan sponsors would cap the number of letters requested at 49 per year to avoid paying any fees, leaving IRS to cover the costs of the work.

Information Provided to U.S. Workers on Unclaimed Retirement Accounts Is Often Outdated and Incorrect

Certain information U.S. workers receive on unclaimed workplace retirement accounts based on data reported to IRS by plan sponsors is not reliable because plan sponsors are not updating the data over time as required. SSA maintains data on vested, unpaid retirement benefits left behind in workplace retirement plans by separated participants in its pension benefit record database.[79] The information, including the name of the plan, the value of the benefit, and the contact information of the plan administrator, is reported by plan administrators to IRS, and IRS provides it to SSA. When an individual retires and claims Social Security benefits, SSA sends the individual a Notice of Potential Private Pension Benefit Information.[80] The notice informs the recipient that they may have an unclaimed retirement account from a former employer and suggests that they may want to make an effort to determine whether or not the benefit actually does exist. SSA mails about 90,000 notices to new Social Security claimants each month. Separated participants can often find that no benefit exists, according to DOL and SSA documentation and stakeholders we interviewed. A TPA executive also told us separated participants are not always able to determine what happened to their accounts.[81]

---

[79] Administrators of workplace retirement plans covered by the vesting standards of section 203 of ERISA are required to report to IRS each year on Form 8955-SSA certain information on participants who separated from service, and are covered under the plan and entitled to vested deferred benefits that were not paid during the year. IRS is required to transmit this information to SSA. 26 U.S.C. § 6057(a), (d). Each month, SSA checks the name and Social Security Number of each new claimant for Social Security benefits to determine whether the claimant is listed in SSA's pension benefit record database, and mails one or more notices to each new claimant listed. SSA also sends these notices to individuals upon request and to claimants of a lump-sum death payment or hospital insurance coverage under Title XVIII of the Social Security Act. 42 U.S.C. § 1320b-1(a); 20 C.F.R. § 422.122.

[80] Participants can request this information earlier, but that fact is not publicized, and not many do so.

[81] ERISA contains certain requirements relating to the maintenance of records for reporting and disclosure purposes and for determining the pension benefits to which participants and beneficiaries are or may become entitled. For example, section 107 requires that records pertaining to required reports must be maintained for at least six years, and section 209 requires employers to maintain records sufficient to determine benefits that are or may become due to each employee. In addition, under the IRC and Treasury regulations, any person subject to income tax is required to keep certain relevant records and retain them so

IRS and SSA have a memorandum of understanding (MOU) in place establishing their agreements for collecting and managing these data. In the MOU, IRS and SSA agree to pursue improvements to the reporting process. The MOU states that, where appropriate and consistent with IRS directives, IRS will assess penalties under the IRC on plan sponsors who fail to file Form 8955-SSA according to instructions. The agencies have also agreed to contact and receive information from filers as necessary and appropriate to follow up regarding missing, incomplete, or incorrect information requested on the form.

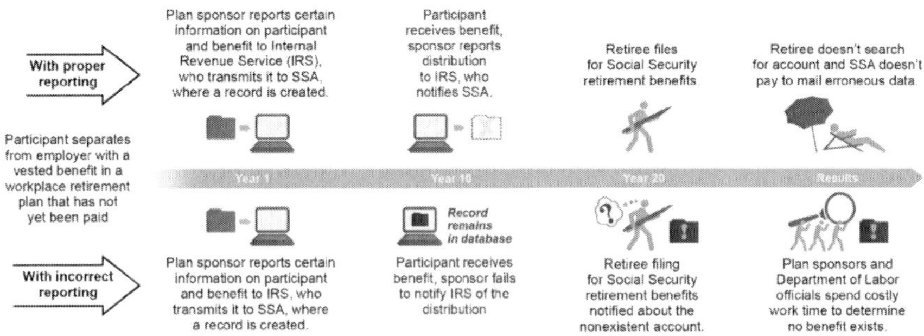

Source: GAO analysis of agency and retirement industry interviews and agency documents. | GAO-18-19.

Note: These reporting requirements apply only to plans covered by the vesting standards of the Employee Retirement Income Security Act of 1974 (ERISA), as amended. Years shown are hypothetical; these events could happen on a different timeline. Retirees may also experience a burden to research the letter received from SSA that incorrectly indicates that a retirement benefit may be due.

Figure 2. One Way Erroneous Information on Unclaimed Workplace Retirement Accounts Accumulates in the Social Security Administration (SSA) Pension Benefit Record.

According to the Form 8955-SSA instructions, plan sponsors are required to report when benefits previously reported are paid, and therefore no longer due, to plan participants. Such updates allow the pension benefit record database at SSA, used to generate the Notice of Potential Private Pension Benefit Information, to reflect the fact that those benefits are no

long as they may become material in the administration of any internal revenue law. 26 U.S.C. § 6001, 26 C.F.R. § 1.6001-1.

longer due. IRS officials said the data can be inaccurate because plan sponsors are not consistently reporting distributions, resulting in erroneous records of accounts accumulating in the database (see Figure 2).

An executive at one TPA told us that plan sponsors generally remember to put participant names on Form 8955-SSA, but often fail to take the names off after benefits are paid. According to the TPA executive, if there are 1,000 names on the list of separated participants with vested benefits in the plan, 999 will have been paid by the time they receive the notice from SSA. Nonetheless, participants will generally inquire about a benefit when they receive the SSA notice because it is from the government, and they trust the notice and think the money is there, according to one TPA with whom we spoke.

IRS officials told us that enforceable penalties can be imposed on plan sponsors for not including all required information on the form. The IRS website lists four possible actions related to incorrectly filing Form 8955-SSA that are subject to a penalty;[82] however, a failure to report distributions is not on the list. IRS officials said if the agency were to add the failure to report distributions to the list the penalty would likely encourage some sponsors to update the data as required.[83]

IRS officials told us they do not currently know which plans are not reporting distributions. The Notice of Potential Private Pension Benefit Information leaves the responsibility for determining whether a benefit exists up to the participant and the agencies do not ask the participant for the results of their inquiries. SSA includes a note at the bottom of the notice encouraging new retirees to contact DOL with complaints, but the participant is not asked to follow up with IRS or SSA to identify plans associated with inaccurate data. Having this information would help IRS select plans to audit in order to update and improve the quality of data in

[82] The four listed actions include: (1) failure to file an annual registration statement, (2) failure to file notification of a change in the status of the plan, (3) failure to furnish a statement to a plan participant or furnishing a fraudulent statement, and (4) late filing.

[83] IRS officials told us that Form 8955-SSA currently requires that a plan administrator provide updated information for participants who have previously been reported on the Form 8955-SSA, even though 26 C.F.R. § 301.6057-1(c) suggests that providing updated information is voluntary. IRS told us that this issue will be evaluated as part of its guidance project on IRC section 6057 reporting requirements listed on its 2017-2018 Priority Guidance Plan.

SSA's pension benefit record database. SSA could modify the notice participants receive to encourage them to inform IRS if they determine the information on the notice to be erroneous. DOL benefits advisers, who field calls from inquiring individuals after they receive a notice about a potential benefit that no longer exists, also have information on plans that may not be reporting distributions to separated participants on Form 8955-SSA as required.[84] DOL officials told us they would need a formal MOU in place to facilitate such information sharing. Figure 3 illustrates these possible options for identifying plans not reporting distributions as required.

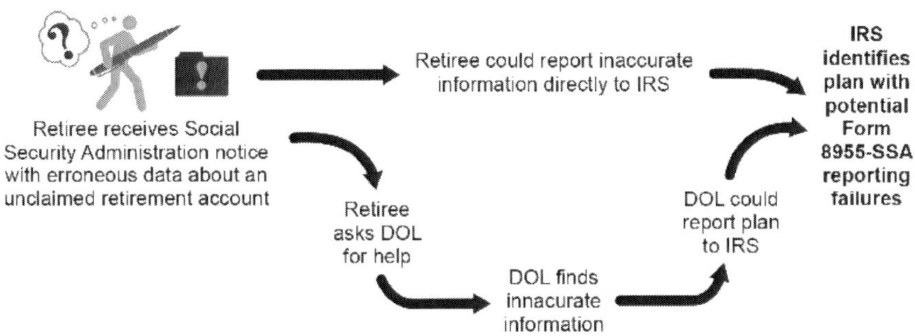

Source: GAO analysis of Department of Labor (DOL) and Internal Revenue Service (IRS) documentation. | GAO-18-19.

Figure 3. Two Options that Could Identify Workplace Retirement Plan Sponsors with Form 8955-SSA Reporting Failures.

Standards for internal control in the federal government state that agencies should communicate quality information externally so that external parties can help agencies achieve their objectives.[85] Although IRS and SSA have agreed in the MOU to work together to promote efforts to improve internal controls, they are not collaborating to improve the

[84] DOL already has this information in summaries of some participant phone calls in some cases. We previously reported that one of the reasons these data are poorly managed is that responsibility for the data and their reporting is spread across three agencies. In addition to these steps required of IRS and SSA, DOL assists those who need help with the notice. We previously recommended Congress consider providing DOL authority to centralize these data. See GAO-14-92.

[85] See GAO, *Standards for Internal Control in the Federal Government*, GAO-14-704G (Washington, D.C.: September 2014).

likelihood that the Notice of Potential Private Pension Benefit Information will correspond to an actual benefit in the future. While IRS has authority over implementing and enforcing the Form 8955-SSA reporting requirements, IRS officials do not have access to SSA's pension benefit record database to update records.[86] IRS officials told us at one point they discussed with SSA a possible project that would allow plan sponsors to update all the records associated with their plan at once. SSA officials told us they could collaborate with IRS to update the data in the pension benefit record database. By working together, IRS and SSA can increase the likelihood that the Notice of Potential Private Pension Benefit Information corresponds to actual workplace retirement benefits in the future.

Complex Tax Requirements and a Lack of Guidance Can Hinder U.S. Individuals' Ability to Correctly Report Foreign Retirement Accounts

Stakeholders Told GAO that U.S. Individuals Who Participate in Foreign Workplace Retirement Plans Face Multiple Challenges

U.S. individuals who participate in foreign retirement plans can face a number of challenges with tax reporting requirements on their retirement savings. According to IRS officials and tax preparers with whom we spoke, these challenges are greater for U.S. individuals who live and work abroad full time than for corporate executives on temporary assignment in a foreign country. Individuals sent abroad for limited times by their employer often remain as participants in their employer's U.S. workplace retirement plan and do not need to participate in a foreign workplace plan.

---

[86] IRS officials said that changes they made to the form in 2009 have likely also improved reporting of distributions by plan sponsors. However, we reviewed the 2008 and the 2016 form instructions and found they both instructed plan sponsors to report a participant that has previously been reported under the plan but is no longer entitled to those deferred vested benefits.

According to IRS officials and tax professionals with whom we spoke, many of these executives may have tax filing assistance made available to them by their company, further reducing their reporting burden. Individuals who work in a foreign country may be forced to participate in a mandatory foreign retirement plan, depending on the country and the rules governing residency, according to officials with whom we spoke in our case study locations. In these instances, according to IRS officials, the individuals have no choice but to comply with U.S. tax reporting rules on their foreign retirement accounts. Those who live abroad long-term due to family or personal ties naturally accumulate foreign assets and savings, such as foreign retirement accounts.

Tax preparers in all five case study locations we reviewed, as well as IRS officials, indicated that preparing a U.S. tax return for a participant in a foreign retirement plan is more complex than preparing a comparable U.S. tax return that does not include foreign assets. We were told that attempting to categorize a foreign retirement account for tax reporting under the IRC can be challenging because such accounts may be reported as one of several different designations that may or may not be eligible for tax-deferral in the United States.[87] This contrasts with U.S. individuals participating in U.S. retirement plans that meet the criteria for tax-qualified status under the IRC, who generally receive a Form W-2 Wage and Tax Statement that automatically deducts retirement account contributions from gross wages.[88] In addition, participating in a foreign retirement plan can

[87] The tax treatment of a foreign retirement plan depends on various factors, including the characteristics of the plan and the provisions of any relevant tax treaties. For example, according to tax experts with whom we spoke, many foreign workplace retirement plans qualify as an employees' trust, and the taxation of contributions and earnings from these plans are governed by section 402(b) of the IRC. Whether and when contributions and generated income from a section 402(b) trust are taxable as income to the participant depends on various factors, including whether the contributions are "substantially vested" and whether the participant is a highly compensated employee. See 26 U.S.C. §§ 402(b), 83(a). As another example, according to one commercial tax publication for U.S. expatriates, a Canadian Registered Retirement Savings Plan is considered to be a simple grantor trust, and unless an election is made under the U.S./Canada Income Tax Treaty, the earnings of the plan are subject to tax. See: http://www.nysscpa.org/news/publications/the-tax-stringer/stringer-article-for-authors/taximplications-of-foreign-pension-plan-participation#sthash.fRJ9Ikjf.dpuf [accessed on 4/14/17.]

[88] A U.S. individual participating in a workplace retirement plan that meets the criteria for tax-qualified status under the IRC may generally defer paying income taxes on contributions

initiate a complex set of U.S. reporting requirements on retirement assets, such as participants having to report contributions and earnings or having to file additional forms and schedules for their retirement account, which is typically not required of taxpayers with U.S.- based retirement plans. IRS officials told us that the onus is on U.S. individuals who participate in foreign retirement plans to comply with these complex reporting requirements. As a result, these participants often need to turn to expert tax preparers to prepare their U.S. tax return even if they ultimately do not have to pay taxes.

Statutory changes on reporting foreign assets have further affected U.S. individuals who participate in foreign retirement plans. Stakeholders told us that reporting requirements under the Foreign Account Tax Compliance Act (FATCA) can increase the cost of tax preparation for U.S. individuals who participate in foreign retirement plans.[89] For example, according to IRS guidance, these participants in foreign retirement plans must gather and examine monthly retirement account statements, convert the account balance to U.S. dollars, and determine if the total value of the account at the end of the year or anytime during the year caused the individual's total asset value to exceed the reporting threshold. If the total assets meet the reporting threshold, the participant must report the value of their retirement account even if they are no longer contributing to the account. In contrast, participants in U.S. plans generally are not required to report the value of their U.S. workplace retirement accounts under FATCA or IRC section 6038D, according to IRS. We were also told of other

until he or she receives the benefits. For example, if an employee chooses to contribute to a 401(k) account, those contributions, earnings within the account, and any employer contributions on the individual's behalf are not included in the calculation of wages, tips, and other compensation on the Form W-2 Wage and Tax Statement provided by the employer to their employee. For example, an individual filing a 1040-EZ simply puts the wage amount from the Form W-2 onto his or her tax return, thus automatically receiving tax-deferral on retirement contributions.

[89] According to IRS, FATCA is commonly used to refer to sections 501 and 511 of the Hiring Incentives to Restore Employment Act (codified at 26 U.S.C. §§ 1471-1474 and 26 U.S.C. § 6038D, respectively). Our discussions with stakeholders used the term "FATCA;" however, stakeholders did not specify which provisions were being referred to. In this case, these reporting requirements fall under IRC section 6038D, according to IRS officials. IRC section 6038D requires individual U.S. taxpayers to report foreign financial assets that exceed a certain threshold amount.

consequences of FATCA for U.S. individuals abroad, such as a reduction in available financial services, as some banks refuse to do business with U.S. individuals because of FATCA's reporting requirements.

Lastly, once an individual decides to change jobs in a foreign country, transferring foreign retirement savings can be difficult. For example, in several of the case study locations we reviewed foreign officials and tax preparers told us that plans automatically transfer a retirement account to a different account within the plan or to a location outside the plan when an employee separates from their employer, which can have U.S. tax implications. Stakeholders said that existing U.S. tax law does not provide these participants with tax-deferral if they transfer their foreign retirement savings from one foreign workplace retirement plan to another—a benefit granted to U.S. participants in qualified U.S. retirement plans who make such transfers.[90] This condition may act as a disincentive for U.S. individuals abroad to consolidate foreign retirement accounts and can cause challenges when individuals change jobs or are required by their retirement plan or employer to transfer their account.

IRS Guidance Is Unclear Regarding How to Report Foreign Retirement Accounts

While IRS has issued guidance providing information regarding foreign assets and pensions, IRS officials told us that the guidance is not specific on how foreign workplace retirement plans should be treated under the IRC, nor does it provide guidance for specific countries.[91] One source

---

[90] IRS officials told us that transfers from one account to another may be taxable; specifically whether such transfers are taxable depends on whether the amounts are considered constructively received, which depends on the facts and circumstances on whether the individual had control over the amounts in the account and whether receipt of the amount is subject to a substantial limitation or restriction. For example, officials said that if a foreign jurisdiction would impose a penalty tax for withdrawing before a certain age, then that could be a substantial limitation or restriction preventing constructive receipt.

[91] IRS officials told us that tax issues involving foreign retirement plans are more complicated than with U.S. plans. Even without treaties, according to IRS officials, the tax treatment of foreign retirement plans (even those within the same country) is not uniform, and treaty provisions are not uniform.

of guidance is Publication 54, Tax Guide for U.S. Citizens and Resident Aliens Abroad, which discusses special tax rules for U.S. citizens and resident aliens who work abroad or who have income earned in foreign countries. Another source of guidance in the International Tax Gap Series describes how foreign pensions and annuity distributions are taxed. While both guidance sources provide taxpayers with some information on how to report foreign assets, neither describes in detail how taxpayers are to determine if their foreign workplace retirement plan is eligible for tax deferred status, or how to account for contributions, earnings, or distributions on their annual U.S. tax return, particularly whether and when contributions and earnings should be taxed as income.

IRS also directs taxpayers to review tax treaties, if applicable, for provisions related to pensions, but IRS officials told us these treaties can vary from country to country and said that they can be difficult for non-experts to understand.

For example, Treasury officials told GAO that the tax treaties for two of the five[92] case study locations we selected have pension clauses and certain provisions that apply to U.S. residents of those countries saving for retirement that afford some tax protection. However, Treasury officials said that two of our other case study locations have treaties that do not provide tax protections for U.S. individuals on their foreign retirement accounts (one of our case study locations does not have an income tax treaty with the United States.)[93] Tax preparers and IRS officials we spoke with indicated that it is difficult for U.S. individuals to know how to correctly apply tax treaty provisions to their foreign workplace retirement

---

[92] See income tax treaties between the United States and Canada, and the United States and the United Kingdom, respectively.

[93] See the 1996 Convention between the United States of America and the Swiss Confederation for the Avoidance of Double Taxation with Respect to Taxes on Income and the 1982 Double Taxation Taxes on Income Convention between the United States and Australia. IRS' Publication 54 describes the "saving clause" that is typically included in most tax treaties. The "saving clause" provides that the treaties do not affect how the United States taxes its own citizens and residents. As a result, U.S. individuals generally cannot use the treaty to reduce their U.S. tax liability. However, the guidance notes that most treaties provide exceptions to the saving clause that allow certain provisions of the treaty to be claimed by U.S. individuals, and that it is important that taxpayers examine the applicable saving clause to determine if an exception applies.

savings. In addition, these IRS officials and other retirement experts said a U.S. individual abroad without expertise in the IRC and tax treaties would have difficulty reporting their foreign retirement account correctly.

Example from the Income Tax Treaty between the United States and Switzerland

This is an example of the type of language that U.S. individuals may need to read and understand in order to correctly file their income tax return if they hold a foreign pension. According to Department of the Treasury (Treasury) officials, Article 18 of the U.S.-Switzerland tax treaty (excerpt below) does not provide U.S. individuals with tax relief on their pensions if they are living in Switzerland, despite the language stating pensions shall be "taxable only in that State" in which the individual lives. Treasury officials said that since this language is not part of a specific exception to the "saving clause" (Paragraph 3, Article 1 of the treaty), the United States may still tax U.S. individuals on Swiss retirement account contributions and earnings, even if they have already paid tax in Switzerland on these savings.

"Pensions and Annuities

1. Subject to the provisions of Article 19 (Government Service and Social Security), pensions and other similar remuneration beneficially derived by a resident of a Contracting State in consideration of past employment shall be taxable only in that State.
2. Subject to the provisions of Article 19 (Government Service and Social Security), annuities derived and beneficially owned by a resident of a Contracting State shall be taxable only in that State. The term "annuities" as used in this paragraph means a stated sum paid periodically at stated times during a specified number of years or for life, under an obligation to make the payments in return for adequate and full consideration (other than services rendered)."

Source: Treasury officials and the 1996 Convention between the United States of America and the Swiss Confederation for the Avoidance of Double Taxation with Respect to Taxes on Income. | GAO-18-19.

Existing IRS guidance does not alleviate the confusion faced by U.S. individuals who participate in foreign retirement plans. Confusion regarding how to report foreign retirement accounts to IRS on a U.S. tax return or elsewhere is inconsistent with U.S. taxpayers' rights, as described in the Taxpayer Bill of Rights, to pay no more than the correct amount of tax and to know what they need to do to comply with tax laws. Disagreement exists among the professional tax preparers with whom we spoke about the correct method for reporting foreign retirement accounts on a U.S. tax return. IRS officials told us that U.S. tax law generally does not recognize foreign retirement plans as tax-qualified and IRS does not recognize any retirement accounts outside the United States as having tax-qualified status. IRS officials we spoke to said that only plans meeting the specific requirements of 401(k) or other requirements describing retirement plan qualification may achieve tax-qualified status in the United States. As a result, according to IRS guidance, U.S. individuals participating in foreign workplace retirement plans generally cannot deduct contributions to their account from their income on their U.S. tax return. This is true even if the retirement account is considered a tax-deferred retirement account in the country where the individual works, and even if the account is similar in nature to those found in a U.S.-type retirement plan, such as a 401(k) plan. IRS officials told us that it should generally be unnecessary to file a foreign retirement account as a Passive Foreign Investment Company (PFIC) if the foreign retirement plan is covered by a tax treaty with the United States, but acknowledged that some tax advisors in foreign countries advise their U.S. clients to consider their interest in such plans as an investment in a PFIC. For example, in one of the case study locations we reviewed, a tax preparer said that he advises U.S. individuals who participate in such plans to report their foreign retirement account as a PFIC in their U.S. tax filing, and that contributions and earnings are subject to be taxed at the higher tax rate generally applicable to PFICs.[94]

[94] An online guide from a tax preparation firm that serves U.S. expatriates characterizes PFICs as pooled investments registered outside the United States that may include mutual funds, hedge funds, money market funds, insurance products, and non-U.S. retirement plans. According to this guide, PFICs are potentially subject to the top individual tax rate. See https://www.taxesforexpats.com/guides/passive-foreigninvestment-company-8621.html.

Other tax preparers we spoke to in that location said that this is a matter of some discussion among tax preparers and that they reported retirement plans as an employees' trust. The National Taxpayer Advocate told us that receiving incorrect tax advice from a foreign tax preparer may not be a sufficient mitigating circumstance to avoid penalties for reporting a foreign retirement account incorrectly on a tax return. While reasonable reliance on a tax professional with respect to the details of a return is generally a mitigating circumstance for errors on a return, according to the National Taxpayer Advocate, tax preparers in other countries are usually not considered qualified preparers by IRS.[95] U.S. taxpayers who file an incorrect tax return can lose money by accruing penalties.

IRS officials told us that individual taxpayers are responsible for understanding their filing requirements and for determining how to correctly file their tax returns, regardless of whether they live in a foreign country or the United States. In its mission to help taxpayers meet their tax responsibilities, IRS could issue guidance concerning how U.S. individuals are to correctly report their foreign retirement assets. The Taxpayer Bill of Rights states that as part of the right to a fair and just tax system, taxpayers have a right to expect that system to consider circumstances that affect their ability to provide timely information. IRS officials told us they had been considering issuing improved guidance in some areas pertaining to the taxation of foreign retirement accounts. However, without clearer specific guidance from IRS describing how to correctly report foreign retirement assets on a U.S. tax return, U.S. individuals who participate in foreign workplace retirement plans continue to run the risk of filing incorrect returns due to confusion over how to properly classify and report their accounts. Clarifying how U.S. individuals who participate in foreign workplace retirement plans should report their retirement assets on their

[95] Any person with an IRS preparer tax identification number (PTIN) is authorized to prepare federal tax returns. However, tax preparers have differing levels of skills, education, and expertise. For example, Enrolled Agents take a comprehensive exam and are required to complete ongoing education requirements to maintain their credential. Not all PTIN holders have additional credentials and may not have the authority to represent their clients before the IRS.

annual U.S. tax return will help ensure these taxpayers can meet their tax reporting obligations.

Complying with Reporting Requirements Can Be Costly for U.S. Individuals Who Participate in Foreign Workplace Retirement Plans

Federal law requires U.S. individuals to report specified foreign financial assets, including any applicable retirement and pension accounts they own, if these assets, in the aggregate, are above the regulatory threshold.[96] Similarly, the Report of Foreign Bank and Financial Accounts (FBAR) requires information with respect to foreign accounts above a certain amount.[97] As a result, U.S. individuals who participate in foreign retirement plans may need to hire tax preparers to prepare returns in compliance with these U.S. laws, and, according to tax preparers with whom we spoke, the cost for having a complete tax return professionally prepared for an individual holding a foreign retirement account ranges from $1,800 to as high as $16,000.

Determining how a foreign retirement account should be reported is time consuming even for experts. Tax preparers must prepare multiple items, including the tax return itself, and additional schedules and forms pertaining to the retirement account, according to the preparers with whom

[96] According to IRS, FATCA is commonly used to refer to sections 501 and 511 of the Hiring Incentives to Restore Employment Act (codified at 26 U.S.C. §§ 1471-1474 and 26 U.S.C. § 6038D, respectively). Section 511 establishes reporting requirements for individuals, while section 501 (generally referred to in this report as FATCA) establishes reporting requirements for foreign financial institutions and certain other foreign entities. However, in describing our discussions with stakeholders, we use the term "FATCA" if stakeholders used this term but did not specify which provisions were being referred to.

[97] Pursuant to the Bank Secrecy Act and Treasury regulations, U.S. individuals who have financial interests in or signature authority over foreign financial accounts must file an FBAR if the maximum aggregate value of those accounts exceeds $10,000 at any time during the calendar year. This would generally include any foreign workplace retirement accounts, but foreign financial accounts held by or on behalf of tax-qualified retirement plans are exempted. 31 U.S.C. § 5314, 31 C.F.R. §§ 1010.306(c), 1010.350(g)(4). The FBAR is not filed with an individual's tax return, but is filed separately and directly with the Treasury. Failure to file an FBAR when required to do so may result in civil penalties, criminal penalties, or both. 31 U.S.C. §§ 5321-5322.

we spoke. For example, Form 3520 may be required if the account is being reported as a foreign trust. In addition to preparing tax forms, one tax preparer we spoke to said that preparers may have to spend time trying to obtain other documents necessary to prepare a U.S. tax return, for example, detailed retirement account statements.

Foreign Account Tax Compliance Provisions and Internal Revenue Code (IRC) section 6038D Reporting

Foreign account tax compliance provisions, including Internal Revenue Code (IRC) section 6038D, were enacted as part of the Hiring Incentives to Restore Employment Act to reduce tax evasion by creating greater transparency of offshore accounts and entities held by U.S. individuals and by providing IRS with tools to further enforce tax laws, according to IRS. Foreign account tax compliance provisions under IRC sections 1471-1474 generally require foreign financial institutions to report to IRS on foreign financial accounts held by U.S. taxpayers and IRC section 6038D requires individual U.S. taxpayers to report foreign financial assets that exceed a certain threshold amount. Taxpayers who fail to comply with reporting requirements under IRC section 6038D may be subject to penalties, including a $10,000 failure to file penalty, an additional penalty of up to $50,000 for continued failure to file after IRS notification, and a 40 percent penalty on an understatement of tax attributable to non-disclosed assets.

Source: Internal Revenue Service. | GAO-18-19.

Since the implementation of IRC section 6038D, individuals have increased exposure to penalties, and failure to report a foreign retirement account when required may bring significant financial penalties, even if no taxes were due on the retirement account in question.[98] For example, according to the IRS website, failure to report foreign financial assets on Form 8938 as required may result in a penalty of $10,000 and an additional penalty of up to $50,000 for continued failure to report after IRS sends the

---

98 Although discussions with stakeholders generally used the term "FATCA;" stakeholders did not specify which provisions they were referring to. In this case, the reporting requirements for U.S. individuals fall under IRC section 6038D, according to IRS.

individual a notification of failure to report.[99] As a result of this reporting requirement, U.S. individuals who participate in workplace retirement plans abroad may incur substantial costs to correctly file their returns and risk diminishing their retirement security if they fail to correctly report their foreign retirement assets.

Even in cases where the individual owes no U.S. tax, tax preparation can costs thousands of dollars. Three tax preparers and representatives of one investment firm that provides pension advice with whom we spoke noted that even if a U.S. individual who participates in a foreign workplace retirement plan did not ultimately owe any taxes, they are required to report their foreign retirement assets under both FATCA[100] and FBAR. Tax preparers in four of our case study locations[101] as well as in the United States mentioned FATCA's requirements as an added challenge when reporting foreign retirement accounts on U.S. tax returns.[102] Additionally, one investment industry association representative we interviewed said that FATCA casts a wide net and that many "accidental Americans"[103] and U.S. individuals abroad were challenged to comply with its requirements.[104] Some of the tax preparers we spoke with said many individuals taking steps to come into tax compliance as a result of FATCA may happen to

---

[99] 26 U.S.C. § 6038D. However, if the failure to report the information is shown to be due to reasonable cause and not due to willful neglect, no penalty will be imposed. See 26 C.F.R. § 1.6038D-8(e). In addition, individuals may also be subject to a 40 percent penalty on any understatement of tax attributable to non-disclosed assets. 26 U.S.C. § 6662(j)(3). See https://www.irs.gov/businesses/corporations/summary-of-key-fatca-provisions.

[100] Stakeholders generally used the term "FATCA" to describe the reporting requirements for U.S. individuals of their foreign financial accounts and assets. In this case, these requirements fall under IRC section 6038D, according to IRS officials.

[101] The case study locations were Australia, Canada, Hong Kong, Switzerland, and the United Kingdom.

[102] Although our discussions with stakeholders generally used the term "FATCA," these reporting requirements fall under IRC section 6038D, according to IRS.

[103] "Accidental American" is used colloquially to describe citizens of other countries who acquired U.S. citizenship through their parents' ties to the United States rather than their own choices, for example, through a U.S. citizen parent who emigrated abroad, or because they were born in the United States but left as young children. Such individuals may have never lived or worked in the United States as adults, and according to tax preparers with whom we spoke, many such individuals are surprised to learn of their U.S. tax obligations.

[104] Although our discussions with stakeholders generally used the term "FATCA," these reporting requirements fall under IRC section 6038D, according to IRS.

have U.S. citizenship but may never have lived or worked in the United States as adults.[105]

The National Taxpayer Advocate told us that the high cost of tax preparation amounted to an "advanced penalty" for U.S. individuals who live abroad. In a written testimony to Congress in 2015, she stated that FATCA has created unique challenges for U.S. taxpayers abroad[106] and presented evidence in Volume 1 of the Taxpayer Advocate Service Fiscal Year 2016 Objectives Report to Congress that there was little evidence that foreign filers are any more likely to be non-compliant than taxpayers in the general taxpayer population.[107] The National Taxpayer Advocate specifically identified concerns with FATCA as an area of focus in the Fiscal Year 2016 Objectives Report to Congress, and stated that taxpayers' rights to a fair and just tax system, and to pay no more than the correct amount of tax, are being adversely affected by FATCA.[108]

---

[105] Although our discussions with stakeholders generally used the term "FATCA," these reporting requirements fall under IRC section 6038D, according to IRS.

[106] See the written statement of Nina E. Olson, National Taxpayer Advocate, the hearing on the Internal Revenue Service Fiscal Year 2016 Budget Request before the Subcommittee on Financial Services and General Government, Committee on Appropriations, United States Senate. Available at https://www.irs.gov/pub/tas/NTA_Testimony_030315.pdf. See also the National Taxpayer Advocate Fiscal Year 2016 Objectives Report To Congress, Volume 1, available for download at https://taxpayeradvocate.irs.gov/reports/fy-2016-objectives-report-tocongress/full-report. IRS officials noted that the National Taxpayer Advocate was likely referring to reporting requirements for U.S. individuals under IRC section 6038D.

[107] The National Taxpayer Advocate analyzed data from the IRS Compliance Data Warehouse, Individual Return Transaction File Entity, and Individual Master File Status History Tables, and found that 19 of every 1,000 Form 8938 filers did not file their return timely, as compared to 16 of every 1,000 in the general population. They also found that 24 of every 1,000 Form 8938 filers did not pay taxes timely, as compared to 59 of 1,000 general population taxpayers. See also the National Taxpayer Advocate Fiscal Year 2016 Objectives Report to Congress, Volume 1, available for download at https://taxpayeradvocate.irs.gov/reports/fy-2016-objectives-report-to-congress/full-report.

[108] The Taxpayer Bill of Rights adopted by the IRS includes 10 fundamental rights afforded by the Internal Revenue Code (IRC). IRC section 7803(a)(3) requires the IRS Commissioner to ensure that IRS employees are familiar with and act in accordance with these 10 taxpayer rights. The National Taxpayer Advocate has expressed concern that, "without statistically valid evidence or analytical justification, the IRS has adopted a coercive approach to international taxpayers, reflecting an assumption that all such taxpayers are suspect of fraudulent activity." See National Taxpayer Advocate, "Objectives Report to Congress – Fiscal Year 2017, Volume 1" https://taxpayeradvocate.irs.gov/reports/fy-2017-objectives-report-to-congress/full-report. IRS officials noted that the National Taxpayer Advocate was likely referring to reporting requirements for U.S. individuals under IRC section 6038D.

IRS officials we spoke with indicated they are aware of the difficulties some taxpayers are experiencing with these reporting requirements, but said the agency is required to implement the law. They also said that retirement accounts are usually the primary asset for individuals abroad and that from an individual enforcement perspective, these reporting requirements help to ensure a "line of sight" year over year on participants' foreign pension arrangements. IRS officials expressed concern that unless U.S. individuals are required to report foreign retirement accounts via Form 8938, they will seek to avoid proper reporting on their tax returns when distributions are made.

IRS officials told us they have had extensive conversations about providing a possible exemption from reporting requirements under IRC section 6038D for certain U.S. individuals in foreign countries.[109] IRS decided the ability to review a taxpayer's foreign retirement data each year through filing a Form 8938 would allow regulators to evaluate whether contributions, earnings, and distributions were being identified and reported accurately. IRS officials stated that the agency's goal is to build a database with Form 8938 information on individual taxpayers with foreign assets.

IRS officials told us that, unlike individuals, foreign financial institutions in many countries are exempt from reporting retirement accounts under FATCA.[110] IRS officials said this is because such foreign retirement accounts are typically at low risk for tax evasion and Treasury officials told us that the exemption for foreign financial institutions was provided to reduce burden on such institutions. This sentiment was echoed by foreign government officials and retirement experts abroad, who said a retirement account is generally at low-risk for tax evasion both because

---

[109] According to IRS, FATCA is commonly used to refer to sections 501 and 511 of the Hiring Incentives to Restore Employment Act (codified at 26 U.S.C. §§ 1471-1474 and 26 U.S.C. § 6038D, respectively). Section 511 establishes reporting requirements for individuals, while section 501 (generally referred to in this report as FATCA) establishes reporting requirements for foreign financial institutions and certain other foreign entities. However, in describing our discussions with stakeholders, we use the term "FATCA" if stakeholders used this term but did not specify which provisions were being referred to.

[110] For example, Intergovernmental Agreements (IGAs), negotiated by Treasury, which have been concluded with 113 countries to date, may establish such exemptions.

governments regulate retirement accounts and individuals attempting to evade taxes through a retirement account would have to wait many years before seeing any benefit. With respect to IRC section 6038D, according to IRS officials and Form 8938 instructions, if a fair market value is not readily available for a foreign workplace DB plan, it does not have to be included in the taxpayer's calculation of the aggregate foreign assets used to determine whether the taxpayer meets the threshold to file Form 8938.[111] If other foreign financial assets, in the aggregate, exceed the threshold, IRS officials said an individual must list their DB plan on Form 8938, but may list a zero balance if no distributions have been made. Given that IRS does not always require reporting of foreign retirement plans on Form 8938 if the plans cannot be readily valued, providing a broader exemption for other types of workplace plans or for other appropriate circumstances from the calculation of the foreign asset threshold could help ease the reporting burden on U.S. individuals. This would assist those individuals who hold most of their wealth in the form of foreign retirement savings in other types of workplace retirement plans, to avoid potentially high penalties that could diminish their retirement savings.

IRS has not systematically analyzed data from Form 8938 on foreign retirement accounts owned by U.S. individuals. As a result, they may not have evidence showing the effect of these reporting requirements on U.S. individuals who participate in foreign workplace retirement plans, for instance, how many enforcement actions related to retirement accounts resulted from filing Form 8938. Without IRS systematically analyzing Form 8938 data on foreign retirement accounts owned by U.S. individuals, the agency will continue to lack an understanding of how these accounts change over time and if they are definitively low-risk for tax evasion. Understanding the effects of these reporting requirements can provide IRS with information to consider whether IRS could offer individuals some

---

[111] According to IRS officials, this was done because it is difficult to determine the value of unvested benefits in a DB plan. When determining the value of an individual's interest in a foreign estate, foreign pension plan, or foreign deferred compensation plan, the IRS instructions for Form 8938 state that if the individual received no distributions during the tax year and does not know or have reason to know based on readily accessible information the fair market value of his or her interest, to use a value of zero. See also 26 C.F.R. § 1.6038D-5.

form of exemption from reporting on their foreign retirement accounts. Currently, there is no way for IRS to clearly distinguish different types of accounts being reported on Form 8938. To do so would require the Form 8938 to be revised in order to allow taxpayers to clearly specify that the account being reported is a foreign retirement account or pension.[112] In addition, U.S. individuals participating in foreign workplace retirement plans, many of whom count their retirement savings as their primary financial asset, according to IRS officials, will continue to be caught up in IRS' enforcement efforts aimed at catching tax evaders. These U.S. individuals may continue to face potentially high tax preparation fees to complete the filing of Form 8938 and may be liable for penalties for failure to report foreign retirement accounts that may pose little or no risk for tax evasion.

Absent Specific Treaty Provisions, Current U.S. Tax Law Does Not Exempt from Taxation Transfers in Foreign Workplace Retirement Plans

IRS officials told us that U.S. individuals who participate in foreign workplace retirement plans may not realize that a routine transfer of their foreign retirement assets within plans[113] or from one plan to another should

[112] The instructions for Form 8938 currently direct taxpayers to report their interest in a foreign pension plan or foreign deferred compensation plan in Part VI of the form. The instructions further direct taxpayers to enter a description of the specified foreign financial asset being reported in this section for assets that are not maintained in a financial account.

[113] For example, according to officials, when a participant (i.e., scheme member) terminates employment with their employer in Hong Kong, the balance of their retirement account, referred to as a "contribution account," will be automatically transferred after 3 months following the receipt of the notice of the employment cessation from the member's former employer to a "personal account" within the same scheme (i.e., plan). Personal accounts preserve the benefits in respect of previous employments but do not accept employee or employer contributions, according to officials. Further, officials said that the employee can elect to transfer the accrued benefits to his personal account under another scheme of his own choice, or to transfer the accrued benefits to the contribution account of his new employment. However, they said if no action is taken by the employee the benefits accumulated during previous employment will be moved from a contribution account to a personal account under the scheme of the former employer. See appendix III for additional information on Hong Kong's retirement system. In this report, we refer to this type of

be reported as a taxable event, resulting in an incorrect filing and/or potential penalties. Changing jobs and transferring, or "rolling over" retirement savings to another qualified retirement plan is generally a tax-protected transaction for participants in U.S.-based retirement plans.[114] However, IRS officials told us that a U.S. individual who participates in a foreign retirement plan may owe U.S. taxes for similar transfers within or between foreign workplace retirement plans. Retirement plans in some countries routinely initiate administrative transfers of a participant's retirement savings between accounts within the plan, to the employee's new plan, or to a designated institution outside the plan when the participant separates from their employer, according to officials in several of our case study locations. However, IRS officials told us the IRC does not recognize foreign retirement plans as tax-qualified plans,[115] and because these plans are not able to meet the criteria for qualification,[116] tax-deferred transfers or rollovers may not be possible unless a tax treaty provides otherwise. IRS generally considers routine administrative transfers of retirement assets that occur between or within foreign retirement plans to be distributions to the participant and therefore taxable income.

---

transfer as a transfer "within" the foreign workplace retirement plan. By contrast, transfers of investments within a plan, such as changing from one mutual fund investment to another, would not be taxable, according to IRS.

[114] In a direct rollover, a qualified workplace retirement plan makes a payment directly to another qualified plan or an IRA. In an indirect rollover, the plan makes a payment directly to the participant, who subsequently deposits it into another qualified retirement plan or IRA within 60 days. Indirect rollovers are subject to mandatory 20 percent withholding, so participants would have to use other funds in order to roll over the full amount. Rollovers are subject to other IRC requirements. See 26 U.S.C. § 402(c).

[115] In the United States, pre-retirement distributions from a qualified retirement plan can generally be "rolled over" by depositing the amount in another qualified retirement plan or IRA within 60 days. Financial institutions or plans may also directly transfer distributions to another plan or IRA. These rollovers are generally not taxed until money is withdrawn from the new plan. The rollover mechanism allows individuals to save for the future and have their money continue to grow tax-deferred.

[116] For example, among other things, for a 401(k) plan in the United States to be tax-qualified, it must meet minimum distribution requirements that generally require distributions to begin by the time the participant is 701/2 years old or retires, whichever is later. 26 U.S.C. § 401(a)(9). Foreign workplace retirement plans may not meet these requirements. For example, according to officials with whom we spoke, the United Kingdom has no required minimum distribution age.

According to IRS officials with whom we spoke, the transfer of retirement assets within or between plans implies that the participant has some access to and control over their retirement funds. Tax preparers and regulators in three of our case study locations told us that such transfers routinely take place (see appendix III). In these situations, IRS officials told us that deferring taxes on retirement contributions and earnings under IRC section 402(b) pertaining to foreign trusts would no longer be applicable because that section of the IRC does not cover transfers—only contributions and earnings within a given foreign trust. Instead, according to IRS officials, the transfer would generally constitute a "constructive receipt of funds"[117] by the participant and would be reportable and taxable. As a result, a U.S. individual who participates in a foreign retirement plan could owe U.S. tax on the entire amount of their retirement savings when they separate from their employer and their account is transferred to another account within the plan or to a different workplace retirement plan (see Figure 4).

Treasury officials said they have been aware of this issue for some years, having discussed it in multiple negotiations with other countries, and have taken steps to incorporate a solution in U.S. model income tax conventions dating as far back as 1996.Treasury officials told us that the 2016 U.S. Model Income Tax Convention includes a clause that would generally exempt from U.S. income tax such transfers if they qualify as tax-deferred transfers under the laws of the other country. According to Treasury officials, few of the treaties currently in force address this issue and many countries do not have tax treaties with the United States.[118]

---

[117] In general, gains, profits, and income are to be included in gross income for the taxable year in which they are actually or constructively received by the taxpayer. 26 C.F.R. § 1.451-1(a). Under Treasury regulations, income although not actually reduced to a taxpayer's possession is constructively received by him in the taxable year during which it is credited to his account, set apart for him, or otherwise made available so that he may draw upon it at any time, or so that the taxpayer could have drawn upon it during the taxable year if notice of intention to withdraw had been given. However, income is not constructively received if the taxpayer's control of its receipt is subject to substantial limitations or restrictions. See 26 C.F.R. § 1.451-2. In some circumstances, according to IRS officials, workplace retirement funds may become technically available to U.S. individuals during the transfer of foreign retirement accounts between plans when the individual changes jobs or separates from his or her employer even though the individual takes no action to access the funds.

[118] See Article 17, paragraph 2 of the 2016 U.S. Model Income Tax Convention

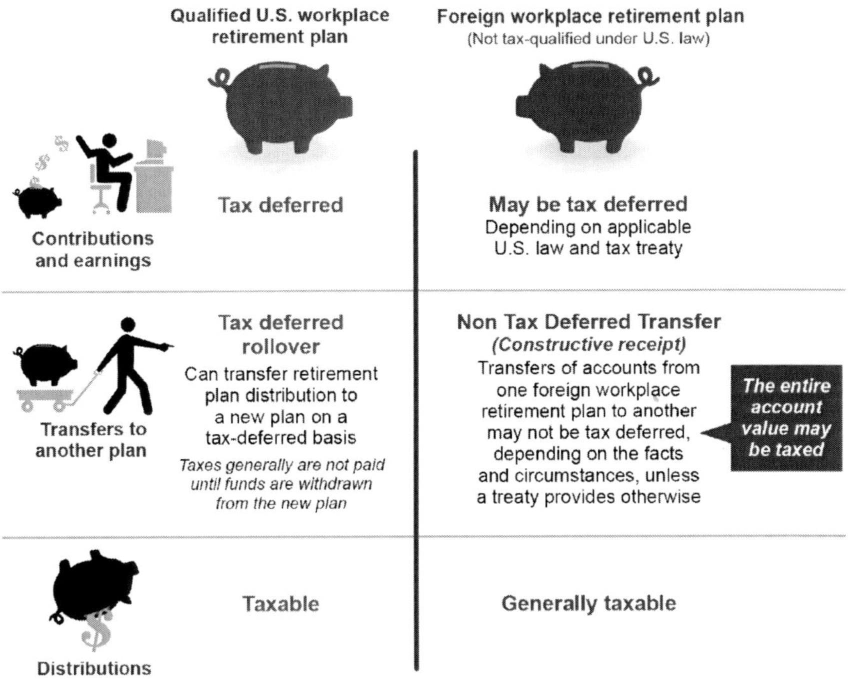

Source: GAO analysis of information provided by IRS officials. | GAO-18-19.

Figure 4. U.S. Taxation of Transfers between Defined Contribution Workplace Retirement Plans.

IRS officials told us that if no treaty exists between the United States and the country where the U.S. individual is participating in a foreign workplace retirement plan, or the treaty does not specify how to treat these transfers, there is generally no form of transfer that will receive U.S. income tax-deferral. In these situations, IRS officials said, there is no way that the plan can structure the transfer to prevent the U.S. individual who is transferring assets within or between foreign plans from receiving a distribution and being subject to tax liability. Even in cases where a tax treaty is in place, the treaty may not provide special treatment for the transfer of retirement assets. This would be the case in at least two of the five case study locations we examined, where despite a tax treaty in place, we were unable to identify any provisions that address these types of transfers. In these cases, according to IRS, the U.S. individual must fall back on the IRC, which does not provide tax-deferral on such transfers. As a result, a U.S. individual who participates in a foreign workplace plan would lose any tax-deferrals on the transfer.

2016 U. S. Model Income Tax Convention Language Would Exempt Certain Transfers of Foreign Retirement Assets from Taxation

The Department of the Treasury developed the U. S. Model Income Tax Convention to be the starting point for negotiating tax treaties with other countries. Language in an actual treaty results from that negotiation and therefore may not include this language. According to Department of the Treasury officials, few treaties currently contain this language.

"2016 United States Model Income Tax Convention, Article 17, Paragraph 2(b)

Where a citizen of the United States who is a resident of ______ is a member or beneficiary of, or participant in, a pension fund established in _____, the United States may not tax the income earned by the pension fund as income of the individual unless, and then only to the extent that, it is paid to, or for the benefit of, that individual from the pension fund (and not transferred to another pension fund established in _______ in a transfer that qualifies as a tax-deferred transfer under the laws of_______)."

Source: Department of the Treasury. | GAO-18-19.

IRS officials and tax preparers told us that the transfer issue can cause tax consequences for holders of foreign retirement assets, but one tax preparer we spoke with noted that U.S. tax laws were not written with foreign retirement plans in mind. As a result, tax preparers said it can be difficult to determine how to report foreign workplace retirement assets under the IRC, making routine administrative transactions[119] costly for U.S. individuals who participate in these plans. They said this is because some or all of the account balance may be subject to tax and retirement account asset growth would be lower due to the loss of tax-deferral. Each

[119] An example of this type of administrative transaction is described earlier in this report with reference to routine administrative transfers of retirement accounts that can occur in Hong Kong when participants separate from their employer.

time retirement assets are transferred, the transfer may be viewed as a distribution, and new contributions and growth could be subject to tax and a loss of tax-deferral. IRS officials also told us that the potential taxation of transfers between foreign plans may cause some individuals to avoid consolidating foreign retirement accounts.

Renegotiating a tax treaty can be time consuming and, according to Treasury officials, is unlikely to happen based on one issue, such as the transfer of retirement savings abroad. Treasury officials in the Office of Tax Policy said that the agency's approach to address these transfers would be to evaluate the issue on a treaty-by-treaty basis. However, this approach may not provide relief because there is no guarantee the country negotiating a treaty with the United States will agree to include provisions for transferring retirement savings on a tax-deferred basis. In order to provide more immediate relief, these Treasury officials said Congress could pass legislation that would allow routine account transfers between two foreign workplace retirement plans in the same country to be free from U.S. tax if that country has a tax treaty with the United States. However, they cautioned that such efforts should be focused on foreign retirement plans that have already been examined by Treasury, for example, through the process of negotiating a tax treaty or as defined in FATCA IGAs, in order to avoid creating a tax evasion loophole. For example, foreign workplace retirement plans could be defined as those recognized by an existing tax treaty or other plans as deemed appropriate by Treasury's Office of Tax Policy. According to Treasury officials, transfers within or between such plans in the same country could be protected from unnecessary taxation by, for example, modifying Section 402(b) or other provisions of the IRC. Officials said that without legislation, U.S. individuals who participate in foreign workplace retirement plans must follow current law, which does not provide tax-deferral for transfers within or between foreign plans, even those that may be eligible for tax-deferred contributions and earnings in the foreign jurisdiction. However, by changing the IRC, Congress can ensure that U.S. individuals who participate in foreign workplace retirement plans can consolidate their accounts in a tax-deferred manner without being taxed on the entire balance when their account is transferred.

CONCLUSION

Plan participants in the current workplace retirement plan environment can accumulate multiple retirement accounts and possibly lose track of them over their careers. The shift to DC plans and the mobility of the American workforce have led to an increase in the number of workplace retirement accounts, with many workers having multiple accounts over the course of their careers. Yet currently, with millions of small retirement accounts left behind by participants with previous employers, plan sponsors are experiencing challenges locating missing participants. DOL has agreed to evaluate the possibility of convening a taskforce to consider the establishment of a national pension registry, in part to address the difficulty of linking missing participants to their former accounts. However, until this effort brings results or another comprehensive solution to unclaimed accounts emerges, there are a variety of improvements federal agencies may make in the short term to help eliminate the inefficiencies in the current system that may reduce participants' retirement savings. Since DOL audit findings show that ongoing plans have challenges staying in touch with missing participants, and DOL has provided guidance on missing participants for terminating DC plans, providing such guidance for ongoing DC plans will help ensure that separated participants will receive information about their benefits.

In addition, IRS guidance on tax withholding does not address distributions of small unclaimed accounts sent to nonresponsive participants that are not always received by those participants. Some stakeholders mistakenly believe that IRS automatically credits all taxes withheld from such distributions toward taxes due. Following IRS guidance, plans generally withhold taxes on cash-outs from such accounts that the participant may not receive. By reviewing the issue of distributions made to participants who are unlikely to receive them, IRS has an opportunity to issue guidance clarifying the applicable tax withholding requirements in those situations.

IRS also has the potential to offer a service that delivers letters that participants are likely to open, is trusted by plan fiduciaries, and can help connect missing participants with their benefits. IRS was forwarding fewer than 50 letters at a time for plan sponsors at no charge, but decided to stop forwarding letters about unclaimed accounts in 2012. IRS can consider again helping connect participants with unclaimed accounts using the letter forwarding program. Lastly, IRS and SSA can take steps to address situations in which sponsors fail to update data to reflect payment of retirement accounts, rendering the data unreliable. Under the existing agreement between IRS and SSA with respect to the Form 8955- SSA data, the agencies can take steps to ensure participants have a more reliable source of information on their benefits in the future.

U.S. individuals who work abroad and participate in a foreign workplace retirement plan face challenges with reporting their accounts. Managing such accounts can be costly as individuals use expensive tax preparers for reporting their foreign retirement savings to IRS. These U.S. individuals are required to pay taxes on their worldwide income, but can become caught in a web of complex U.S. tax requirements governing how they report their foreign workplace retirement savings. By providing guidance on how to appropriately report foreign workplace retirement accounts, IRS can help U.S. individuals comply with these requirements and minimize their reporting burden.

IRS can also initiate a systematic analysis of Form 8938 data on foreign retirement accounts owned by U.S. individuals. Such data would help IRS gain a better understanding of how these accounts change over time, and to determine if they pose a low-risk for tax evasion. The outcome of this analysis could allow IRS to consider offering these individuals an exemption from reporting requirements on their foreign retirement accounts, further easing the burden U.S. individuals face reporting their foreign retirement assets. Lastly, transferring accounts between foreign retirement plans can have negative tax consequences that threaten the ability of U.S. individuals abroad to save for retirement. Congress may wish to consider whether it can assist U.S. individuals who participate in foreign workplace retirement plans by permitting these individuals to transfer their retirement savings to a different account within the plan or to another foreign workplace retirement plan on a tax-deferred basis when they change jobs or separate from their foreign employer. Doing so would permit these U.S. individuals in foreign workplace retirement plans to receive the tax-deferred benefits available to other U.S. plan participants who reside in the United States and who participate in qualified retirement plans.

MATTER FOR CONGRESSIONAL CONSIDERATION

We are making the following matter for congressional consideration.

Congress should consider legislation modifying the Internal Revenue Code to allow routine account transfers within the same foreign workplace retirement plan or between two foreign workplace retirement plans in the same country to be free from U.S. tax in countries covered by an existing income tax treaty that provides for favorable U.S. tax treatment of foreign workplace retirement plan contributions.

RECOMMENDATIONS

We are making a total of seven recommendations, including one to DOL, five to IRS, and one to SSA.

a) The Secretary of Labor should issue guidance on the obligations under ERISA of sponsors of ongoing plans to prevent, search for, and pay costs associated with locating missing participants. (Recommendation 1)
b) The IRS Commissioner should review taxation issues relating to distributions involving incorrect participant addresses and

uncashed benefit checks and clarify for the public the Internal Revenue Code's requirements in these circumstances. (Recommendation 2)

c) The IRS Commissioner should consider revising the letter forwarding program in a cost-effective manner to again provide information on behalf of plan sponsors on unclaimed retirement accounts to participants. (Recommendation 3)
d) The IRS Commissioner should clarify how U.S. individuals are to report their foreign retirement accounts. The clarification could include addressing how these accounts should be designated and how the taxpayer should report contributions, earnings, and distributions made from the account. (Recommendation 4)
e) The IRS Commissioner should systematically analyze data reported through Form 8938 filings on foreign retirement accounts owned by U.S. individuals with the goal of developing an evidence-based understanding of how these accounts change over time and what level of risk these accounts pose for tax evasion. To assist with this analysis, IRS should consider revising Form 8938 to more clearly distinguish between retirement accounts and other types of accounts or assets being reported by taxpayers under current reporting requirements. (Recommendation 5)
f) The IRS Commissioner should take steps to improve the likelihood that the Notice of Potential Private Pension Benefit Information corresponds to actual retirement benefits in the future, for example, by working with the Social Security Administration as necessary. (Recommendation 6)
g) The Social Security Administration Commissioner should take steps to improve the likelihood that the Notice of Potential Private Pension Benefit Information corresponds to actual retirement benefits in the future, for example, by working with IRS as necessary. (Recommendation 7)

AGENCY COMMENTS AND OUR EVALUATION

We provided a draft of this chapter to the Department of Labor, the Department of the Treasury, the Internal Revenue Service, the Social Security Administration, the Pension Benefit Guaranty Corporation, and the U.S. Department of State. DOL, Treasury and IRS, and PBGC provided technical comments, which we have incorporated where appropriate. DOL, IRS, SSA, and PBGC also provided formal comments, which are reproduced in appendices IV, V, VI, and VII, respectively. State did not have any comments. DOL agreed with our recommendation that additional guidance may be helpful to aid plan sponsors and plan fiduciaries of ongoing plans in meeting their existing fiduciary obligations to search for missing participants and to pay benefits. SSA agreed with our recommendation to take steps to improve the likelihood that the Notice of Potential Private Pension Benefit Information corresponds to actual retirement benefits in the future, for example, by working with IRS as necessary.

In its written comments, IRS stated that it generally agreed with the report and its findings. IRS specifically cited that the report identifies several challenges for participants to manage their retirement savings, such as updating former employers with address changes to continue receiving information about retirement plan accounts with former employers and responding to former employers regarding retirement plan accounts. IRS also stated that U.S. individuals participating in foreign retirement plans often do not know how to correctly report foreign retirement accounts and associated income due to complex federal requirements and treaty provisions governing the taxation of foreign retirement accounts. This recognition by IRS of the complex federal requirements and treaty provisions governing the taxation of foreign retirement accounts is in line with GAO's concerns about U.S. individuals with foreign workplace retirement accounts having trouble with routine account transfers within the same foreign workplace retirement plan or between two such plans in the same country. We have asked Congress to consider modifying the Internal Revenue Code to allow routine account transfers within the same foreign workplace retirement plan or between two foreign workplace retirement plans in the same country to be free from U.S. tax in countries covered by an existing income tax treaty that provides for favorable U.S. tax treatment of foreign workplace retirement plan contributions. Congress' ability to modify the Internal Revenue Code in such a way can help U.S. individuals participating in foreign workplace plans to better save for retirement by allowing them to consolidate accounts in a tax-deferred manner without being taxed on the entire balance when their account is transferred.

IRS agreed with two of our recommendations to improve the management of retirement savings. Specifically, IRS agreed to review taxation issues relating to distributions involving incorrect participant addresses and uncashed benefit checks and to clarify for the public the Internal Revenue Code's requirements in these circumstances. We believe that IRS' consideration of this recommendation and any subsequent actions the agency takes to clarify the issue will help to address questions about tax withholding from distributions in situations where the participant may be missing or where a distribution check remains uncashed after a period of time. IRS also agreed to work to improve the likelihood that the Notice of Potential Private Pension Benefit Information corresponds to actual retirement benefits in the future, and agreed to take steps to ensure that the data reported on Form 8955-SSA are accurate and to advise plan sponsors of any changes to reporting these data. We commend IRS for recognizing the importance of addressing this issue for taxpayers and for its willingness to take steps to ensure the accuracy of data reported by plans in the United States on vested benefits belonging to separated employees.

Lastly, IRS agreed with our recommendation to clarify how U.S. individuals are to report their foreign retirement accounts, which could include how the taxpayer should report contributions, earnings, and distributions made from the account. We encourage IRS to take the necessary steps to dispel any confusion U.S. individuals may have over how to properly classify and report their foreign retirement accounts on a U.S. tax return—such clarification should help ensure that these taxpayers can meet their tax reporting obligations.

IRS disagreed with two of our recommendations, citing the limited number of IRS staff and resources needed for the agency to implement these recommendations. First, IRS disagreed with our recommendation to consider revising the letter forwarding program in a cost-effective manner to again provide information on behalf of U.S. plan sponsors on unclaimed retirement accounts to participants. IRS commented that the IRS address of record for a participant would likely be of no greater value than addresses available through alternatives such as commercial locator services. However, our report does not cite the accuracy of IRS addresses, but rather other benefits that make a program revision worth considering, specifically the likelihood that individuals will open IRS correspondence, and the trust DOL places in the service as way for plan fiduciaries to meet their obligations. IRS also stated that the limited number of IRS staff and resources impact the feasibility of reinstating this program for plan participants. GAO continues to believe that expanding the letter forwarding program would be beneficial, and we encourage IRS to consider cost-effective ways to do so.

IRS also disagreed with our recommendation to analyze data provided through Form 8938 filings on foreign retirement accounts owned by U.S. individuals with the goal of developing an evidence-based understanding of how these accounts change over time and what level of risk these accounts pose for tax evasion. Our recommendation further stated that IRS should consider revising Form 8938 to assist with this analysis. In its comments, IRS did not disagree with this recommendation on its merits; IRS only cited a lack of resources to implement the recommendation. Specifically, IRS noted that although the modification to the Form 8938 suggested in this recommendation may seem minor, systemically collecting and analyzing the data would require resources beyond those currently available to IRS. However, as we describe in the report, IRS indicated to us that they already collect foreign account filing data through the Form 8938 and that the current reporting requirements help the agency to "keep a line of sight" on U.S. individuals' foreign pension arrangements. IRS told us that without such data being reported, U.S. individuals with foreign retirement accounts may seek to avoid proper reporting on their tax returns when distributions are made. However, without agreeing to take steps to analyze these data reported by taxpayers, the question remains why IRS continues to collect such information—which we show in the report to present a substantial reporting burden on taxpayers—if the agency has no plan to analyze the data in order to make an informed decision about the risk for tax evasion that such accounts present. It is also unclear to us how IRS would maintain a line of sight on foreign retirement accounts belonging to U.S. individuals without analyzing the data reported by taxpayers on such accounts. While we recognize that resource limits can impede an agency from taking on additional work and projects, we continue to believe that when staff and resources become available, IRS should modify the form and conduct a systematic analysis of these data—data that current law requires taxpayers to report—in order to assess the risk of tax evasion that foreign retirement accounts pose. Without such an analysis, IRS will have no basis to reach an evidence-based understanding of how these accounts change over time and what level of risk they pose for tax evasion. Further, as we have shown in the report, this reporting can be costly for U.S. individuals and could potentially lead to a decrease in their retirement savings. Without such an analysis by IRS, U.S. individuals who own foreign retirement accounts will continue to face these substantial reporting burdens without the knowledge that the data they are required to provide will be put to good use by the federal government.

Sincerely yours,
Charles A. Jeszeck, Director
Education, Workforce, and Income Security Issues

APPENDIX I: IRS INSTRUCTIONS ON REVIEWING TAX TREATY PROVISIONS RELATED TO FOREIGN RETIREMENT ACCOUNTS

IRS advises U.S. taxpayers to review tax treaty provisions carefully to better understand how to report their foreign income, including the distribution of savings from foreign retirement accounts.[120] IRS specifically advises taxpayers to read the residency article in a tax treaty to find any special rules pertaining to reporting and taxing foreign income, including distributions from foreign workplace retirement plans. When deciding whether a tax treaty applies to a taxpayer, the taxpayer should first identify their tax residency (Article 4 under most treaties). According to IRS, a taxpayer's residency determines how treaty articles on pensions and annuities will be applied and taxpayers should use the domestic laws of each country to identify residency. If, after applying the domestic law of each country, the taxpayer determines they are a resident of both countries, the tiebreaker rules of the applicable treaty are applied to determine residency based on the country in which the taxpayer has closer personal and economic relations, the country of habitual abode for the taxpayer, or the country in which the taxpayer is a national, according to IRS. If none of the above tiebreaker rules apply, the treaty generally provides that residency will be decided by the competent authorities of each country upon request by the taxpayer. Taxpayers are also advised to read all the protocols of the treaty to see if the residency rules have been amended by a later protocol. As a general rule, according to IRS, the pension/annuity articles of most tax treaties allow the country of residence (as determined by the residency article) to tax the pension distribution or annuity under its domestic laws, unless the tax treaty provides an exception to that rule. According to IRS, some treaties, for example, provide that the country of residence may not tax amounts that would not have been taxable by the other country if the individual was a resident of that country. There also may be special rules for lump-sum distributions. If the taxpayer is a U.S. citizen, IRS guidance provides that they also may need to refer to the "saving clause" (typically found in Article 1) for special rules that allow the United States to tax income in some cases as if the treaty had not entered into force.

---

[120] The information in this appendix was gathered from the IRS' International Tax Gap Series, The Taxation of Foreign Pension and Annuity Distributions and through discussion with IRS officials.

APPENDIX II: ESTIMATED NUMBER OF U.S. CITIZENS LIVING ABROAD

Researchers and federal officials have identified a range of estimates for U.S. citizens living outside the United States.[121] (See Figure 5).

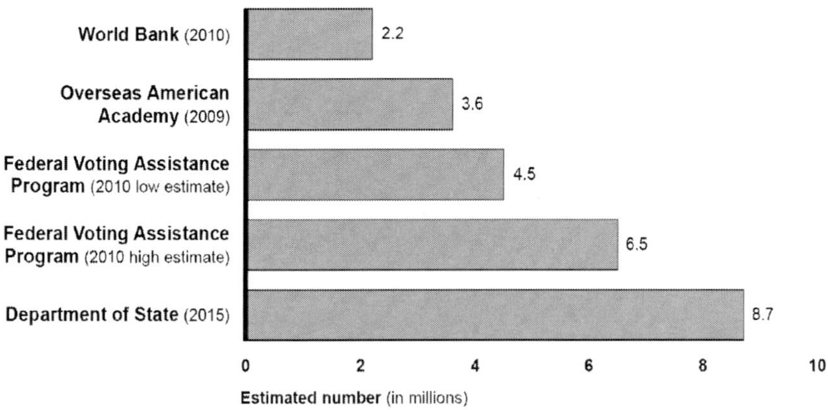

Source: Migration Policy Institute and the U.S. Department of State. | GAO-18-19.

Figure 5. Estimates of U.S. Citizens Living Abroad.

Table 2. U.S. Citizens Abroad by Geographic Region as of April 21, 2015

Region	Africa	East Asia and the Pacific	Europe and Eurasia	The Near East	South and Central Asia	Western Hemisphere	Total
Total Private and Official U.S. Citizen residents	231,854	1,135,114	2,027,914	1,019,457	618,772	3,706,577	8,739,688

Source: U.S. Department of State. | GAO-18-19.

[121] See Migration Policy Institute, *Counting the Uncountable: Overseas Americans*. Joe Costanzo, Amanda Klekowski von Koppenfels; May 17, 2013.

The U.S. Department of State (State) estimates that as of April 2015, 8.7 million U.S. citizens live abroad. Table 2 shows estimates of the number of U.S. citizens living abroad by geographic area that State's Bureau of Consular Affairs recently released to the Federal Voting Assistance Program.[122]

APPENDIX III: EFFORTS TO LINK PARTICIPANTS TO DORMANT OR UNCLAIMED RETIREMENT ACCOUNTS IN CASE STUDY LOCATIONS

We gathered the information in this appendix for each case study location by reviewing relevant documentation, publicly available research and reports, and interviewing relevant stakeholders, including government officials, plan sponsors, and service providers. We did not conduct an independent legal analysis to verify the information provided about the laws or regulations in the locations we selected for this study. Instead, we relied on appropriate secondary sources and interviews with relevant officials to support our work. We provided this information to appropriate officials in each case study location for their confirmation.

In the five case study locations we reviewed, participants, including U.S. individuals working in those locations, stay connected to their foreign workplace retirement savings through centralized institutions, direct contact with plans or government agencies, or through public pension registries. The low prevalence of unclaimed retirement accounts that we found in these locations is likely due, in part, to participants using these mechanisms to stay connected to their retirement savings.

---

[122] The Federal Voting Assistance Program is tasked with assisting U.S. citizens abroad with voting.

Unclaimed Retirement Accounts Are Maintained within Centralized Institutions or a Participant's Former Employer's Plan

In two of the five locations we reviewed, Australia and Switzerland, plans transfer dormant accounts belonging to separated employees to a centralized institution that is actively monitored by regulators. These accounts generally remain within these institutions until claims for benefits are made by the participant. For example, Swiss officials told us that in the event of a change of employment, the pension scheme (i.e., plan) of an insured person (i.e., participant) transfers the accumulated assets on behalf of that person to the pension scheme of the new employer. Vested benefits institutions are used to hold the assets when a person ceases to be subject to occupational benefits (workplace retirement) plans owing to termination of employment, e.g., in connection with a career break or being laid off.[123] In these cases, the pension scheme mandatorily transfers the assets to a vested benefits institution. This procedure ensures that the accumulated assets remain blocked in the pension cycle until the insured person joins a new pension scheme or an insured event occurs (old age, disability, or death). Once the person recommences employment and thus becomes subject to mandatory occupational benefits plans again, the termination benefits must be transferred by the vested benefits institution to the new pension scheme. If the pension scheme member or insured person does not become re-employed, the vested benefits institution keeps the assets until an insured event occurs (retirement, disability, or death). Further, if a separated employee fails to inform their former plan that they have a new employer, the participant's former plan automatically transfers the account after 6 months and within 2 years to the Substitute Occupational Benefit Institution.[124] This institution is a nonprofit entity that the Swiss federal

[123] Vested benefits institutions are subject to government regulation and are supervised by regional organized public authorities and registered in a directory. All regional authorities are under the supervision of a federal Occupational Pension Supervisory Commission.

[124] Plans also can receive instructions from separated employees to transfer their benefits to a "vested benefits institution"—typically a bank or an insurance company. These transferred benefits will reside within a vested benefits account at a bank or a vested benefits policy at

government commissioned in 1985; it works closely with the Swiss federal government to maintain Swiss retirement assets for participants and is charged with certain governmental responsibilities.[125] For retirement assets transferred to the Substitute Occupational Benefit Institution, account balances are not merely preserved until claimed or transferred, but grow according to returns on Switzerland's central fund investments. Figure 6 describes how accounts of separated employees in Switzerland are transferred to designated locations when they become dormant or unclaimed.

Swiss plans also transfer accounts belonging to separated employees to the employee's new plan once they receive instruction from the employee. This transfer along with account transfers to the Substitute Occupational Benefit Institution or a vested benefits institution, such as a bank or insurance company, contributes to the low prevalence of lost retirement accounts in Switzerland[126] because participants do not accumulate multiple retirement accounts with different plans when changing jobs throughout their career.

---

an insurance company until claimed by the participant or transferred with instructions from the participant to their new account set up with their new employer. Swiss officials said that after a period of ten years from the normal retirement age, any balances on accounts or on vested benefits policies shall be transferred to the Guarantee Fund. Claims for benefits that have not been made shall become statute-barred (i.e., no longer subject to benefits claims) when the member (participant) turns or would have turned 100. The assets shall be used for financing the 2nd Pillar Central Office, which oversees occupational benefits plans in Switzerland.

[125] The Substitute Occupational Benefit Institution is an occupational benefits organization supported by major employee and employer organizations. In January 1995, the Swiss government commissioned these organizations to take responsibility for organizing and managing vested benefit retirement accounts for participants. The Substitute Occupational Benefit Institution reports to the Swiss Supervision Commission for Occupational Pensions. The Commission is a supervisory authority responsible for ensuring uniform supervisory practices across the Swiss occupational pension system. The Commission oversees the supervisory authority of the nine regional supervisory authorities and is the licensing authority for occupational pension experts and asset managers in occupational pension plans.

[126] As of January 2016, the Substitute Occupational Benefit Institution had reported that more than 2.97 billion francs (approximately $3.1 billion USD) in unclaimed retirement benefits were held in approximately 632,000 dormant accounts. These funds represent less than 1 percent of total assets held in Swiss pensions. Following a survey of the Swiss pension system, Aon Hewitt reported that for 2013/14, the Swiss pension system held $642 billion USD in pension assets. Willis Towers Watson has reported that the Swiss pension system held $817 billion USD in 2016.

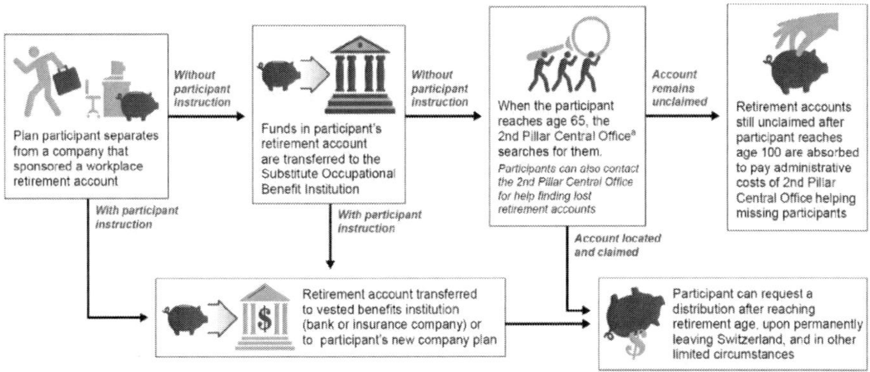

Source: GAO analysis of Switzerland's occupational benefits system. | GAO-18-19.

Note: We did not conduct an independent legal analysis to verify the information provided about the laws or regulations in the locations we selected for this study. Instead, we relied on appropriate secondary sources and interviews with relevant officials to support our work.

[a]The 2nd Pillar Central Office is a government entity that oversees occupational benefits plans in Switzerland.

Figure 6. Transfer Process for Dormant Workplace Retirement Accounts Belonging to Separated Employees in Switzerland.

In Australia, plans (also referred to as schemes or super funds) transfer unclaimed super accounts belonging to lost members (e.g., separated employees) to a centralized government institution, the Australian Taxation Office (ATO). These accounts generally remain within the ATO until claims for benefits are made by the member. While their money is being held by the ATO it earns interest at the consumer price index rate.

In three of the five locations GAO reviewed—Canada,[127] Hong Kong, and the UK—the participant's former employer's plan maintains dormant accounts until claimed or transferred to a new plan. For example, in Hong Kong, according to its retirement schemes (plan) regulator, the Mandatory

[127] An exception to this is found in several of Canada's provinces. Specifically, Alberta, British Columbia, and Quebec have unclaimed property legislation and regimes that provide for the transfer of unclaimed property, including retirement accounts, to an unclaimed property fund. For example, in Alberta, accounts within a registered retirement savings plan, registered education savings plan, or other tax-deferral plan will be considered unclaimed and prone to transfer 3 years after an attempted or required distribution is made to the participant.

Provident Fund Schemes Authority (MPFA),[128] whenever employees, including U.S. individuals working in Hong Kong, change to a new employer, they need to open a new Mandatory Provident Fund (MPF) "contribution account" under the MPF scheme in which the new employer participates to accumulate MPF contributions in respect of the new employment. If an employee who has ceased employment with an employer does not take action to transfer the benefits accrued from the previous employment to the new "contribution account" with their new employer's scheme (i.e., plan) or a "personal account" in an MPF scheme of the employee's choice, their former employer's scheme will automatically transfer their accumulated MPF benefits from the contribution account to a personal account[129] within the original scheme for continuous investment. Government officials told us that MPF schemes keep the benefits of the scheme members (i.e., plan participants) within the scheme until the scheme member returns to make a claim or to issue instructions to transfer benefits in the account to another MPF scheme. The MPFA advises scheme members that failing to consolidate the MPF benefits accumulated from previous employments can result in accumulating multiple MPF accounts that can be difficult to manage—this can result in accounts becoming lost over time. To address this challenge, the MPFA conducts regular publicity programs and publishes pamphlets reminding scheme members that when they change employers they should consolidate the benefits under the previous employment to any existing personal accounts or to the new contribution account under the MPF scheme of their new employer.

---

[128] The MPFA is a statutory body established in 1998 to regulate and supervise the operations of Hong Kong's Mandatory Provident Fund retirement plans and occupational retirement plans. The MPFA's mission is to regulate and supervise privately managed provident fund retirement plans; to educate the working population about saving for retirement and the role of the MPF system as one of the pillars supporting retirement living; and to lead improvements to provident fund retirement plans to make them more efficient and user-friendly, and better meet the needs of the working population. The Mandatory Provident Fund system is a mandatory retirement program for Hong Kong residents; it has been in place in Hong Kong since 2000. The objective of this mandatory retirement system is to provide secured retirement benefits for the workforce of Hong Kong.

[129] The primary difference between these accounts is that personal accounts do not accept any contributions from employees or employers.

In two of the five locations we reviewed—Australia and Switzerland—plans are required to regularly report to regulators on unclaimed accounts, missing participants, and account transfers made for separated employees, including those made on behalf of U.S. individuals. For example, in Australia, plans are required to communicate information on unclaimed accounts to the ATO.[130] Specifically, every 6 months plans are required to identify and report members who meet the definition of "lost"[131] and unclaimed accounts considered "uncontactable or inactive" to the ATO. Further, plans are also required to transfer unclaimed accounts to the ATO when certain unclaimed super money criteria are met.[132] In Switzerland, before the end of January each year, occupational benefits institutions and institutions that manage vested benefits accounts or policies are required to report to the 2nd Pillar Central Office all persons for whom assets were held in December of the previous year.

Plans in two of the locations we reviewed provide separated participants information on account transfers that can help them stay connected to their retirement savings. For example, in Hong Kong, MPF schemes (plans) provide a transfer statement to members once the transfer

---

[130] In Australia, a lost member's plan will transfer unclaimed retirement accounts to a centralized government institution (the ATO) after the member is uncontactable or inactive and these accounts meet the definition of 'unclaimed super money'. For example, this can occur if the missing participant turns 65, or if the balance of the dormant account is under the small lost member account dollar threshold (currently $6,000 AUD). As a result, participants, including U.S. citizens with an Australian retirement account, know where to search for their lost accounts or unclaimed benefits, and participants can claim this money at any time.

[131] Australian officials told us that a participant becomes "lost" when the superannuation provider has lost contact with the participant or has not received a contribution or rollover from that participant within the last 5 years. However, a participant would not be considered lost if the superannuation provider has no reason to believe any address held is incorrect or if the participant indicated or notified the superannuation provider of their existence.

[132] Plans are required to transfer 'unclaimed super money' to the ATO for (a) members aged 65 or older; non-member spouses; or deceased members, (b) small lost member accounts and insoluble lost member accounts (when participant has lost touch with the plan or the account has not been used for 5 years), and (c) if unclaimed super money belonging to former temporary residents who are eligible to claim the "Departing Australia Superannuation Payment" have not done so, and a minimum of at least 6 months has elapsed since they departed Australia and their visa ceased to be effect—in this case, the holding super fund is required to transfer the unclaimed super money to the ATO.

of benefits to another MPF scheme is completed.[133] The MPF scheme that receives the transfer must, as soon as practicable after receiving the transferred benefits, provide the member written notice confirming the transfer and stating the monetary value of those benefits. In Switzerland plans must regularly contact their participants and if unable to do so, must inform the 2nd Pillar Central Office, who will try to reestablish contact between the plan and their participants.[134]

Unclaimed Retirement Accounts Are Accessed Through Contact with Government Agencies or Through Public Pension Registries

Participants in three of the five locations we reviewed can access information on their retirement accounts by contacting a government agency. According to government and retirement plan officials in Australia, participants can access their retirement account details by logging onto the myGov platform, which is a secure way to access government online services. Participants, including U.S. individuals, who have registered online via myGov and have their personal accounts linked to ATO online services can view their retirement accounts online and can claim their money at any time. For those that choose not to register for myGov, they can use the Departing Australia Superannuation Payment online service to claim their super funds once they have departed Australia and their visa has ceased to be in effect. In Hong Kong, MPFA officials told us that scheme members seeking information on their personal accounts or on unclaimed retirement benefits with any MPF scheme (plan)

---

[133] The transfer statement should include, among other things, the following details: name of transferring trustee; name of scheme and account number of the account from which the transfer was made; name and address of the scheme member; amount of accrued benefits transferred; name of scheme to which the benefits have been transferred; and date on which the transfer was made.

[134] The 2nd Pillar Central Office also handles inquiries from participants or their heirs, compares personal data with notifications received from occupational benefits institutions, and communicates the results to those making the inquiry, who can then claim their benefits from the institution in question.

can approach MPFA to request a search of the Personal Accounts Register[135] or Unclaimed Benefits Register,[136] respectively. The MPFA's website includes instructions for initiating these inquiries. In Switzerland, government officials told us that participants, including U.S. individuals, can directly contact the 2nd Pillar Central Office, which can locate all the institutions holding vested benefits on the participant's behalf.

In two of the five case study locations, Australia and the UK, participants can access information on their retirement accounts by using pension registries or other government supported services.[137] For example, in the UK, the government provides all participants, including U.S. individuals with a UK retirement account, access to the Pension Tracing Service to help them locate their lost retirement accounts.[138] The UK government has also established other organizations and services to help participants locate their lost retirement accounts. The Pensions Advisory Service is an independent organization that is funded by the UK

---

[135] The MPFA maintains a Personal Account Register for scheme members to check for free. Information available includes whether a member has any personal accounts and, if so, the name and contact number of the scheme maintaining the personal account(s). MPF scheme members, including U.S. individuals, who would like information to help them identify and locate their personal accounts, contact the MPFA for assistance.

[136] The MPFA maintains an Unclaimed Benefits Register for members of the public to check for free. Information available includes whether a participant has any unclaimed benefits and, if so, the name and contact number of the plan where the benefits reside. Participants must directly communicate with MPFA and make an inquiry about their benefits. Participants can make an inquiry into their unclaimed benefits by sending relevant forms to MPFA via fax or mail or by visiting MPFA in person. In pension clauses and certain provisions, under the following special circumstances, a participant's accrued benefits may be classified as "unclaimed benefits" if: (1) the participant reaches the age of 65 but has not withdrawn his/her accrued benefits from the plan and remains unreachable despite attempts by the plan to search and locate the participant; or (2) a participant requests a distribution from their plan for accrued benefits; the plan issues a check but the check remains uncashed after 6 months from the issue date and the participant remains unreachable despite search attempts by the plan sponsor to locate the participant.

[137] For information on how participants use a pension registry in Australia to access information on unclaimed retirement accounts, see GAO, *401(k) Plans: Greater Protections Needed for Forced Transfers and Inactive Accounts*, GAO-15-73 (Washington, D.C.: Nov. 21, 2014).

[138] To do so, participants provide the service with personal and employment information and the service will trace and identify contact details of the retirement plan in question— this is similar to services provided to participants in the United States by DOL's benefits advisors. The service can only put an individual in contact with a lost retirement plan and does not have access to private retirement account details—the participant must contact their former plan directly once it has been traced in order to find out what their retirement account is worth.

government.[139] Officials told us that the service was implemented because retirement accounts and pensions in the UK had become excessively complicated. The service sometimes receives questions from participants living abroad, such as in the United States, or from U.S. individuals living in the UK. Service officials told us that it is particularly challenging for these foreign participants to know how to repatriate their retirement benefits and to locate missing retirement accounts. Government officials told us that the UK government is committed to ensuring that members of the public can access good-quality, free-to-client, impartial financial guidance and debt advice which is currently provided by three different organizations. These officials said that a bill was introduced in June 2017 that would set up a new single financial guidance body to provide guidance and information on all matters relating to occupational and personal pensions. Officials said they expect that this single financial guidance body to go live no earlier than October 2018.

The UK government is also currently developing a new pension online tool, the Pensions Dashboard. The dashboard is being developed as a joint project between the UK government and the country's retirement industry; 17 of the UK's largest pension firms developed a prototype demonstrating that the technology for the dashboard works.[140] The goal of the dashboard is to allow participants to log into one portal to locate all of their pension data, including information on the value and the location of different retirement savings accumulated throughout their career.[141] Currently, a UK

---

[139] The Pension Advisory Services receives grants from the UK's Department for Work and Pensions. The service provides people with free professional, independent and impartial assistance with their retirement accounts. The service offers information and guidance to participants through a variety of channels including a telephone helpline, web chat, written inquiries, online inquiries, and the service's website. The service is delivered by in-house retirement specialists and a nationwide network of volunteer advisers who have typically worked in the retirement industry in roles that have required a high level of technical knowledge. The service answers thousands of calls a year from participants about any aspect of their retirement benefits. Officials said that in 2016, the service received about 250,000 calls, and about 1 in 6 of those calls was about a lost retirement account. A fair proportion of those calls are due to participant migration to and from other countries.

[140] These pension firms include Abbey Life, Aon, Aviva, Fidelity International, HSBC, L&G, LV=, NEST, NOW, People's Pension, Phoenix, Prudential, Royal London, Scottish Widows, Standard Life, Willis Towers Watson, and Zurich.

[141] According to the UK government, on average, a person can have 11 employers over their working life, which means that they could end up with almost a dozen retirement accounts

ID verification system is available to UK residents to review their tax bills and other financial information online, and officials are considering permitting participants to use this system with proper credentials to access the dashboard.[142] In time, UK government officials said that the dashboard may replace the UK's Pension Tracing Service, but not for many years. Other officials added that they are uncertain whether the dashboard will include all plans. One concern is that many lost accounts may be with old defined benefit plans or small defined contribution plans that do not have online systems that can be integrated into the dashboard. As a result, some of the plans most likely to have lost participants may also be the least likely to participate in the dashboard.

APPENDIX IV: COMMENTS FROM THE DEPARTMENT OF LABOR

U.S. Department of Labor

Employee Benefits Security Administration
Washington, D.C. 20210

November 28, 2017

Charles A. Jeszeck
Director, Education, Workforce, and Income Security
United States Government Accountability Office
Washington, DC 20548

---

by the time they retire. At the moment there is no way for people to see the value of all of their retirement accounts in one place and research has shown that over a third of people approaching retirement find it difficult to keep track of their retirement accounts. The dashboard aims to also provide a link to "lost" retirement accounts with previous employers and could help release the £400 million worth of retirement savings that the UK's Department for Work and Pensions estimates is currently unclaimed.

142 These credentials could include use of a UK resident's National Insurance number, their UK passport number, and the resident's verified UK address. For U.S. individuals wanting to access the dashboard, UK officials told us that they would at least need to use their National Insurance number as a credential, but it is likely that additional information would be required of U.S. individuals and it is unknown if they could access the system from outside the UK.

Dear Mr. Jeszeck:

Thank you for the opportunity to review the Government Accountability Office (GAO) draft report entitled "Workplace Retirement Accounts: Better Guidance and Information Could Help Plan Participants at Home and Abroad Manage Their Retirement Savings" (GAO-18-19). The draft report recommends that the Department of Labor (Department) issue guidance on the ERISA obligations of sponsors of ongoing plans to prevent, search for, and pay costs associated with locating missing participants.

As your report notes, large numbers of participants of retirement age are not receiving their retirement income when due as the result of out-of-date mailing addresses, failure to maintain accurate records, and inadequate searches for missing participants. In an effort to help plan officials meet their fiduciary obligations under ERISA to reunite missing participants with their benefits, the Department's Employee Benefits Security Administration (EBSA) has issued the following guidance:

- 29 CFR § 2550.404a-2 - Safe Harbor for Automatic Rollovers to Individual Retirement Plans relating to mandatory cash-outs ($5,000 or less) from ongoing defined benefit and defined contribution plans;
- 29 CFR § 2550.404a-3 - Safe Harbor for Distributions from Terminated Individual Account Plans;
- 29 CFR § 2578.1 –Termination of Abandoned Individual Account plans; and
- Field Assistance Bulletin (FAB) 2014-01 – Fiduciary Duties and Missing Participants in Defined Contribution Plans, which sets out search steps for finding missing participants that EBSA would treat as meeting the fiduciary requirements of section 404 of ERISA.

More recently, the Department worked closely with the Pension Benefit Guaranty Corporation (PBGC) on its final rule regarding missing participants under section 4050 of ERISA.[1] After PBGC publishes its final rule, EBSA expects to revisit its guidance under 29 CFR § 2550.404a-3, 29 CFR § 2578.1, and FAB 2014-01 to facilitate the use of the PBGC missing participants program. EBSA also provided input to the Internal Revenue Service on its October 19, 2017 memorandum to its Employee Plans Examination employees regarding missing participants and minimum required distributions. Finally, EBSA currently is engaged in a major enforcement initiative (the "Terminated Vested Participant Project" or "TVPP") examining whether plan officials are meeting their fiduciary obligations under section 404 of ERISA to find missing participants and pay them their benefits.[2] As noted in the GAO report, the TVPP uncovered a number of failures to update addresses, maintain records, and adequately search for missing participants. As the result of the problems uncovered by the TVPP, EBSA is considering the need for additional guidance regarding the duty of plan fiduciaries to maintain updated addresses and other records.

With regard to GAO's recommendation, EBSA agrees that additional guidance may be helpful to aid plan sponsors and plan fiduciaries of ongoing plans in meeting their existing fiduciary obligations to search for missing participants and to pay benefits.

We appreciate having had the opportunity to review and comment on the draft report. Please do not hesitate to contact us if you have any questions concerning this response or if we can be of further assistance.

Sincerely,

Jeanne Klinefelter Wilson

Jeanne Klinefelter Wilson
Deputy Assistant Secretary for Policy

---

[1] PBGC's final rule is currently under review by OIRA.

[2] Under ERISA section 404(a)(1) a plan fiduciary must "discharge his duties with respect to a plan solely in the interest of the participants and beneficiaries and— (A) for the exclusive purpose of:
(i) providing benefits to participants and their beneficiaries; and (ii) defraying reasonable expenses of administering the plan; [and] (B) with the care, skill, prudence, and diligence under the circumstances then prevailing that a prudent man acting in a like capacity and familiar with such matters would use in the conduct of an enterprise of a like character and with like aims …."

APPENDIX V: COMMENTS FROM THE INTERNAL REVENUE SERVICE

DEPARTMENT OF THE TREASURY
INTERNAL REVENUE SERVICE
WASHINGTON, D.C. 20224

DEPUTY COMMISSIONER

December 14, 2017

Charles A. Jeszeck, Director
Education, Workforce, and Income Security
United States Government Accountability Office
441 G Street, NW, Room 5968
Washington, DC 20548

Dear Mr. Jeszeck:

Thank you for the opportunity to review the draft report of the Government Accountability Office entitled "WORKPLACE RETIREMENT ACCOUNTS: Better Guidance and Information Could Help Plan Participants at Home and Abroad Manage Their Retirement Savings" (GAO-18-19). We generally agree with the report and its findings. The focus of the report is to identify steps that federal agencies can take to assist participants in complying with federal reporting and withholding requirements and managing their retirement savings. The Department of the Treasury, the Internal Revenue Service (IRS), the Department of Labor, the Department of State, the Pension Benefit Guaranty Corporation, and the Social Security Administration (collectively, the Agencies) regulate these requirements.

The IRS is committed to helping U.S. taxpayers understand and meet their tax responsibilities. The draft report identifies several challenges to managing those savings, such as updating former employers with address changes (to continue receiving information about retirement plan accounts with former employers) and responding to former employers regarding retirement plan accounts. In addition, U.S. individuals participating in foreign retirement plans often do not know how to correctly report foreign retirement accounts and associated income due to complex federal requirements and treaty provisions governing the taxation of foreign retirement accounts.

The report provides several recommendations to the Agencies that are aimed at facilitating the linking of missing participants to their retirement plan accounts and clarifying how to appropriately report foreign workplace retirement accounts. With that as background, enclosed are comments on the draft report's recommendations directed to the IRS.

We appreciate having the opportunity to review and comment on the draft report. Please do not hesitate to contact us if you have questions concerning this response or if we can be of further assistance.

Sincerely,

Kirsten B. Wielobob
Deputy Commissioner for
Services and Enforcement

Comments on the GAO Recommendations directed to the IRS

Recommendation 2:
The IRS Commissioner should review taxation issues relating to distributions involving incorrect participant addresses and uncashed benefit checks and clarify for the public the Internal Revenue Code's requirements in these circumstances.

Comment:
The IRS agrees with this recommendation and will take steps to review these taxation issues and clarify the Internal Revenue Code's requirements for the public.

Recommendation 3:
The IRS Commissioner should consider revising the letter forwarding program in a cost-effective manner to again provide information on behalf of plan sponsors on unclaimed retirement accounts to participants.

Comment:
The IRS disagrees with the recommendation. The premise behind the Letter Forwarding Program is based on a belief that the IRS address of record is a better source of information than what could be found with the use of other alternatives. With advances in web-based technology and the widespread use of commercially available locator services, the address available from the IRS would likely be of no greater value than what could be obtained without a Letter Forwarding process. In fact, the guidance the Department of Labor issued in 2014 affirms the steps plan administrators can take to locate missing participants which is based on the availability of alternative sources of information. Based on the limited IRS staff and resources and the many commercially available services, it is not feasible to reinstate this program.

Recommendation 4:
The IRS Commissioner should clarify how U.S. individuals are to report their foreign retirement accounts. The clarification could include addressing how these accounts should be designated and how the taxpayer should report contributions, earnings, and distributions made from the account.

Comment:
The IRS agrees with this recommendation and will take steps to provide additional information on the Internal Revenue Code's requirements for U.S. individuals reporting their foreign retirement accounts.

Recommendation 5:
The IRS Commissioner should systematically analyze data reported through Form 8938 filings on foreign retirement accounts owned by U.S. individuals with the goal of developing an evidence-based understanding of how these accounts change over time

and what level of risk these accounts pose for tax evasion. To assist with this analysis, IRS should consider revising Form 8938 to more clearly distinguish between retirement accounts and other types of accounts or assets being reported by taxpayers under current reporting requirements.

Comment:
The IRS disagrees with the recommendation. The modification to the Form 8938 suggested in this recommendation may seem minor, but systemically collecting and analyzing the data would require resources beyond those currently available to IRS.

Recommendation 6:
The IRS Commissioner should take steps to improve the likelihood that the Notice of Potential Private Pension Benefit Information corresponds to actual retirement benefits in the future.

Comment:
The IRS agrees with this recommendation and will take steps to ensure that the data reported on Form 8955-SSA is accurate. As IRS takes such steps, plan sponsors will be advised.

Appendix VI: Comments from the Social Security Administration

SOCIAL SECURITY

Office of the Commissioner

November 9, 2017

Mr. Charles Jeszeck
Director, Education, Workforce, and Income Security
United States Government Accountability Office
441 G Street, NW
Washington, DC 20548

Dear Mr. Jeszeck:

Thank you for the opportunity to review the draft report, "WORKPLACE RETIREMENT ACCOUNTS: Better Guidance and Information Could Help Plan Participants at Home and Abroad Manage Their Retirement Savings" (GAO-18-19). Please see our enclosed comments.

Sincerely,

Stephanie Hall

Stephanie Hall
Acting Deputy Chief of Staff

COMMENTS ON THE GOVERNMENT ACCOUNTABILITY OFFICE DRAFT REPORT, "WORKPLACE RETIREMENT ACCOUNTS: BETTER GUIDANCE AND INFORMATION COULD HELP PLAN PARTICIPANTS AT HOME AND ABROAD MANAGE THEIR RETIREMENT SAVINGS" (GAO-18-19)

GENERAL COMMENTS

We are committed to improving the "*Potential Private Retirement Benefit Information*" notice (Form 8955-SSA), as we understand the importance of the information it may provide individuals as they prepare for retirement. We will continue our partnership with the Internal Revenue Service (IRS) and meet with them on a bi-monthly basis to discuss the Employee Retirement Income Security Act of 1974 related activities. In addition, to improve the accuracy of the notice, we plan to meet with the IRS starting next month with the objective to review Form 8955-SSA to ensure we are capturing the necessary information on the form and update instructions as necessary.

Recommendation 1

The Social Security Administration Commissioner should take steps to improve the likelihood that the Notice of Potential Private Pension Benefit Information corresponds to actual retirement benefits in the future, for example, by working with the IRS as necessary.

Response

We agree.

APPENDIX VII: COMMENTS FROM THE PENSION BENEFIT GUARANTY CORPORATION

PBGC
Protecting America's Pensions

Pension Benefit Guaranty Corporation
1200 K Street, N.W., Washington, D.C. 20005-4026

Office of the Director

December 8, 2017

Charles A. Jeszeck
Director, Education, Workforce, and
Income Security Issues
U.S. Government Accountability Office
441 G Street NW
Washington DC 20226

RE: Workplace Retirement Accounts: Better Guidance and Information Could Help Plan Participants at Home and Abroad Manage Their Retirement Savings

Dear Mr. Jeszeck:

Thank you for your helpful report on the challenges American workers face when attempting to claim earned retirement benefits from previous employers. We are grateful for the opportunity to work with GAO on this important issue. We've provided brief technical comments on the draft under separate cover.

The draft report states that from 2004 through 2013, over 25 million participants in workplace plans separated from employment and left at least one retirement account behind. Many of these participants lose track of those accounts or their plans lose track of the participants. PBGC is proud to provide one part of the solution through its current Missing Participants Program, and we are expanding that solution so that many more workers and retirees can be united with their benefits in the future.

For more than 20 years, PBGC's Missing Participants Program has connected people who were missing when their pension plans terminated to their retirement benefits. Currently the program is open only to terminated PBGC-insured single-employer plans. On September 20, 2016, PBGC issued a proposed rule that would expand its existing Missing Participants Program to cover terminated 401(k) and other defined contribution plans and certain defined benefit plans that aren't currently covered by the program. PBGC anticipates having the expanded program available in 2018 (for plans that terminate after 2017).

We're looking forward to offering our missing participants program to a new group of customers, and we believe this program will be a great resource for employers and workers alike.

GAO's continued exploration of these important issues is certainly welcome, and we look forward to continued collaboration.

Sincerely,

WTReeder

W. Thomas Reeder
Director

INDEX

C

D

E

F

J

L

M

N

O

P

Q

R

S

T

U

V

W